Work, Learning and Transnational Migration

As the globalisation of migration intensifies, many countries have joined the international competition for the most talented, skillful and resourceful workers. More recently, migration has shifted from international to transnational, characterised by its multiple and circular flows across transnational spaces rather than singular or unidirectional movement. When transnational migrants arrive in a new country, many of them face multifaceted barriers when it comes to transitioning into work and learning in the host society.

Work, Learning and Transnational Migration examines the non-linear transition of work and learning for transnational migrants; the multiple barriers facing migrants in the process of transition; tensions between mobility, knowledge and recognition; issues of language, power and transnational identity; and how socio-cultural differences have been used to entrench social inequality in migrants' transition. The rich international contexts and global perspectives provided across all chapters enrich our understanding about the changing nature of work and learning in the age of transnational migration.

This book was originally published as a special issue of *Globalisation, Societies and Education*.

Shibao Guo is Professor in the Werklund School of Education, University of Calgary, Canada. He specialises in citizenship and immigration, race and ethnic relations, adult and lifelong education, and comparative and international education. His research had been funded by a number of organisations, including the Social Sciences and Humanities Research Council, International Organisation for Migration, and Education International. He is a former president of the Canadian Association for the Study of Adult Education (2009–2011), and currently he serves as president of the Canadian Ethnic Studies Association and co-editor of *Canadian Ethnic Studies*.

Work, Learning and Transnational Migration

Opportunities, challenges and debates

Edited by
Shibao Guo

LONDON AND NEW YORK

First published 2016
by Routledge
2 Park Square, Milton Park, Abingdon, Oxon, OX14 4RN, UK

and by Routledge
711 Third Avenue, New York, NY 10017, USA

Routledge is an imprint of the Taylor & Francis Group, an informa business

© 2016 Taylor & Francis

All rights reserved. No part of this book may be reprinted or reproduced or utilised in any form or by any electronic, mechanical, or other means, now known or hereafter invented, including photocopying and recording, or in any information storage or retrieval system, without permission in writing from the publishers.

Trademark notice: Product or corporate names may be trademarks or registered trademarks, and are used only for identification and explanation without intent to infringe.

British Library Cataloguing in Publication Data
A catalogue record for this book is available from the British Library

ISBN 13: 978-1-138-92617-2

Typeset in Times New Roman
by RefineCatch Limited, Bungay, Suffolk

Publisher's Note
The publisher accepts responsibility for any inconsistencies that may have arisen during the conversion of this book from journal articles to book chapters, namely the possible inclusion of journal terminology.

Disclaimer
Every effort has been made to contact copyright holders for their permission to reprint material in this book. The publishers would be grateful to hear from any copyright holder who is not here acknowledged and will undertake to rectify any errors or omissions in future editions of this book.

Contents

Citation Information vii
Notes on Contributors ix

1. Introduction: work, learning and transnational migration 1
   Shibao Guo

2. The changing face of work and learning in the context of immigration: the Canadian experience 7
   Shibao Guo

3. Complicating the entrepreneurial self: professional Chinese immigrant women negotiating occupations in Canada 32
   Hongxia Shan

4. The making of the 'precarious': examining Indian immigrant IT workers in Canada and their transnational networks with body shops in India 49
   Srabani Maitra

5. Becoming transnational: exploring multiple identities of students in a Mandarin–English bilingual programme in Canada 65
   Yan Zhang and Yan Guo

6. Language, institutional identity and integration: lived experiences of ESL teachers in Australia 85
   Sepideh Fotovatian

7. Between the nation and the globe: education for global mindedness in Finland 101
   Vanessa de Oliveira Andreotti, Gert Biesta and Cash Ahenakew

8. Constructing a theory of individual space: understanding transnational migration through the experience of return Chinese immigrants from Canada in Beijing 115
   Yueya Ding

9. 'Talent circulators' in Shanghai: return migrants and their strategies for success 131
   Yedan Huang and Khun Eng Kuah-Pearce

Index 151

Citation Information

The following chapters were originally published in *Globalisation, Societies and Education*, volume 13, issue 2 (June 2015). When citing this material, please use the original page numbering for each article, as follows:

Chapter 1
Introduction: work, learning and transnational migration
Shibao Guo
Globalisation, Societies and Education, volume 13, issue 2 (June 2015) pp. 171–176

Chapter 3
Complicating the entrepreneurial self: professional Chinese immigrant women negotiating occupations in Canada
Hongxia Shan
Globalisation, Societies and Education, volume 13, issue 2 (June 2015) pp. 177–193

Chapter 4
The making of the 'precarious': examining Indian immigrant IT workers in Canada and their transnational networks with body shops in India
Srabani Maitra
Globalisation, Societies and Education, volume 13, issue 2 (June 2015) pp. 194–209

Chapter 5
Becoming transnational: exploring multiple identities of students in a Mandarin–English bilingual programme in Canada
Yan Zhang and Yan Guo
Globalisation, Societies and Education, volume 13, issue 2 (June 2015) pp. 210–229

Chapter 6
Language, institutional identity and integration: lived experiences of ESL teachers in Australia
Sepideh Fotovatian
Globalisation, Societies and Education, volume 13, issue 2 (June 2015) pp. 230–245

CITATION INFORMATION

Chapter 7
Between the nation and the globe: education for global mindedness in Finland
Vanessa de Oliveira Andreotti, Gert Biesta and Cash Ahenakew
Globalisation, Societies and Education, volume 13, issue 2 (June 2015) pp. 246–259

Chapter 8
Constructing a theory of individual space: understanding transnational migration through the experience of return Chinese immigrants from Canada in Beijing
Yueya Ding
Globalisation, Societies and Education, volume 13, issue 2 (June 2015) pp. 260–275

Chapter 9
'Talent circulators' in Shanghai: return migrants and their strategies for success
Yedan Huang and Khun Eng Kuah-Pearce
Globalisation, Societies and Education, volume 13, issue 2 (June 2015) pp. 276–294

The following chapter was originally published in the *Journal of Education and Work*, volume 26, issue 2 (April 2013). When citing this material, please use the original page numbering for each article, as follows:

Chapter 2
The changing face of work and learning in the context of immigration: the Canadian experience
Shibao Guo
Journal of Education and Work, volume 26, issue 2 (April 2013) pp. 162–186

For any permission-related enquiries please visit:
http://www.tandfonline.com/page/help/permissions

Notes on Contributors

Cash Ahenakew is a First Nations' scholar at the University of British Columbia, Vancouver, Canada, whose research experience and interests focus on the areas of international indigenous studies in education, indigenous curriculum and pedagogy, and indigenous health and well-being. He has been a research associate in international research projects on global citizenship education, international indigenous networks and critical intercultural education at the universities of Oulu, Finland and Canterbury, New Zealand. His doctoral dissertation, 'The Effects of Historical Trauma, Community Capacity and Place of Residence on the Self-Reported Health of Canada's Indigenous Population' interprets quantitative data through indigenous theories. He is Plains Cree and his family comes from Ahtahkakoop Cree Nation.

Vanessa de Oliveira Andreotti is Canada Research Chair in Race, Inequalities and Global Change at the University of British Columbia, Vancouver, Canada. Her research examines political economies of knowledge production, and discusses the ethics of international development and of ideals of globalism and internationalisation in education and in global activism, with an emphasis on representations of and relationships with marginalised communities. Her teaching scholarship engages with the use of social cartographies in curriculum and pedagogy and with the interface between political and existential approaches to questions of justice and conviviality. She is a research fellow at the University of Oulu, Finland, where she was chair of Global Education from 2010 to 2013.

Gert Biesta is Professor of Educational Theory and Policy at the Department of Education, Brunel University London, UK, and Visiting Professor at ArtEZ Institute of the Arts, The Netherlands. His work focuses on the theory and philosophy of education, and the theory and philosophy of educational and social research, with a particular focus on democracy and democratisation. His latest book, *The Beautiful Risk of Education* (2014) won the 2014 Outstanding Book Award of the American Educational Research Association (Division B).

Yueya Ding is an Associate Professor of Anthropology and Education at the National Academy of Education Administration in Beijing, China. She received an MA from the University of Calgary, Canada, and a PhD in Anthropology of Education from Minzu University of China. Her research interests include ethnic minority, multicultural education and migration. She is also a Board Member of the China Council on Anthropology of Education, China Union of Anthropological and Ethnological Sciences.

Sepideh Fotovatian has a PhD in Education from Monash University, Melbourne, Australia.

NOTES ON CONTRIBUTORS

Her research focuses on internationalisation of higher education, English as an international language, international student experiences, globalisation, transition and institutional identity negotiation, mobility and integration. She is a Lecturer at Simon Fraser University, Vancouver, Canada. She has taught different graduate courses including: Seminar in Second Language Teaching, Sociocultural Perspectives on Education and Identity, Second Language Learning and Schooling. Her research has been published in journals such as *Higher Education Research and Development*, *Globalisation, Societies and Education* and *Teaching in Higher Education*.

Shibao Guo is Professor in the Werklund School of Education, University of Calgary, Canada. He specialises in citizenship and immigration, race and ethnic relations, adult and lifelong education, and comparative and international education. His research had been funded by a number of organisations, including the Social Sciences and Humanities Research Council, International Organisation for Migration, and Education International. He is a former president of the Canadian Association for the Study of Adult Education (2009–2011), and currently he serves as president of the Canadian Ethnic Studies Association and co-editor of *Canadian Ethnic Studies*.

Yan Guo is Associate Professor of Language and Literacy in the Werklund School of Education at the University of Calgary, Canada. Her research interests include critical perspectives in teaching English as an Additional Language (TEAL), immigrant parent engagement, intercultural communication, language and identity, and language policy. Her recent publications have appeared in *Canadian Journal of Education*, *Language and Education*, *Intercultural Education*, *Canadian Ethnic Studies* and *Journal of Contemporary Issues in Education*. Her latest books are *Spotlight on China: Changes in education under China's market economy* and *Spotlight on China: Chinese education in the globalized world*.

Yedan Huang received her BA in American Studies and Sociology, and MPhil in Sociology at the University of Hong Kong. She was a visiting scholar at UCLA, Los Angeles, CA, under the sponsorship of Fulbright Scholarship Program by the Bureau of Educational and Cultural Affairs, Department of State of United States in 2009–2010. Her research interests include return Chinese migrants and Buddhist philanthropy.

Khun Eng Kuah-Pearce is Professor and Head of the School of Arts and Social Sciences, Monash University, Malaysian Campus. Her research focus is on Chinese Diaspora-Mainland Connections; and Buddhism, politics and philanthropy. She is the author of two books, editor/co-editor of seven edited books, guest editor/co-editor of four journal issues and numerous journal articles and book chapters. She is working on two books based on research on Buddhist philanthropy, and China's emerging philanthropic landscape.

Srabani Maitra is an Eyes High Post-doctoral fellow in the Werklund School of Education at the University of Calgary, Canada. She specialises in immigration, workplace learning/training, South Asian diaspora, race, racism and transnational service work. Her research has been funded by organisations such as Social Sciences and Humanities Research Council and appeared in journals including *Studies in Continuing Education*, *Canadian Journal for the Study of Adult Education*, *Journal of Workplace Learning* and *Qualitative Inquiry*.

NOTES ON CONTRIBUTORS

Hongxia Shan is an Assistant Professor in the Department of Educational Studies at the University of British Columbia, Vancouver, Canada. She specialises in (im)migrant studies, work and learning, knowledge transfer, and gender, race and class analysis. Her work has appeared in journals such as *International Journal of Lifelong Education*, *Comparative Education*, *Canadian Journal for the Study of Adult Education*, *Journal of Workplace Learning*, *Work, Employment and Society* and *International Journal of Health Promotion*.

Yan Zhang holds a PhD in Teaching English as a Second Language from the University of Calgary, Canada. She has more than fifteen years' experience teaching in language and literacy development in China and Canada. Her research interests include literacy, identity development, poststructuralism, second language acquisition, multilingualism and so on. Her doctoral dissertation focuses on multilingual children and looks specifically at the complexity of their language acquisition and literacy development, balancing poststructural perspectives of literacies and identities as processes of becoming.

Introduction: work, learning and transnational migration

Shibao Guo

University of Calgary, Canada

This book examines the changing nature of work and learning in the age of transnational migration. Fuelled by globalisation, the integration of the world economy and advanced transportation technologies has greatly enhanced the mobility of people across national boundaries. In 2015, the number of international migrants worldwide reached 244 million from 175 million in 2000 and 154 million in 1990 (United Nations 2015). As globalisation intensifies, unidirectional 'migration to' is now being replaced by 'asynchronous, transversal, oscillating flows that involve visiting, studying, seasonal work, temporary contracts, tourism and sojourning' (Cohen 2008, 123). In this view, migration has shifted from '*inter*-national' to '*trans*-national' and 'multiple, circular and return migrations, rather than a singular great journey from one sedentary space to another, occur across transnational spaces' (Lie 1995, 304). As such, migrants are no longer expected to make a sharp and definitive break from their homelands.

Portes, Guarnizo, and Landolt (1999) propose three criteria for identifying a transnational phenomenon: the process involves a significant proportion of persons in the relevant universe, the activities of interest possess certain stability and resilience over time and the content of these activities is not captured by some pre-existing concept. When analysing transnationalism, individuals and their support networks are regarded as the proper units of analysis. Unlike early transnationalism, which was often limited to the movement of elites, contemporary grass-roots transnational activities have commonly developed in reaction to the negative effects of government policies or in response to the condition of dependent capitalism foisted on weaker countries. In such cases, transnational movement serves to circumvent the permanent subordination of immigrants and their families. As Lie (1995) explains, 'the idea of transnationalism challenges the rigid, territorial nationalism that defines the modern nation-state; the dividing line is replaced by the borderlands of shifting and contested boundaries' (304).

Castles and Miller (2009) identify six trends in contemporary migration. The first is the 'globalisation of migration' – increasing numbers of countries are affected by migratory movements with entrants from a broad spectrum of economic, social and cultural backgrounds. The 'acceleration of migration' shows that the international movement of people is growing in volume in all regions. The third trend, the 'differentiation of migration', indicates that more countries have diversified their intake of immigrants to include a whole range of types. The 'feminisation of migration', the fourth trend identified by Castles and Miller, demonstrates that, particularly since the 1960s, women play a significant role in all regions and in most types of migration. The growing 'politicisation of migration' suggests that domestic politics, bilateral and regional relationships, and national security policies of states are increasingly affected by international migration. The last of these trends is the 'proliferation of migration transition' that occurs when traditional lands of emigration become lands of transit for both migration and immigration. Taken together, these trends highlight the links between migratory flows and economic, political and cultural change in the context of globalisation.

When transnational migrants arrive in a new country, many of them face multi-faceted barriers in transition into work and learning in the host society. In the context of Canada, for example, despite the fact that immigrants bring significant human capital resources to the Canadian labour force, my research has shown that many highly educated immigrant professionals experienced deskilling and devaluation of their prior learning and work experience upon arrival (Guo 2009, 2013a, 2013b). As a consequence, many have suffered unemployment and under-employment, poor economic performance and downward social mobility. Recent immigrants' negative experience in Canada can be attributed to a *triple glass effect*, including *a glass gate, glass door* and *glass ceiling*, which may converge to create multiple structural barriers and affect immigrants' new working lives at different stages of their integration and transition processes (Guo 2013b). While a *glass gate* denies immigrants' entrance to guarded professional communities, a *glass door* blocks immigrants' access to professional employment at high-wage firms. Finally, *the glass ceiling* prevents immigrants from moving into management positions because of their ethnic and cultural differences.

Against this backdrop, it becomes imperative for this book to focus on the changing nature of work and learning in the age of transnational migration. The collection contains eight outstanding contributions by established and emerging scholars in five different countries. Shibao Guo, the book editor, opens the discussion with an analysis of the transition experience of Chinese immigrants in Canada. Under Canada's knowledge-based economy, recent immigrant selection practices have placed more weight on education and skills, favouring economic immigrants over family class immigrants. Among recent arrivals in Canada, many came from China. Through the accounts of the experience of recent Chinese immigrants in Canada, Guo's study reveals that recent arrivals from China were young, well-educated and experienced professionals. Unfortunately, many of them faced multi-faceted barriers in transition into work and learning in Canada, with language and employment as the most frequently cited barriers. Guo's analysis shows that their educational qualifications failed to yield high occupational and economic achievements because their Chinese educational qualifications and prior work experience were not recognized by professional associations or employers in Canada. It seems evident that immigrants' international credentials and experience have been racialised on the basis of ethnic and national originals demonstrating how racial and socio-cultural differences have been used to entrench social inequality in immigrants' transitions. The findings also show the precarious nature of work and learning for recent immigrants, characterised by part-time employment, low wages, job insecurity, high risk of poor health, and limited social benefits and statutory entitlements. Through the process of deskilling and reskilling, learning has become a vehicle to colonising immigrants into dominant norms and values of the host society.

In Chapter 3, Hongxia Shan focuses on how female Chinese immigrant professionals negotiate occupations in Canada in the context of neoliberalism and entrepreneurialism. At the outset of the chapter Shan argues that the ideology of the entrepreneurial self has been mobilised as a model of governance in the era of neoliberalism. Through an analysis of the transition processes of immigrants in reorienting their career trajectories and employment opportunities, the study examines how the neoliberal subjectivity of an entrepreneurial self is produced for immigrant women in Canada. Shan's analysis displays how a credential and certificate regime reproduces and naturalises the existing social order in the labour market. The study challenges the problematic notion of the entrepreneurial self that acts as an ideological device reinforcing gender roles and gendered segmentation through deskilling and subsequent training and reskilling.

In the fourth chapter, Srabani Maitra continues with the examination of immigrants' transition experience, with a focus on Indian immigrant professionals in Canada. Similar to the experience of Chinese immigrant professionals in the previous study, Indian immigrants in Canada also encountered devaluation and denigration of their prior learning and work experience after immigrating to Canada. Many of them had to turn to India-based 'body shopping' agencies for job placement in the global labour market. The author conducted semi-structured interviews with 15 Indian immigrant IT workers in Canada who used such services and five global recruiters in India. Maitra's analysis reveals how global body shops are turning immigrant professionals into a globally circulating and precarious workforce subject to multiple insecurities of severe regulations and flexible work patterns of the recruitment agencies. The findings also demonstrate how Indian immigrant IT professionals in Canada are being increasingly drawn to these body shops to find jobs in their own areas of expertise because of racialised and gendered labour market barriers and the failure of Canadian Government in providing necessary support to ameliorate the challenging transitions of recent immigrants.

With the next chapter Yan Zhang and Yan Guo explore how immigrant children negotiate identities in transnational contexts in Canada. More specifically, the study examines how a group of multilingual students in a Mandarin-English bilingual programme become transcultural and transnational in their multiple literacy practices and identity negotiation. Informed by post-structural perspectives, Zhang and Guo treat identity formation as processes of becoming; identity is conceived of as provisional and relational. In applying this framework, the authors analyse how transnational and transcultural identities are formed through the use of language and other symbolic systems. To this end, Zhang and Guo collected multiple forms of data, including observations, interviews and documents and performed rhizoanalysis. Following Deleuze and Guattari (1987), the authors adopted rhizome as an inductive approach to analyse how immigrant students articulated their multi-dimensional and multidirectional growth and identity. The results show that multilingual children negotiate their multiple identifications in transnational and translingual spaces by incorporating different aspects of varying cultures through a process of transculturation. The findings challenge the dominant discourse of fixed and essentialised identities with profound implications for developing a pedagogy of flow in fostering multiple ways of being, learning and belonging.

In Chapter 6, Sepideh Fotovatian takes up some of Zhang and Guo's themes of identity formation and negotiation through the use of language. She provides us with an account of the processes of non-native English teachers' engagement in social interactions, network building and taking agentive actions in and through daily interactions to negotiate professional and institutional identities in Australia. Fotovatian defines institutional identity as identities legitimised through membership in an institution and dynamically constructed, negotiated and renegotiated in and through interactions with other institutional members and claim social and professional representations associated with legitimate membership in the institution. The author argues that everyday interactions are important avenues for negotiations of language, identity and power. As in Canada, minority groups in Australia often feel reprimanded and devalued for the language, social and cultural capitals that they bring to their new contexts. In documenting the negotiations of institutional identities through everyday engagement in institutional interactions, Fotovatian contests the monolingual and monocultural ideologies that promote linguicism and accenticism resulting in marginalising non-native English speakers and minority groups in Australia. She calls on members of host institutions to take action to recognise newcomers as legitimate members of the institution.

In Chapter 7, Vanessa de Oliveira Andreotti, Gert Biesta and Cash Ahenakew focus on conceptual and theoretical issues as they examine education for global mindedness in the context of Finland. Foregrounded by a discussion of the wider sociopolitical history of Finland, the authors first analyse the tensions facing the country as an example of a small modern state at the interface of nationalist and global orientations and the growing racism and xenophobia as a result of the intensified hostility towards difference. As the last Nordic country to open its borders to immigration, Finland recently developed national strategies to promote international mindedness through education. These are limited by a binary, one-dimensional representation of global mindedness; a linear understanding of developmental processes focusing on individual capacities towards situated contextual modes of engagement and narrow cognitive approaches of knowledge acquisition about cultural otherness and difference. Drawing on post-structuralist, post-colonial and (neo) pragmatist perspectives of ethics, otherness and transnational engagements, the authors develop an alternative framework that conceives of global mindedness as a multi-dimensional construct. They argue that the issue is neither about cognition and understanding nor about empathy and relationships, but ultimately is about modes of existence and exposure. This framework challenges humanist and universalist approaches to the formation of global mindedness and helps host populations to engage ethically and productively with difference within and outside of their national borders.

The last two chapters examine transnational migration in terms of the multiple, circular and return migrations that Cohen (2008) and Lie (1995) spoke of earlier. In Chapter 8, Yueya Ding investigates transnational migration through the experience of return Chinese immigrants from Canada in Beijing, China. At the outset of the chapter, Ding highlights the important role that China has played in transnational migration as an important source and host country. She points out that as one of the top source countries, China has sent a large number of highly skilled migrants to different parts of the world, particularly to developed countries. China's recent economic boom, however, is attracting some of them back. Guided by transnationalism as a theoretical framework, Ding conducted life history research with return Chinese immigrants from Canada. Through accounts of their stories and experiences, different integration and reintegration strategies are explored, including self-adjustment, lifelong learning and flexible citizenship. Informed by Lefebvre's theory of space and Faist's transnational social space, a theory of individual space is constructed. Ding's analysis displays that transnational migration is a process of constant construction and reconstruction of migrants' expected individual space in various societies involving a negotiation between internal and external worlds about the relationships among the self, others and external society.

In the final chapter of the collection, Yedan Huang and Khun Eng Kuah-Pearce from the University of Hong Kong continue the discussion of transnational migration with a focus on the return migration to Shanghai of Chinese expatriates from Australia, Canada, France, Germany, Singapore and the USA. Rapid economic development and preferential social policies have lured many 'talent circulators' to Shanghai, people who circulate freely between the diasporic Chinese community and their homeland. Huang and

Kuah-Pearce group recent returnees into two categories: the 'golden collars', who are considered part of an economic and social elite possessing desirable technological, management and financial skills, and the 'golden plated', who are less successful. Huang and Kuah-Pearce analyse how talent circulators readapt and reestablish their career and social life in Shanghai through the deployment of their social capital and *guanxi* networks. Their analysis demonstrates that many talent circulators adopt a pragmatic approach towards flexible citizenship and multiple territorialities where they view Shanghai as one stop on their transnational migration journey.

Taken as a whole, this book examines the non-linear transition of work and learning for transnational migrants; the multiple barriers facing migrants in the process of transition; tensions between mobility, knowledge and recognition; issues of language, transition and transnational identity and how sociocultural differences have been used to entrench social inequality in migrants' transition. The foregoing contributions demonstrate that transnational migration has brought significant changes to the demographics and sociocultural fabric of receiving societies with profound implications for immigrant's work and learning. The rich national contexts and global perspectives provided across all nine chapters enrich our understanding about the changing relationship between work, learning, knowledge, mobility, citizenship and identity in the context of globalisation and transnational migration. As the book editor, I wish to thank all of the authors for their outstanding contributions.

References

Castles, S., and M. Miller. 2009. *The Age of Migration: International Population Movements in the Modern World*. New York: The Guildford Press.
Cohen, R. 2008. *Global Diaspora: An Introduction*. 2nd ed. London: Routledge.
Deleuze, G., and F. Guattari. 1987. *A Thousand Plateaus: Capitalism and Schizophrenia*. London: Athlone Press.
Guo, S. 2009. "Difference, Deficiency, and Devaluation: Tracing the Roots of Non/recognition of Foreign Credentials for Immigrant Professionals in Canada." *Canadian Journal for the Study of Adult Education* 22 (1): 37–52.
Guo, S. 2013a. "The Changing Face of Work and Learning in the Context of Immigration: The Canadian Experience." *Journal of Education and Work* 26 (2): 162–186. doi:10.1080/13639080.2011.630657.
Guo, S. 2013b. "Economic Integration of Recent Chinese Immigrants in Canada's Second-tier Cities: The Triple Glass Effect and Immigrants' Downward Social Mobility." *Canadian Ethnic Studies* 45 (3): 95–115. doi:10.1353/ces.2013.0047.
Lie, J. 1995. "From International Migration to Transnational Diaspora." *Contemporary Sociology* 24 (4): 303–306. doi:10.2307/2077625.
Portes, A., E. I. Guarnizo, and P. Landolt. 1999. "The Study of Transnationalism: Pitfalls and Promise of an Emergent Research Field." *Ethnic and Racial Studies* 22 (2): 217–237. doi:10.1080/014198799329468.
United Nations. 2015. *Population Facts, No. 2015/4*. New York: United Nations.

The changing face of work and learning in the context of immigration: the Canadian experience

Shibao Guo

Workplace & Adult Learning, Faculty of Education, University of Calgary, Calgary, Canada

> Through the accounts of the experience of recent Chinese immigrants in Canada, this study examines the changing nature of work and learning in the context of immigration. Its findings reveal the precarious nature of work and learning for immigrant professionals, characterised by part time, low wages, job insecurity, high risks of ill health and limited social benefits and statutory entitlements. The study also shows that immigrants' foreign credentials and knowledge have been racialised on the basis of ethnic and national origins. As a consequence, they suffered unemployment and underemployment, poor economic performance and downward social mobility. The racialised experience of Chinese immigrants demonstrates how racial and socio-cultural differences have been used to entrench social inequality in immigrants' transitions. Through the process of deskilling and re-skilling, learning has become a vehicle to colonising immigrants into the dominant norms and values of the host society. The study urges government organisations, professional associations, educational institutions and prior learning assessment agencies to adopt an inclusive framework which fully embraces all human knowledge and experience, no matter which ethnic and cultural backgrounds they emerge from.

Introduction

A number of Canadian scholars highlight the changing nature of work and learning under Canada's knowledge-based economy (Fenwick 2006; Livingstone, Mirchandani, and Sawchuk 2008; Rubenson and Walker 2006). Driven by forces of global capitalism, much work has become temporary, low-pay and precarious, and learning has been reduced to an instrument used to help Canada to increase its competitiveness and productivity in a global economy. What particularly concerns critical Canadian scholars is the ways in which rhetoric about skilled labour shortages, and a narrowly focused skills agenda obscure these darker consequences of the 'new economy'. Introduced by the Canadian government in the early 1990s, the innovation strategy promoted up-skilling and re-skilling for the development of a competitive and flexible workforce (Rubenson and Walker 2006). Following this, Canada unleashed its essential skills initiative in the mid-1990s to increase citizens' employability and productivity, despite critiques that the skills-based approach is an individualistic, decontextualised, fragmented and gendered approach to human knowledge and learning processes (Fenwick 2006). Further, this dominant discourse typically equates work with paid employment, and learning with formal education. A more expansive view of work and learning challenges these conventional perspectives, maintaining that work can be both paid and unpaid and that learning occurs in both formal and informal situations (Livingstone, Mirchandani, and Sawchuk 2008).

Largely missing from this animated discussion has been considerations of the impact of these evolving conditions of work and learning on Canada's immigrants. Immigration has played an important role in transforming Canada into an ethno culturally diverse and economically prosperous nation. Between 2001 and 2006 alone, 1.1 million new immigrants moved to Canada, 57% of whom were in the prime working age group of 25–54 (Statistics Canada 2007). However, little is known about their new life in Canada. Drawing on the experience of recent Chinese immigrants in Calgary, Canada, this study aims to explore the changing face of work and learning in the contexts of immigration and cultural diversity. It begins with a review of changing immigration policies in Canada, followed by an examination of research on immigrants' transitions from the perspectives of the politics of difference. The research design and findings are presented. The study concludes with policy recommendations. It urges government organisations, professional associations, educational institutions and prior learning assessment agencies to adopt an inclusive framework which allows us to work towards recognitive justice that balances freedom of migration with recognition and full membership in Canada.

Context of Canada's immigration policy

The driving forces behind immigration are social, political, economic and demographic. In the nineteenth century, massive immigration was used as a strategy to develop Western Canada, and served the economic and demographic interests of the country. Immigration has also functioned as a means of cultural domination and social control. In deciding which immigrant groups are most desirable and admissible, the state sets parameters for the social, cultural and symbolic boundaries of the nation, as manifested in historically racist Canadian immigration policies. From the Confederation of Canada in 1867 until the 1960s, the selection of immigrants was based on their racial background. British and Western Europeans were the most 'desirable' citizens, Asians and Africans the 'unassimilable' and, therefore, 'undesirable'. After the Second World War, Canadian immigration policy continued to be 'highly restrictive', despite external and internal pressures for an open-door policy (Knowles 1997).

In the mid-1960s, Canada was experiencing 'the greatest postwar boom' (Whitaker 1991, 18). Skilled labour was required to help Canada build its rapidly expanding economy. Europe, Canada's traditional source of immigrants, could not meet this need as it was undergoing its own economic recovery. The Canadian government thus turned its recruitment efforts to such traditionally restricted areas as Asia. In 1967 a 'point system' was introduced by the Liberal government, which based the selection of immigrants on their 'education, skills and resources' rather than racial and religious backgrounds (Whitaker 1991, 19). According to Whitaker (19), this new system represented 'an historic watershed', and 'establish[ed] at the level of formal principle that Canadian immigration policy is "colour blind"'. However, the new selection method was criticised for being 'in favour of some racial groups and against others' (Matas 1996, 100). Despite these criticisms, the 'point system' was successful in shifting the pattern of immigration to Canada away from Europe, and towards Asia and other Third World regions. By the mid-1970s, Canada accepted more immigrants from the Third World than from the developed world. The largest number of these later immigrants arrived from Asia, followed by the Caribbean, Latin America and Africa.

In general, immigrants come to Canada under one of three major categories: economic class, family class and refugees. The economic class is comprised of skilled workers and business immigrants. Skilled workers are admitted under a point system using prescribed selection criteria based on education, occupation, language skills and work experience. Canada has three classes of business immigrants: *investors*, *entrepreneurs* and *self-employed persons*, each with separate eligibility criteria. Family class immigration reunites close family members of an adult resident or citizen of the hosting country, such as children, parents and spouse or common-law partner. Refugee protection is usually offered to those who fear returning to their country of nationality or habitual residence because of war, fear of persecution, torture or cruel and unusual treatment or punishment.

Since the mid-1990s, given Canada's pursuit of a knowledge-based economy, immigrant selection practices have placed more weight on education and skills, favouring economic immigrants over family class immigrants and refugees. As Li (2003) notes, this new shift was based on the assumption that economic immigrants bring more human capital than family class immigrants and refugees, and are therefore more valuable and desirable. According to Li (2003), economic-class immigrants made up more than half of all immigrants admitted throughout the late 1990s. Among them there were a considerable number of highly educated professionals, particularly scientists and engineers. In the year 2000, of the total 227,209 immigrants and refugees admitted, 23% (52,000 individuals) were admitted as skilled workers (Couton 2002). It is imperative to find out how they are doing in Canada.

Research on immigration and integration

This study employs the politics of difference as its theoretical framework in the analysis. First, at the centre of this analysis are immigrants themselves. It is important to review what this term means. According to Li (2003), the notion of 'immigrant' is socially constructed. He argues that it is often associated with people of non-white origin. Descendants of mostly white early European settlers, now long-established Canadians, do not think of themselves as immigrants. Li (2003) thus argues that the term 'immigrant' has, in its present context become a codified word for people of colour, who come from a different racial and cultural background, who do not speak fluent English, and who work in lower position jobs. Li maintains that the social construction of 'immigrant' uses skin colour as the basis for social marking. Immigrants' real and alleged differences are claimed to be incompatible with the cultural and social fabric of 'traditional' Canada, and these individuals are therefore deemed undesirable. Immigrants are also often blamed for creating urban social problems and racial and cultural tensions in the receiving society (Li 2003). The social construction of 'immigrant' places uneven expectations on immigrants to conform over time to the norms, values and traditions of the receiving society.

Current immigration policies in Canada's new economy have primarily focused on Canada's labour force shortages and on the interests of the state. Policies largely ignore barriers faced by immigrants as they try to transition to life in Canada. Research shows that immigrants moving to a new country are likely to encounter barriers in the process of adapting to a new society. They need assistance with language, employment, housing, daycare, education, health, counselling, legal and social services. A number of studies have identified one such barrier as lack of access to mainstream social services (Leung 2000; Nguyen 1991; Reitz 1995; Stewart et al. 2008). Other studies identify employment barriers, including the devaluation and denigration of immigrants' foreign credentials and prior work experience, as new challenges facing immigrants. Despite Canada's expressed preference for highly skilled immigrants, and despite the fact that immigrant professionals bring significant human capital resources to the Canadian labour force, a number of studies have shown that many highly educated immigrant professionals experience deskilling and devaluation of their prior learning and work experience after immigrating to Canada (Basran and Zong 1998; Henry et al. 2006; Krahn et al. 2000; Mojab 1999; Ng 1999). As Henry et al. (2006) note, there is little recognition in Canada of the professional qualifications, credentials and experiences of immigrants. Some immigrants experience major shifts from prior occupations in sciences, engineering, business and management to occupations in sales, services and manufacturing. As a result, they suffer wage losses and downward social mobility. Highly educated refugees encounter similar barriers (Krahn et al. 2000). The situation for immigrant women is even worse. Many argue that in the labour force, the category of 'immigrant women' has served to commodify these women in the eyes of employers (Mojab 1999; Ng 1999). Their already lower class positions are reinforced when they provide cheap, docile labour to the state under exploitive conditions, often permeated with racism and sexism (Mojab 1999; Ng 1999). As a result, both immigrants themselves and Canadian society as a whole suffer severe economic impacts (Li 2001; Reitz 2001).

Why do such inequities occur in a democratic society like Canada where democratic principles are upheld and where immigrants are 'welcome'? Non-recognition of foreign credentials and prior work experience can be attributed to a deficit model of difference which led us to believe that differences are deficiency, that the knowledge of immigrant professionals, particularly for those from the Third World countries, is incompatible and inferior, and hence invalid (Guo 2009). One of the articulations of Canadian society lies in its commitment to cultural pluralism; however, a number of commentators argue that Canada endorses pluralism only in superficial ways (Cummins 2003; Dei 1996; Fleras and Elliott 2002; Ghosh and Abdi 2004). In reality, Canada tends to prefer 'pretend pluralism', which means that we 'tolerate rather than embrace differences' (Fleras and Elliott 2002, 2). In practice, differences have been exoticised and trivialised. While minor differences may be gently affirmed in depoliticised and decontextualised forms such as food, dance and festivities, substantive differences that challenge hegemony and resist being co-opted are usually perceived by many Canadians as deficient, deviant, pathological or otherwise divisive (Guo 2009). Clearly, one of the hurdles that prevent us from fully recognising immigrants' educational qualifications and professional experiences is the politics of difference. As to the knowledge possessed by immigrants, it is deemed inferior because their real and alleged differences are claimed to be incompatible with the cultural and social fabric of the 'traditional' Canada. In fact, the hierarchy of knowledge and power is rooted in Canada's ethnocentric past, where immigrants from Europe and the USA were viewed the most desirable, and those from the Third World countries as undesirable. Although Canada's commitment to the point system as immigration policy does not permit the recruitment of immigrants on the basis of racial and national origins, it is insufficient to move Canadian society beyond diffuse racial and national preferences. As Dei (1996) notes, the power relations are embedded in social relations of difference. In fact, the negative attitudes and behaviours towards immigrants coexist with Canada's commitments to democratic principles such as justice, equality and fairness. The coexistence of these two conflicting ideologies can be referred to as 'democratic racism'

(Henry et al. 2006). Democratic racism prevents the government from fully embracing differences or making any changes in the existing social, economic and political order, and from supporting policies and practices that might ameliorate the low status of immigrants because these policies are perceived to be in conflict with and a threat to liberal democracy.

Research methods

Two data gathering strategies were employed in this study: questionnaires and personal interviews. Questionnaires provided a useful starting point by allowing me to maximise the number of responses within a reasonably short time period. The questionnaires were divided into four sections: (i) basic demographic information; (ii) motivation for immigrating to Canada; (iii) the integration experience of Chinese immigrants including their level of satisfaction with Canada and its employment situation and (iv) concluding remarks. The questionnaire was made available in both English and Chinese. Records from Canada's Landed Immigrant Data System guided a purposeful selection of economically active, Chinese-born Canadian immigrants, aged 20–65. Participants were recruited through immigrant service organisations and churches where Chinese immigrants were more likely to congregate, including the Calgary Chinese Community Service Association, Calgary Centre for Newcomers, Calgary Catholic Immigrant Society and Immigrant Services Calgary. A total of 131 completed questionnaires were received. The survey, while small, is representative of the People's Republic of China (PRC) Chinese immigrant population in Calgary (Guo and DeVoretz 2006a).

Questionnaires do not, however, allow for in-depth accounts of lived experiences of immigrants. To further probe some of the responses received in the questionnaires, I conducted personal interviews with a number of the questionnaire respondents. The interviews allowed me to talk to immigrants in detail about the barriers they faced in their transition to life in Canada. Eight questionnaire respondents were interviewed. In selecting participants for this phase of the research, I tried to strike a balance among people of different ages, genders, educational backgrounds, lengths of stay, employment and citizenship status. Each interview lasted about 1 h. Participants were selected from those who had, in the questionnaire, expressed interest being interviewed. Because not everyone might have felt comfortable to be interviewed in English, participants were offered a choice between English and Chinese. In the end, only one person chose to be interviewed in Chinese, but some interviewees also used Chinese where they needed it most.

All interviews were taped and transcribed verbatim for analysis, which was an ongoing process. For example, questionnaires were analysed as they were collected, and interviews were built on what was learned from the survey results. Further, each interview was conducted after the previous one was transcribed, and a preliminary analysis was completed. This helped me to adjust my interview strategies and enhance the quality of each, subsequent interview. All data were collected between October 2005 and June 2007. The study focused on the experience of immigrants, hence the perspectives of employers were not represented here. Future research needs to be conducted to explore what employers could do to help immigrants with their transition process.

Report of findings

Profile of recent immigrants: young, well-educated and experienced professionals

Among all questionnaire responses received, 56% were female and 44% male. Most were married. The age of the participants ranged from 20 to 60, with the majority (77%) aged between 31 and 42 and a mean age of 34. The sample reflects the younger cohorts, which are the focus of Canadian immigrant recruitment. The participants came from all over China, with the three largest groups hailing from Beijing, Tianjin and Shanghai. The majority came to Canada as skilled workers (79%) and only a small portion (16%) came under family reunion, which again reflects recent trends in Canada's immigrant selection practices with their emphasis on economic immigrants (Li 2003). Participants were predominantly recent arrivals to Canada, having resided in Calgary for less than five years (70%). Only 22% had been in Canada 5–10 years, and 8% had been in Canada more than 10 years. The length of stay was reflected in their participants' citizenship status – only 29% were Canadian citizens. The rest were permanent residents.

In terms of their educational background, the majority (79%) arrived in Canada with a university degree or higher. Fifty-three per cent held bachelor degrees, 19% had masters degrees and 7% held doctorates (see Figure 1). The sample is thus representative of the broader demographic of recent Chinese immigrants to Canada, particularly those from PRC since the

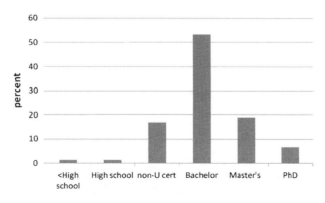

Figure 1. Highest level of education.

mid-1990s (Guo and DeVoretz 2006a; Lindsay 2007). In comparison to the 40% of Canadian adults aged 25–64 who held college or university qualifications in 2000 (Livingstone 2008), clearly, this was a highly educated group. Most received their highest education from institutions in China (89%) and a smaller portion from Canada (9%). Regarding their level of English language proficiency, more than half (52%) of the surveyed stated that they had intermediate or advanced English language skills.

To help better understand the survey data, three cases from the personal interviews are presented here to illuminate the demographic information. Of the eight people interviewed for this study, Ying Liu had lived in Calgary the longest. She moved to Calgary in 1991 to join her husband, who was studying at the University of Calgary for his master's degree in petroleum engineering. They became landed immigrants in 1993. She was in her early 40s, living with her husband and two children. She held a master's degree in economics. In the 15 year since she had moved to Calgary, Ying had held jobs as a retail salesperson, waitress and bank teller before reaching her current position as financial sales representative at one of the largest banks in Canada.

Xuehan Jiang moved to Calgary directly as new immigrant in 2001, along with his wife. He received a bachelor's degree in petroleum engineering from a prestigious university in China. Prior to moving to Calgary, he had worked for Sinopec (China Petroleum and Chemical Corporation) for nine years as a Process Engineer. He is now working for an engineering company in Calgary as a 'Process Specialist', a codified word for non-recognised engineers working in engineering positions. Xuehan was in his mid-30s when he came to Canada, and was the ideal Canadian immigrant recruit – young, well-educated and experienced. He has one daughter who was born in Calgary in 2004. He chose Calgary because of its booming oil industry.

Among all interviewees, Tianhai Wang was the most recent immigrant, having resided in Calgary for almost a year at the time of his interview. His immigration application took five years, and cost him US$5000. Believing there would be a brighter future in Canada, he moved to Calgary with his wife and a three-year-old daughter. He had many years of experience working as an equipment maintenance engineer in China. Now, he works as a restaurant dishwasher in the evenings, and attends English classes during the day. He and his wife take turns caring for their daughter.

Motivations for moving to Canada

People moved to Canada for a number of reasons. Unlike earlier waves of immigrants who moved primarily for economic reasons (Li 1998; Tan and Roy 1985), the most frequently cited motivations among these recent arrivals were Canada's natural environment (62%) and children's education

(52%), followed by seeking new opportunities (27%) and living in Canadian culture (23%). Only a small proportion stated obtaining Canadian citizenship or permanent residency (18%) as a major motivation for immigrating to Canada. This finding is significant because it illustrates that there is a breadth and complexity of motivations to migrate to Canada well beyond traditionally noted economic motivations.

In the personal interviews, I further explored these motivations with the participants. Meiyu Wang, who moved to Calgary in 2004 as an accountant, commented:

> At first, I think here is very good for my daughter, for her future. In China, competition is too heated. Moreover, environment in China, not only the natural environment but also the social and political environment, is not good. People feel pressure living in China.

Another participant, Bing Lin who moved to Calgary from the UK, explained why he chose Canada:

> Basically my experience told me that Canada is a country in a lot of aspects a lot better than Birmingham in terms of the economics, in terms of the society, in terms of diversity of culture, in terms of the environment. In all those aspects, Canada is a lot better than European countries.

For Xuehan Jiang, immigrating to Canada was his wife's idea and he just followed. He stated:

> I didn't want to come. It's my wife. My wife, you know, she got this information and asked me to come to Calgary. I had a good luck in China. I was an engineer in China. I had a self-business also. So I didn't want to come. But my wife wanted to come here.

It is evident that for Xuehan the household is the key locus of decision-making in determining migration (Van Hear 1998).

When asked if they had achieved their main goals for immigrating to Canada, only 40% indicated that they had. Those who said they had not achieved their goals were less optimistic about the possibility of achieving their goals in the future (33%). The major factors that had prevented them from achieving their goals were: language difficulties (82%), lack of Canadian work experience (69%), non-recognition of Chinese work experience (45%), non-recognition of Chinese qualifications (40%) and lack of social network (39%) (see Figure 2). In the personal interviews, several respondents talked about language as a major obstacle. Yaohua Wu stated:

> One of the important things is our language skill. You know in the engineer position, not only you just working, working, working, use your hand, use

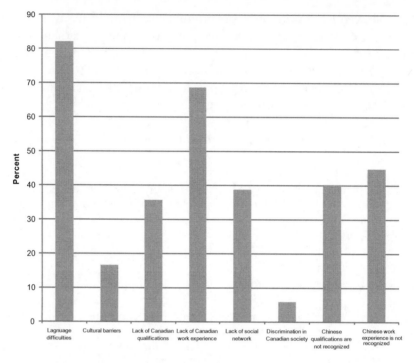

Figure 2. Obstacles for achieving main goals.

your head to do something, you have to communicate with others. You don't have enough communicate skills.

The language issue is puzzling. As reported earlier, more than half (52%) of the respondents indicated that they arrived with intermediate or advanced English skills. It is not clear if their original assessment of their own skills was too high, or if some elements of language (such as accent) are not being accepted by the host society. For others, the problem clearly lies in the devaluation of their international experiences and qualifications. Bing Lin highlighted two major issues facing immigrant professionals:

> One, a lot of people think the recognition of foreign education is still not as fair as local degree. Secondly, a lot of experience that you have had in, back to your country, in China or whatever, is not recognised fully as the engineering experience in Canada.

Several immigrant interviewees noted that the process of foreign credentials recognition was a lengthy, costly, mysterious and frustrating process. In his interview Xuehan Jiang told me that he applied for Association of Professional Engineers, Geologists and Geophysicists of Alberta (APEGGA) membership in 2006, and passed the mandatory ethics and law exam in February 2006. In June 2006, he got the evaluation result from APEGGA, which required him to take additional eight exams from APEGGA, or eight courses from university. He pointed out that the evaluation was not fair at all because he had already taken most of these courses in his undergraduate programme in China.

Another obstacle facing participants was the need for Canadian work experience. According to APEGGA membership regulations, those who have gone through a Canadian university education in engineering are qualified for membership after fulfilling a four-year work experience requirement. Internationally educated engineers, however, have to have at least 10 years of international experience, plus one year of Canadian experience. Even for Bing Lin, the only interviewee who has gone through the APEGGA membership application successfully, the evaluation of international qualifications and experiences remained a mysterious process. He stated:

> In terms of how they look at your particular experience, we certainly don't know how they evaluate. Because sometimes you will see my friends who have very very good experience, graduated from very very well-known university of China, however, they were asked to take technical exams, even though they have more than 10 years experience. So it's difficult to say how they evaluate.

Ironically, despite the fact that they are not recognised as engineers, many of them in fact perform engineers' duties. Xuehan Jiang was one of them who worked as a Process Specialist rather than a Process Engineer. The differences between a specialist and an engineer, according to Xuehan, are that engineers can stamp, date and sign on documents, whereas specialists cannot. Accordingly, engineers have legal responsibilities, whereas specialists do not. Of course, engineers are better paid than specialists, although the income gap can be small. Bing Lin also talked about the significance of being recognised as an APEGGA member. He stated:

> The membership, in some degree, is a milestone for a lot of practicing engineers. Because with a membership, certainly you are allowed or you are qualified to stamp all those drawings, all your designs. Without that even the work is done by yourself, you still have to ask someone to do the stamping, which in some degree, it's not recognising your work.

From talking to the participants, I learned that 'specialists' and 'consultants' were often used as codified words for internationally educated engineers who do engineer's work, but not paid or recognised as such.

Multiple barriers facing immigrant's transition

Participants were also asked to describe barriers they faced in their transition to life in Canada. Many of the responses in this section overlapped the obstacles participants described in relation to their goal attainments.

Respondents were asked about their employment experiences, their social life and their level of satisfaction with life in Canada. When asked if they had encountered any major difficulties since arriving in Canada, a majority indicated they had. Difficulties cited included language barriers (83%), employment (45%), cultural adjustment (42%), lack of social network (40%) and being a foreigner (19%). The findings correspond with the previous question regarding the obstacles which prevented immigrants from achieving their main goals. The results also support findings from a number of other studies concerning the challenges faced by immigrant professionals in accessing the Canadian job market (Basran and Zong 1998; Henry et al. 2006; Mojab 1999; Ng 1999).

While some of the questionnaire participants experienced only one major difficulty (23%), many encountered multiple barriers. In the interviews, the participants discussed some of these barriers in greater detail. Several accounts illustrate that barriers extend well beyond those directly related to the labour market. For some, a major challenge was navigating a new system that was very different from their home culture. Xuehan Jiang commented:

> When we arrived here in Calgary, I remembered I lived in a motel for one week. I didn't know renting apartment that you can only move in early of the month, not later of the month. So we had to live in the motel for one week and cost about 600 dollars. It's big money.

Accessing information was another difficulty identified by several participants. This is how Ying Liu described it:

> I think the major problem lay in people who try to find an active professional job. They don't have much information or right channel to find information. Because when they first come, your social circle is always limited. It is what your friends or whatever they know. Information, for me, is the major barrier.

For Hong Zhu, lack of confidence prevented her from pursing her professional career. She stated:

> In my opinion, I always think my English is not good enough. So I don't have enough self-confidence to find this kind of [professional] job ... The most important thing I think is to help us build the self-confidence.

Despite the multiple barriers reported, surprisingly a large portion of the survey respondents (64%) felt Canada was 'better' or 'much better' than expected. In the personal interviews, people were invited to identify three aspects of life in Canada that they were satisfied with. Bing Lin had this to say:

> First thing, I think, is freedom, freedom in speech, freedom almost in everything, and you feel you are free without any pressure from society, or from

other people, people's view or whatever. That gives you the room to perform best, which I might not be able to perform in China ... Second one, I guess, is equality. Regardless of the wealth or poor, usually, you will be treated equally in Canada, which will not happen in a lot of countries, even in Singapore. That makes you feel very comfortable about that. Third ... is the environment ... At least we have clean air, clean water, and all those kind of things. And we are not afraid about pollutions and the government is doing whatever they can to improve the environment in Canada.

One area of disappointment for these Chinese Canadians was their lack of social life. Several immigrants reported that they lived in isolation. Ying Liu, having lived in Calgary for 15 years, said she has made many friends, but she also pointed out: 'I have to say that my circle of friends are still Chinese, majority. I don't have many Caucasian friends'. When I probed her about what, given that she did not have language barriers, prevented her from making non-Chinese friends, she replied:

I think in terms of friendship, you have to have that friend who is really willing to know you. We have one couple here we are really close to. They are Caucasians. Actually, she was born in Hong Kong, but her husband was Caucasian. They were really in this kind of relationship that would like to know you and make relationship growing.

Participants' stories suggest that recent Chinese immigrants can experience multiple barriers in the process of transition to Canadian life, including language difficulty, lack of information, cultural adjustment and lack of a social network (see also Guo and DeVoretz 2006b).

Immigrant's work and learning

Employment was by far the most serious barrier for most immigrants. When asked to compare their employment situations in Canada with previous employment in China, only 28% indicated improvement (see Figure 3).

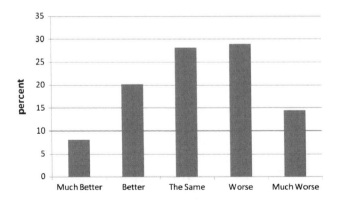

Figure 3. Employment situation in Canada.

I conducted a comparative analysis to further examine the changes in employment between pre- and post-arrival in Calgary. The findings reveal that prior to moving to Canada, more than half (52%) held jobs in natural and applied sciences, forming the largest occupational group among the surveyed. Next were professionals in social sciences and education (18%), followed by those in finance, business and administration (10%) and managerial positions (8%). For many, after arriving in Calgary, employment situations took a marked downturn. The groups experiencing the most significant negative changes were scientists and social scientists, and teachers and professors, with dramatic declines of 16 and 12%, respectively. Given increased participation in other occupations, it seems clear that many of them might have gone to construction, trades and labour work (7%), or some simply did not have a job (17%) (see Table 1).

The most worrisome group was the unemployed, which, in this study, reached a dramatic 17%. The change of employment directly affected participants' annual household income. More than one-third (38%) reported a poverty level income of less than $20,000. This poverty rate is significantly higher than the 16% low-income cut-off rate for the overall Canadian population, and 26% for the Chinese population in Canada (Lindsay 2007). The annual immigrant earnings deficit caused by skill underutilisation is assessed at $2.4 billion nationally (Reitz 2001). Further, these figures were drawn as the unemployment rate reached its lowest in 33 years, both nationally and in the province of Alberta. We need to ask: Who benefited from the economic boom in Canada? What is the situation like under the current economic conditions, which are far more difficult than those five years ago?

Table 1. Change of occupation before and after immigration.

Occupational categories	Occupation before immigration Frequency	Occupation before immigration Valid percentage	Occupation after immigration Frequency	Occupation after immigration Valid percentage
Occupation in natural and applied sciences	65	52	39	35.8
Professional occupation in social science, education and government services	22	17.6	6	5.5
Professional occupation in finance, business and administration	14	10.2	8	7.4
Middle and other management	10	8	0	0
Students	3	2.4	7	6.4
Construction, trades and labourers	0	0	8	7.3
Unemployed	0	0	19	17.4
Total	114	83	87	79.2

The pre- and post-immigration occupational changes and poor economic performance confirm the findings of a number of studies, including the government-sponsored Longitudinal Survey of Immigrants to Canada (Statistics Canada 2003), which reveal that 60% of new immigrants did not work in the same occupational field as they had before arriving in Canada. Many immigrant professionals experienced major, downward shifts from prior occupations in natural and applied sciences and management (for men) and business, finance and administration (for women) to occupations in sales and services and processing and manufacturing. Again, lack of Canadian experience and transferability of foreign credentials were reported as the most critical hurdles to employment.

It is important to note, however, not all foreign credentials are devalued in Canada (Li 2008). According to Li, foreign credentials held by majority member immigrants bring a net earning advantage; only those held by visible minority suffer an earnings penalty. Li's study suggests that foreign credentials of immigrants are racialised since the local market rewards credentials differentially depending on the racial background of the immigrants. In her research with immigrant women, Mojab (1999) finds that access to the job market is not determined by education alone, but is constrained by other factors such as gender, national origin, race and ethnicity. She also points out that systemic racism and ethnicism affects immigrants differently whereby immigrant women from advanced countries (e.g. Australia, Britain, New Zealand or the USA) are treated differently from those originating in the Third World countries. The findings of this study are consistent with Li and Mojab's revealing that the knowledge of immigrant professionals, particularly for those from the Third World countries, has been racialised and materialised in Canada on the basis of gender, ethnicity and national origins. The racialised experience of Chinese immigrants also speaks to the notion of immigrant as social construct, which uses skin colour as the basis for social marking (Li 2003).

We also spent a considerable amount of time in the interviews discussing immigrants' employment situations (see Table 2). Once again, the interview responses illuminated findings from the survey data. Like the larger survey population, the interviewees' experiences were marked by underemployment, downward social mobility and psychological trauma. While some were concerned about getting a professional job commensurate with their training and work experience, many others were simply trying to survive in their new environment. For example, when Yaohua Wu first landed in Calgary, there was no 'honeymoon period' for his new life in Canada. The first thing he did was to get a job as a restaurant dishwasher. He explained: 'I got no money so I could survive in Canada. That's the most important thing for new immigrants'. He then worked in an Irish pub as a waiter, and flipped burgers in a Wendy's restaurant for half a year before securing a job as lab technician. Having settled in gradually, he started to look for a

Table 2. Change of occupation before and after immigration for interviewees.

Interviewee	Gender	Age	Education	Length of stay in Calgary	Occupation before immigration	Occupation after immigration
Meiyu Wang	Female	34–36	Bachelor	1 year	Accountant	Food processing factory worker, hotel chamber maid, steel factory worker
Tianhai Wang	Male	37–39	Bachelor	1 year	Equipment maintenance engineer	Restaurant dishwasher, bread factory worker, unemployed
Hui Liao	Male	34–36	Bachelor	2 years	Computer programmer	Restaurant kitchen helper, waiter, computer technician
Hong Zhu	Female	31–33	Bachelor	3 years	Electrical engineer	Food processing factory worker, Subway clerk, Home Depot cashier, insurance salesperson
Yaohua Wu	Male	31–33	Bachelor	4 years	Petroleum engineer	Restaurant dishwasher, waiter, warehouse stocker, lab technician, research engineer
Xuehan Jiang	Male	34–36	Bachelor	5 years	Process engineer	Drafter, process specialist
Bing Lin	Male	34–36	Master	5 years	Process engineer	Drafter, technologist, process engineer
Ying Liu	Female	40–42	Master	15 years	Economist	Retail salesperson, waitress, bank teller, financial planner

professional job. Even with nine years experience working as an engineer in China, he still failed to find his dream job as an engineer in an oil company. He recalled:

> You know, after the lab, my last job, I tried to find a job in oil companies. I wrote about 600 resumes. I sent out 600 resumes. I got about 10 job interviews, but finally I failed. I didn't get anything. Finally, I found this position as a research engineer at University of Calgary.

Another new immigrant, Tianhai Wang, had very similar experiences. He stated:

> I came to Calgary without much money. So I worked in a restaurant as a labour worker for 3 months at first. I was working as a dishwasher. However, the boss could not hire enough workers so I often took working loads for two. Therefore, my working loads were very heavy. I felt very tired.

Several immigrants mentioned that adjusting the dramatic shift from professional jobs to manual work was mentally and physically draining. In commenting on her devaluation from an economist in China to her first two Canadian jobs as a salesperson in a shoe store and as a restaurant waitress, Ying Liu had this to say:

> There is no match whatsoever. But that's the only thing you can have and it pays the bill. Well, I had a long time to adjust myself mentally and psychologically because you internally were thinking you were lowering your status. You could have a professional job back in your country, but here you were low and really low. It was hard.

Obviously, immigrants had to reposition themselves in their career change. As Shan (2009) notes, in the process of career repositioning, immigrants' perceptions and performances of self significantly informed their employment strategies and practices.

In the process of settling in and adjusting to a new culture and a new society, learning for immigrants has become part of the being, living and becoming that Jarvis (2008) describes. As such, it aligns with Livingstone, Mirchandani, and Sawchuk's (2008) argument in challenging the conventional equation of learning with formal education. Indeed, some immigrants do learn in more structured environments such as English classes, but more often they learn informally at home, in their communities, or at work (see Liu 2007; Schugurensky and Slade 2008). For example, Xuehan Jiang described what he did when he first arrived in Calgary:

> The first thing I did is to take the English test. I went to [one of the local immigrant service agencies]. So I went there and talked to the counsellor and

I also got some information about job seeking, living in Calgary. And I also attended a lot of workshops, not only from immigration services department but also from Alberta Human Resources. From there, I think I know how to find a job in Canada, how to write a resume, how to get interview, learn how to say in the interview, and all the stuff. I learned a lot of stuff in the first month.

Another immigrant, Ying Liu, talked about how she learned from working with her clients in the bank as a financial service representative. She stated:

So I remembered the first few lessons I learned was that you don't judge client. They have the right to decide what's right for them. What you decide is what's right for the bank policy and do the right thing. So you get to make money. Other things are along with cultural difference because when you were included as a sales person, you not exclusively deal with Asian market, you still deal with Caucasians, so that's a lot of cultural crush in terms of understanding privacy.

Ying then gave an example to illustrate what she learned about cultural differences in banking. She continued,

When I first come, you know, Chinese, we didn't have much of products in terms of credit cards or cheques, so it was struggle at first. And then in terms of opening a joint account or a single name account, what's the difference between them? It is really a cultural shock for me because my client would tell me 'No, that's my husband's. That's not mine' or 'That's my wife's. I don't want to deal with that'. I had never thought about that. You cannot assume too much based on your background.

For Ying Liu, learning through experience is an important way of learning in the workplace (Fenwick 2003).

In a context where work has become solely a means of survival, the meaning of learning has also departed from its early notion of voluntary participation (Selman et al. 1998). Instead, it has become something that immigrants were forced to do in order to survive and to comply with dominant norms and standards (Crowther 2004). In particular, when newcomers had to work at survival jobs to make ends meet, learning became a balancing act between work, learning and family. For many of them, this was a real struggle. Tianhai Wang explained:

I took LINC [Language Instruction for Newcomers to Canada] class in the morning and worked in the bread factory from the afternoon to night. It was a full-time job and was tiring, too. I came back home from work late at night. I had no time focusing on my English.

For Tianhai, the fatigue of a hard labour job made it difficult to acquire the learning he needed to transition to professional employment. The problem was compounded because he also needed to consider his wife's equally important work and learning needs:

> Such a situation that I studied and worked whereas my wife stayed at home taking care of our child lasted one LINC term. By the end of last LINC term, I started to think about my wife's job. Her English is obviously poor. But she worked as a tailor in China. There are not many tailors here. She was recommended to current working place by her LINC teacher. The boss likes her very much. I switched my roles with hers. We have a three-year old child. I must stay at home taking care of her.

Tianhai and his wife were able to take turns caring for their child, but this was not an option for Hong Zhu. Her husband worked in Fort McMurray, 700 km away from Calgary. As an insurance salesperson, her work required her to be available to meet with clients in the evenings and during weekends, and childcare was an issue. Unable to resolve this problem, she decided to take her three years old child back to China. She explained:

> Because my husband went to Fort McMurray to work after he worked in Calgary. He finished his laboratory period in Calgary, then he had to go to Fort McMurray, so I sent my son back to China. Then I can start my English course. That's not a good choice. But I don't have time to take care of him. So we have no choice.

Revisiting the three categories of learning barriers identified by Cross (1981) – situational, institutional and dispositional – it is clear that many immigrants are highly motivated to learn; it is the structural barriers that hinder their participation.

One of the questions in the survey asked immigrants where they would go for help when they needed it: government organisations, community members, non-government organisations or friends and family. The majority (65%) chose friends and family as their first choice. It is apparent that government organisations have failed to address issues facing newcomers, despite the fact that immigration falls under federal jurisdiction. However, it is important to note that the process of navigating citizenship as newcomers is not a lone journey. In the interviews, several immigrants discussed how they helped each other. Bing Lin, who volunteers regularly at one of the local immigrant service agencies providing newcomers with job search advice, commented:

> We all feel as an immigrant it's difficult to start life in a country ... You have to take care of yourself and you hope someone can help you. But it's not easy. As a Chinese who has been here for a little bit longer, I feel we should help, do something about that, you know, give a little bit more information,

share some of experience, for those new immigrants, and then we can build a better society here.

Another immigrant, Yaohua Wu, noticed the lack of information for newcomers, so he created a website to help immigrants build an online community to help each other. He said:

> Even after one year I came here, I didn't know the work experience programme. Nobody told me. After one year, I knew there was a programme in Calgary for the job searching. So I decided to create the website to let people know ... We have information such as education, work, and some living, and house. I think you can find everything on my website.

What emerged from these conversations was the systematic way in which the agency of individual immigrants is stifled by structural and institutional constraints. On a more positive note, however, the stories shared by these Chinese immigrants highlight the spirit of mutual support and community building among immigrant communities, and the role of immigrants as agents of social change.

Further, despite all the challenges they have faced in transitioning to life in Canada, many newcomers remain hopeful about their future. Meiyu Wang, for example, commented:

> I am very happy here now but I hope I can get a stable life within two years. I am now renting a room of a single house and busy with my study. Everything seems not stable now. I hope I can get a stable job and then get my own house when my financial conditions get better. Maybe at that time, I will feel life stable. To get a stable life is my goal.

This conversation is truly inspirational! Despite all the setbacks, they demonstrated creativity and persistence in setting and achieving goals. It is evident that they were highly motivated to learn. It is imperative to remove structural barriers which hinder their participation in learning and access to the job market.

Discussion and conclusion

This study set out to explore the transitional experiences of recent Chinese immigrants from the PRC, and through which to examine the changing face of work and learning in the context of Canada's immigration and cultural diversity. The findings reveal that since the mid-1990s, many highly skilled Chinese immigrants arrived in Canada because Canada's knowledge-based economy favoured economic immigrants over family class immigrants and refugees. The study demonstrates that recent Chinese arrivals were young, well-educated and experienced professionals. Some of them held master's and doctoral degrees. Unfortunately, their educational qualifications failed to yield high occupational and economic achievements. Many of them faced multifaceted barriers in transition into work and learning in Canada. Despite Canada's up-skilling and re-skilling agenda (Fenwick 2006; Rubenson and Walker 2006), many Chinese immigrants experienced deskilling and devaluation of their prior learning and work experience after immigrating to Canada. In the process of transition from China to Canada, many of them encountered major difficulties, with language and employment as the most frequently cited barriers. Coupled with the devaluation and denigration of their Chinese educational qualifications and prior work experience, recent immigrants suffered unemployment and underemployment, poor economic performance, downward social mobility and negative effects on families. Non-recognition of Chinese immigrants' foreign credentials and prior work experience can be attributed to a deficit model of difference which led us to believe that differences are deficient and inferior and hence need to be devalued. It seems evident that foreign credentials and knowledge of immigrant professionals, particularly for those from the Third World countries, has been racialised and materialised on the basis of ethnic and national origins. The racialised experience of Chinese immigrants also speaks to the notion of immigrant as social construct which uses skin colour as the basis for social marking. In terms of learning, it has become an assimilation tool rather than facilitating immigrant's adaptation and transition. Through the process of deskilling and re-skilling, learning acts as a vehicle to colonising immigrants into the dominant norms and values of the host society, and by extension a means of social control and subordination (Guo 2010a).

Chinese immigrants' work and learning experiences can be understood from the perspectives of precarious and contingent work. Vosko (2008) defines precarious employment as forms of work involving 'limited social benefits and statutory entitlements, job insecurity, low job tenure, low wages, and high risks of ill health' (160). Full-time, permanent workers, adds Vosko, hold the least precarious positions. Unfortunately, full-time employment jobs became less common over the 1990s and early 2000s in Canada. In fact, forms of employment characterised by insecurity, low income and uncertainty are growing. Vosko points out that the social consequences of these developments are far-reaching, including lack of control over the labour process, stressors and strains and regulatory ineffectiveness. Mirchandani et al. (2008) use the term 'contingent work' to describe the same characteristics of precarious employment, arguing that Canada's *new economy* requires the dismantling of a full-time permanent workforce, and its replacement by a temporary and part-time workforce that can be 'dispensed of or shifted around quickly and expediently by employers' (171). Mirchandani et al.'s study of immigrant women working in Toronto's garment industry, call centres and supermarket chains, found that participants tended to be low waged, seasonally or temporarily employed. Their employment was generally insecure, and provided few employment related benefits.

The experiences of recent Chinese immigrants in this study reflect the characteristics and consequences of precarious or contingent employment described by Vosko (2008) and Mirchandani et al. (2008). As such, learning has become an instrument to regulate and diminish rather than enable and maximise immigrants' potentials.

Another attempt to explain Chinese immigrants' negative experience is *the triple glass effect* which consists of multiple layers of institutional racism including a *glass gate, glass door* and *glass ceiling* (Guo 2010b). The first layer, *the glass gate*, denies immigrants' entrance to guarded professional communities. Among a number of players and institutions that may be blamed for the devaluation of immigrants' foreign credentials and prior work experiences are professional associations and prior learning assessment agencies because immigrant's knowledge and experiences are often deemed different, deficient, and hence need to be devalued. However, successful license does not automatically guarantee a professional job, and immigrant professionals need a professional company to house them. According to Guo, in securing a professional job, many immigrants hit the second layer of glass – *the glass door*, which blocks immigrants' access to professional employment at high-wage firms. At this level, employers are the key players. Employers may refuse to offer immigrants any professional jobs because they do not have Canadian work experience, or their prior work experience is devalued because it is inferior to the Canadian experience. Or, immigrants may not secure any professional job because of their skin colour or their English accents. Guo continues to argue that it is *the glass ceiling* which prevents immigrants from moving up to management positions because of their ethnic and cultural differences. Worse still, some immigrants may work on the same job but be paid less than their white colleagues, creating racialised disparities in earnings. Guo concludes that *glass gate, glass door* and *glass ceiling* may converge to produce *a triple glass effect* that creates multiple structural barriers and affect immigrants' new working lives at different stages of their integration and transition processes.

The findings of this study have important implications for researchers, educators and policymakers. Through the accounts of the experience of recent Chinese immigrants in Canada, the study demonstrates the changing nature of work and learning in the context of immigration and through which the imperative for scholarship towards redefining work and learning. In particular, we need to examine the non-linear work and learning transitions of immigrants, the multiple structural barriers facing immigrants in the process of transitions, and how racial and socio-cultural differences have been used to entrench social inequality in immigrants' transitions. The study urges government organisations, professional associations, educational institutions and prior learning assessment agencies to dismantle barriers by adopting an inclusive framework which allows us to work towards recognitive justice that balances freedom of migration with recognition and full membership in Canada (Guo 2010a). However, we have to acknowledge that the issues facing immigrants are much broader social issues, which require political will. It is time for federal and provincial governments to exercise their legislative roles to introduce bills that will make professional associations and employers accountable for how they treat immigrants.

References

Basran, G., and L. Zong. 1998. Devaluation of foreign credentials as perceived by visible minority professional immigrants. *Canadian Ethnic Studies* 30, no. 3: 6–18.

Couton, P. 2002. Highly skilled immigrants: Recent trends and issues. *Canadian Journal of Policy Research* 3, no. 2: 114–23.

Cross, P.K. 1981. *Adults as learners: Increasing participation and facilitating learning*. San Francisco, CA: Jossey-Bass.

Crowther, J. 2004. 'In and against' lifelong learning: Flexibility and the corrosion of character. *International Journal of Lifelong Education* 24, no. 2: 125–36.

Cummins, J. 2003. Challenging the construction of difference as deficit: Where are identity, intellect, imagination, and power in the new regime of truth? In *Pedagogies of difference: Rethinking education for social change*, ed. P. Trifonas, 41–60. New York, NY: Routledge Falmer.

Dei, G.J.S. 1996. *Anti-racism education: Theory and practice*. Halifax: Fernwood.

Fenwick, T. 2003. *Learning through experience: Troubling assumptions and intersecting questions*. Malabar, FL: Krieger.

Fenwick, T. 2006. Work, learning, and adult education in Canada. In *Contexts of adult education: Canadian perspectives*, ed. T. Fenwick, T. Nesbit, and B. Spencer, 187–97. Toronto: Thompson Educational.

Fleras, A., and J. Elliott. 2002. *Engaging diversity: Multiculturalism in Canada*. Toronto: Nelson Thomson Learning.

Ghosh, R., and A.A. Abdi. 2004. *Education and the politics of difference: Canadian perspectives*. Toronto: Canadian Scholars' Press.

Guo, S. 2009. Difference, deficiency, and devaluation: Tracing the roots of non-recognition of foreign credentials for immigrant professionals in Canada. *Canadian Journal for the Study of Adult Education* 22, no. 1: 37–52.

Guo, S. 2010a. Toward recognitive justice: Emerging trends and challenges in transnational migration and lifelong learning. *International Journal of Lifelong Education* 29, no. 2: 149–67.

Guo, S. 2010b. Understanding immigrants' downward social mobility: A comparative study of economic and social integration of recent Chinese immigrants in Calgary and Edmonton. Working Paper #WP10–12. Edmonton: Prairie Metropolis Centre.

Guo, S., and D. DeVoretz. 2006a. The changing face of Chinese immigrants in Canada. *Journal of International Migration and Integration* 7, no. 3: 275–300.

Guo, S., and D. DeVoretz. 2006b. Chinese immigrants in Vancouver: Quo vadis? *Journal of International Migration and Integration* 7, no. 4: 425–47.

Henry, F., C. Tator, W. Mattis, and T. Rees. 2006. *The colour of democracy: Racism in Canadian society.* Toronto: Thompson Nelson.

Jarvis, P. 2008. *Democracy, lifelong learning and learning society: Active citizenship in a late modern age.* London: Routledge.

Knowles, V. 1997. *Strangers at our gates: Canadian immigration and immigration policy, 1540–1997.* Toronto: Dundurn Press.

Krahn, H., T. Derwing, M. Mulder, and L. Wilkinson. 2000. Educated and underemployed: Refugee integration into the Canadian labour market. *Journal of International Migration and Integration* 1, no. 1: 59–84.

Leung, H.H. 2000. *Settlement services for the Chinese Canadians in Toronto: The challenges toward an integrated planning.* Toronto: Ontario Administration of Settlement and Integration Services.

Li, P.S. 1998. *The Chinese in Canada.* Toronto: Oxford University Press.

Li, P.S. 2001. The market worth of immigrants' educational credentials. *Canadian Public Policy* 27, no. 1: 23–38.

Li, P.S. 2003. *Destination Canada: Immigration debates and issues.* Don Mills: Oxford University Press.

Li, P.S. 2008. The role of foreign credentials and ethnic ties in immigrants' economic performance. *Canadian Journal of Sociology* 33, no. 2: 291–310.

Lindsay, C. 2007. *Profiles of ethnic communities in Canada: The Chinese community in Canada.* Ottawa: Statistics Canada.

Liu, L. 2007. Unveiling the invisible learning from unpaid household work: Chinese immigrants' perspective. *Canadian Journal for the Study of Adult Education* 20, no. 2: 25–40.

Livingstone, D.W. 2008. Mapping the field of lifelong (formal and informal) learning and (paid and unpaid) work. In *The future of lifelong learning and work: Critical perspectives*, ed. D.W. Livingstone, K. Mirchandani, and P.H. Sawchuk, 13–30. Rotterdam: Sense.

Livingstone, D.W., K. Mirchandani, and P.H. Sawchuk. 2008. Introduction: Critical perspectives on learning and work in turbulent times. In *The future of lifelong learning and work: Critical perspectives*, ed. D.W. Livingstone, K. Mirchandani, and P.H. Sawchuk, 1–10. Rotterdam: Sense.

Matas, D. 1996. Racism in Canadian immigration policy. In *Perspectives on racism and the human services sector: A case for change*, ed. C.E. James, 93–102. Toronto: University of Toronto.

Mirchandani, K., R. Ng, N. Coloma-Moya, S. Maitra, S. Rawlings, K. Siddiqui, H. Shan, and B. Slade. 2008. The paradox of training and learning in a culture of contingency. In *The future of lifelong learning and work: Critical perspectives*, ed. D.W. Livingstone, K. Mirchandani, and P.H. Sawchuk, 171–84. Rotterdam: Sense.

Mojab, S. 1999. De-skilling immigrant women. *Canadian Woman Studies* 19, no. 3: 123–8.

Ng, R. 1999. Homeworking: Dream realized or freedom constrained? The globalized reality of immigrant garment workers. *Canadian Woman Studies* 19, no. 3: 10–114.

Nguyen, T.C. 1991. *Report on the Vietnamese community in the city of York.* York: York Community Services.

Reitz, J.G. 1995. A review of the literature on aspects of ethno-racial access, utilization and delivery of social services. http://www.ceris.metropolis.net/Virtual%20Library/other/reitz1.html.

Reitz, J.G. 2001. Immigrant skill utilization in the Canadian labour market: Implications of human capital research. *Journal of International Migration and Integration* 2, no. 3: 347–78.

Rubenson, K., and J. Walker. 2006. The political economy of adult learning in Canada. In *Contexts of adult education: Canadian perspectives*, ed. T. Fenwick, T. Nesbit, and B. Spencer, 173–86. Toronto: Thompson Educational.

Schugurensky, D., and B.L. Slade. 2008. 'Can volunteer work help me get a job in my field?' On learning, immigration and labour markets. In *The future of lifelong learning and work: Critical perspectives*, ed. D.W. Livingstone, K. Mirchandani, and P.H. Sawchuk, 263–74. Rotterdam: Sense.

Selman, G., M. Cooke, M. Selman, and P. Dampier. 1998. *The foundations of adult education in Canada*. Toronto: Thompson Educational.

Shan, H. 2009. Practices on the periphery: Highly educated Chinese immigrant women negotiating occupational settlement in Canada. *Canadian Journal for the Study of Adult Education* 21, no. 2: 1–18.

Statistics Canada. 2003. *Longitudinal survey of immigrants to Canada: Process, progress and prospects*. Ottawa: Statistics Canada.

Statistics Canada. 2007. *Immigration in Canada: A portrait of the foreign-born population, 2006*. Ottawa: Statistics Canada.

Stewart, M., J. Anderson, M. Beiser, E. Mwakarimba, A. Neufeld, L. Simich, and D. Spitzer. 2008. Multicultural meanings of social support among immigrants and refugees. *International Migration* 46, no. 3: 123–59.

Tan, J., and P.E. Roy. 1985. *The Chinese in Canada*. Ottawa: Canadian Historical Association.

Van Hear, N. 1998. *New diasporas: The mass exodus, dispersal and regrouping of migrant communities*. Seattle, WA: University of Washington Press.

Vosko, L. 2008. Precarious employment and 'lifelong learning': Challenging the paradigm of 'employment security'. In *The future of lifelong learning and work: Critical perspectives*, ed. D.W. Livingstone, K. Mirchandani, and P.H. Sawchuk, 157–70. Rotterdam: Sense.

Whitaker, R. 1991. *Canadian immigration policy since confederation*. Ottawa: Canadian Historical Association.

Complicating the entrepreneurial self: professional Chinese immigrant women negotiating occupations in Canada

Hongxia Shan

The Ontario Institute for Studies in Education, University of Toronto, Toronto, Canada

> A core mode of governance in the era of neoliberalism is through the production of 'entrepreneurial self'. This paper explores how the 'entrepreneurial self' is produced for 21 Chinese immigrant women in Canada. The women displayed extraordinary entrepreneurialism by investing in Canadian education. Becoming entrepreneurial, however, is more than an individualised 'choice'. It is imbricated with the ideology of meritocracy cultivated in China, the 'credential and certificate regime' in Canada, and the gendered expectations in the host labour market and at home. Given the ideological confluence, and the material conditions the women lived, a feminized and racialized labour is reproduced.

Introduction

> Defining it in general as 'the conduct of conduct', Foucault presents government as more or less methodical and rationally reflected 'way of doing things', or 'art' for acting on the actions of individuals, taken either singly or collectively, so as to shape, guide, correct and modify the ways in which individuals conduct themselves. (Burchell 1993, 267)

At the end of the 1970s, the economic West witnessed, in the conduct of conduct, a paradigmatic shift from liberalism to neoliberalism, which has since swept the globe (e.g., Dobrowolsky 2008; Harvey 2005; Ong 2007). If during the time of liberalism, laissez-faire state was practised to give free reign to the quasi-natural self-regulating market, and the 'natural, private interest motivated conduct of free market *exchanging* individuals', in the era of neoliberalism, governments have been proactive in constructing the political, institutional and cultural conditions for a free market. In particular, cultivating '*entrepreneurial and competitive* conduct of economic-rational individuals' (Burchell 1993, 271, italicised original emphasis) and encouraging the development of responsible selves have been made a core mode of governance today, particularly in the West.

A founding thesis of neoliberalism is that 'human well-being can best be advanced by liberating individual entrepreneurial freedoms and skills within an institutional framework characterised by strong private property rights, free markets and free trade' (Harvey 2005, 2). Indeed, today, a pro-capital orientation if not an all-encompassing competitive market logic, along with an individualised entrepreneurial culture, has been introduced to different domains of social and economic life, such as welfare provision, public services, taxation, and immigration and education (e.g., Clarke 2004; Olssen and Peters 2005; Ong 2007; Peters 2001). Within such a context, individuals have been moralised and 'responsiblised' to develop entrepreneurial attitudes and skills and ultimately the subjectivity of an entrepreneurial self (Peters 2001).

Studies have long directed criticism towards the impacts that neoliberalism and the entailed entrepreneurial culture have had on women and racialised minorities (e.g., Blackmore 1999, 2002; Grummell, Devine, and Lynch 2009; Morley 1999; Stanley 1997; Theodore 2007; Wilson 2004, 2006). As far as immigrants are concerned, the impacts of neoliberal policies on the regulation of their conditions of entry (e.g., Arat-Koc 1999; Bauder 2008) as well as on their access to services and welfare (e.g., Bhuyan and Smith-Carrier 2012; Matejskova 2012) have been well documented. This paper adds to the expanding scholarship with an examination of how the neoliberal subjectivity of an entrepreneurial self is produced for some professional Chinese immigrant women in Canada. Specifically, based on two studies of 21 Chinese immigrant women in Toronto, Canada, this paper explores how the women tried to reorient their career trajectory and optimise their employment opportunities after immigration. It begins by examining closely the notion of the entrepreneurial self. It then introduces the backgrounds of the studies, followed by the research methods. In the section of research findings, special attention is paid to the production of the entrepreneurial subjectivity for the women. The paper ends with a discussion of the implications of the research findings.

The entrepreneurial self and its production

Developing an entrepreneurial economy is amongst the top priorities in countries such as Canada that operate within a neoliberal ideological and economic framework. Entrepreneurship or entrepreneurialism is a term used by the governments to emphasise the development of behaviours and skills that lead to venture creation, or the development of enterprising attitudes among individuals across disciplines and industrial sectors (see Industry Canada 2010). In this paper, entrepreneurialism is used to reference enterprising attitudes and a culture of self-reliance, or the subjectivity of entrepreneurial self, rather than business-related motivations and behaviours.

While entrepreneurship has an economic and human capital connotation, the notion of an 'entrepreneurial self' is not only economic but also social and even moralistic (Peters 2001). Peters pinpoints that an 'entrepreneurial self' is essentially a relationship that 'one establishes to oneself through forms of personal investment and insurance that becomes the central *ethical* component of a new individualised and privatised consumer welfare economy' (Peters 2001, 60, italicised author's emphasis). Within the discourse of entrepreneurial self, individuals are regarded, not so much as right-based citizens as clients, consumers and entrepreneurs who are accountable to their own well-being (Simons and Masschelein 2006). In the field of training and education, the entrepreneurial culture is best manifested through the lifelong learning discourse that has turned individuals into learners who should be able to recognise opportunities, marshal resources and make appropriate investment to achieve various goals (Gouthro 2002; Reimers-Hild et al. 2005).

Of note, the discourses of 'entrepreneurial self' and 'entrepreneurial culture' are but part and parcel of complex practices of neoliberalisation. According to Harvey (2005), neoliberalisation involves 'creative destruction' and reconfiguration of a range of social policy and practices, including but not limited to 'prior institutional frameworks and powers', 'divisions of labour, social relations, welfare provisions, technological mixes, ways of life and thought, reproductive activities, attachments to the land and habits of the heart' (Harvey 2005, 3). The entrepreneurial culture could be understood as an ideological grip of the heart that lends vitality to various neoliberal practices. In particular, it caters to the flexible regime of production as well as the ensuing contingent culture of work by invoking the image of a rational and responsible self. In other words, we are not only increasingly exposed to the vagaries of the market, we are also expected to become what Hart calls 'generic workers' (1992), who are psychologically, mentally and behaviourally prepared 'for living with instability, and/or being able to think of oneself in terms of renewable, exchangeable and updatable resource rather than in terms of a human being with unique experiences, hopes, wishes and dreams' (87). The central problem with the social evocation of a responsible, generic and entrepreneurial worker, Hart continues to point out, is that:

> the built-in obsolescence and proposed throw-away nature of one's work-related experiences and competencies may seriously conflict with psychological and social need for constancy, or for continuity in one's personal history in order to be able to develop and sustain a sense of self, and a supportive community. (Hart 1992, 87)

In other words, the flexible regime of production and the neoliberal regulation of labour are conditioned on the estrangement of the workers from their intimate selves and social needs as human beings. If this trend of alienation has impacted all workers, communities traditionally marginalised are impacted the most. Research has shown that the policy construct of an entrepreneurial self lies precisely in its rejection of personal identity in the name of rationality, rendering irrelevant the lived reality and needs of socially disadvantaged groups (e.g., Davis 2007; Roberts and Mahtani 2010).

Despite the inherent problems with the discourses of entrepreneurial culture and the entrepreneurial self, they have been readily embraced by many as rational and commonsensical. To explain this myth, Harvey (2005) points out that the ability of neoliberalism as an ideology to penetrate and co-opt some other common-sense ideologies has been crucial. For instance, Harvey (2005) argues that the idea of an entrepreneurial self is appealing to the masses in part because it evokes the democratic value of freedom of choice. In Komulainen, Naskali, and Keskitalo-Foley's study (2011) of pre- and in-service teachers implementing enterprise education in Finland, they point out that the government's mandate to produce enterprising mentality among students resonated well with the traditional ideal that education should produce hard-working and responsible citizens; this is how the 'entrepreneurial culture' found its way into the everyday practices of teachers. In a study of older post-Soviet immigrants in eastern Berlin (Matejskova 2012), the immigrants surrendered themselves to extreme exploitative conditions. Such collective despondency to exploitation, Matejskova argues, has to do with their continued endorsement of work as a practice of social embedding, a legacy of state-socialist structuring of life, which unexpectedly dovetailed with the neoliberal project of work-based integration in Germany. Webb, Gulson, and Pitton (2014) have also recently argued that the neoliberal education policies such as the one that has led to the development of the Africentric Alternative School have also capitalised on a historical concern to care for the self as well as the ideal of freedom of choices for groups of people. Clearly, neoliberalism is harder to challenge precisely because it also rides on other seemingly commonsensical discourses while opening 'the social order to be regulated' (Harvey 2005, 40). This very feature of the neoliberal culture of entrepreneurialism makes it imperative for us to explore processes of neoliberalisation (Peck and Tickell 2002) and to 'identify the material grounding for the construction of consent' (Harvey 2005, 40) through interrogating our everyday lives.

Immigration to Canada

Canada is a country of immigrants. While historically Canada favoured Caucasian immigrants over immigrants of colour (Jakubowski 1997), in 1967, the introduction of the point system officially marked the end to Canada's overt discriminatory immigration practices based on racial and ethnic preferences (Satzewich 1998). Ever since, Canada has experimented with different immigration criteria to attract immigrants that could directly contribute to the Canadian economy. In particular, it has been targeting immigrants with various educational backgrounds, working experiences usable to the Canadian economy as well as a level of proficiency in one of the official languages in Canada.

Concomitant with the shifts in immigration policy is the changing demographic of recent immigrant cohorts. To start with, an increasing percentage of recent immigrants are skilled immigrants experienced in various occupations and professions. In recent years, skilled immigrants account for more than 50% of all immigrants to Canada (CIC 2007). Among these immigrants, a good percentage are from non-traditional immigrant countries in Asia. For instance, the People's Republic of China was the top immigrant source country for Canada between 1998 and 2008 (CIC 2011). As well, the number of immigrant women has been on the rise. Unlike the traditional image of women trailing behind their spouses, many women now come to Canada as skilled immigrants, intending to have a career of their own (Raghuram and Kofman 2004).

In spite of the fact that immigrants come to Canada often by virtue of their educational attainment and work experience, they are typically under- or unemployed after immigration (Guo 2009). Studies have revealed a host of barriers preventing immigrants from succeeding in the Canadian labour market. They range from immigrants' lack of English proficiency (Boyd 1990), cultural capital (Bauder and Cameron 2002) and social capital (Xue 2008), to the devaluation of immigrants' credentials and experience (e.g., Guo 2010; Ng and Shan 2010; Shan 2009a), demands for Canadian work experience (e.g., Chakkalakal and Harvey 2001; Sakamoto, Chin, and Young 2010; Slade 2012) as well as institutionalised racism and sexism (e.g., Ng 1988; Man 2004). With few exceptions (Ng and Shan 2010; Shan 2009a, 2009b, 2012, 2013), little attention has been paid to how immigrants try to manage their employment after immigration. This paper contributes to this void of the scholarship by examining how a group of Chinese immigrant women professionals rebuild their careers and status after migration.

The studies

In view of the barriers immigrants face, a Chinese Professional Women's Reference Group was formed at the Ontario Institute for Studies in Education, University of Toronto, by a number of professional Chinese immigrant women, with the late Dr. Roxana Ng as the facilitator of the group. What the women did in the group was sharing, venting, listening, confiding and most importantly reflecting on their experiences. Although that group was short-lived, in 2005, a study was initiated to explore the ways in which

Chinese immigrant women navigate the gendered and racially segregated Canadian labour market.[1] This led to a larger study that included professional women from India.[2] Interviewees were identified through snowballing, email networks of professional immigrants and organisations serving new immigrants in the city of Toronto, a most popular destination for immigrants in Canada. Ten Chinese women were interviewed in the first study and 11 in the second study.[3] Both studies made use of life-history style interviews as the primary data collection tool in order to give women space to recollect and reflect on their immigration and job search experience. The women were asked to describe their educational backgrounds and occupational experiences prior to immigration, as well as their expectations and knowledge of the Canadian labour market before they immigrated. They then were asked to recount how they attempted to find paid employment after immigration and to contextualise their experience in relation to the social and economic conditions in which they found themselves. The interviews were long: between two to three hours; permission was also asked of the respondents to conduct a second interview or to provide further clarification if needed. In the first study, all but one interview were conducted in Mandarin. All interviews were then transcribed verbatim in the language in which the interviews were conducted – there was no need for translation as all researchers understood both Mandarin and English. In the second study, all but one interview were conducted in English. All interviews were then transcribed verbatim, and the Chinese interview was translated into English to make it accessible to the non-Chinese researchers.

Data analysis was conducted using two simultaneous methods: identifying themes in the interview data and tracing social relations extending beyond the everyday lives of the women; the latter is informed by the method of inquiry of institutional ethnography (IE). For the first part of the analysis, researchers, some of whom shared similar experiences with the research participants, independently coded the data for emerging themes. They then convened and compared their themes to produce a coherent picture and to tease out threads of social relations extending beyond the women's experiences in their everyday lives. IE is a feminist approach developed by Dorothy Smith (1987, 2005), which begins from and takes up the standpoint of people's daily experiences, in this case women's labour market experiences. Researchers interested in tracing the social relations further identified and analysed relevant social practices to map the social happenings constituting people's experiences (see Ng and Shan 2010; Shan 2009a). Preliminary research findings were presented in a community forum where we invited the research participants as well as other stakeholders to hear our findings and provide feedback.

Research findings

In both studies, all the women were confronted with dismal job prospects, and many started their working life in Canada by taking up surviving jobs or what some called 'breaking neck labour' in restaurants and factories. Yet, none was going to settle with their first jobs. All of them, except for one who needed an income to sponsor her family to come to Canada, tried to dig themselves out of these 'menial' labour jobs and to develop a career that would enable them to utilise their prior educational and professional knowledge and experiences. As they strived for new career paths in Canada, the women demonstrated an incredible entrepreneurial spirit. They actively sought information, invested in training and education and negotiated new identities and positionalities in the host labour market. Becoming entrepreneurial, however, is not merely an individualised response on the part of the women to the supremacy of the logic of the market. I argue that it has to do with the women's espousal of meritocracy as an ideology cultivated through the traditionally competitive Chinese education system. It is also inextricably linked to what I call a credential and certificate regime (CCR) that reproduces and naturalises the existing social order in the labour market as well as the gendered ideology at home that may privilege men's careers over women's.

Entrepreneurial investment and the meritocratic educational system in China

All the women were middle-class professionals in China. They all held at least a bachelor degree from China: seven in English, seven in engineering, two in medicine, two in law, two in business and one in library information. In China, they worked as professionals such as medical doctors (paediatrician and surgeon), lawyers, professors, teachers, engineers, customs coordinators and administrators and managers.

To reach the social and professional status that they had in China, the women had to first of all make it through the highly competitive educational system, which has long been regarded as *the* route to social mobility for the masses. Since classical times, Confucianism has emphasised education as more valuable than anything else in the society. Between Sui Dynasty (587 A.D.) and Qing Dynasty (1904 A.D.), an imperial examination system was used as a recruitment mechanism for the state to select government officials (Gan 2008). During the 1950s, a national College Entrance Examination was introduced in Maoist China. This system was put on hold during the Cultural Revolution but was resumed in 1977 (Bai and Chi 2011). Since 1978, when Deng started opening up China to the world, Chinese education system has experienced a drastic process of transformation characterised with marketisation and massification. By 2004, China has transformed its highly selective elite higher education system and became the largest mass higher education provider in the world. That means that after 2004, 15% and more of the university student age cohort could have an opportunity to get into universities. Prior to that, the university admission rate was lower. For instance, it was estimated to be 5% or lower at the end of the 1970s and the beginning of 1980s (Yu and Ertl 2010). This rate does not take into account the number of students who have dropped out of the school system due to reasons such as poverty, which has a disproportionate effect on students from rural areas.

The women respondents in this study entered universities between 1977 and 1993. During this period of time, students who made it into universities were largely 'taken care of' by the state. The majority of them were recruited and posted to jobs on the basis of state quota and centralized state planning. Prior to 1989, no students except for those outside of state quota had to pay tuition. Not only that, all university students were also provided with free accommodation and living allowances. To earn a spot in the university, however, all students within or outside of state quotas had to exercise extraordinary discipline, work hard and succeed in the university entrance exams.

In the studies, no information was solicited from the women about their experiences with the school system. Yet, when they became reminiscent of their professional status in China, some would mention the name of their graduating universities as a way to reaffirm themselves. Some also referred to their experiences of writing college examinations when explaining why they immigrated to Canada. The common sentiment among them is that they would not like their children to go through what they had gone through in order to get into universities. I would also argue that the fact that the women were able to upgrade their life opportunities through surviving or excelling in the meritocratic and highly competitive educational system in China has left imprints in the personal biography of the women. This is manifested the best in their entrepreneurial investment in training and in education after immigration.

In the study, 17 out of the 21 respondents, for instance, attended training and education programmes in Canada – all except for one woman did so with the specific goal of getting a Canadian degree and certificate. One other woman had experiences working and studying in the USA as a visiting scholar before immigration. At the time of the interview, she was conducting self-study to get recertified as a clinical doctor. To a great extent, the two studies corroborate a number of statistical studies that have shown that recent immigrants tend to invest in re-schooling and re-education in Canada (Adamuti-Trache et al. 2011; Banerjee and Verma 2012). A host of factors have contributed to immigrants' decisions to go back to schools, such as gender, age, prior level of education, language proficiency, family obligations, job opportunities, recognition of credentials and financial limitations (Adamuti-Trache et al. 2011; Banerjee and Verma 2012). As a researcher with a Chinese background, I also discerned the women's long-held belief in meritocracy, which was cultivated through the competitive educational system in China of their time, dovetailed with the neoliberal imperative in Canada that immigrants should be self-reliant and 'up and running' upon immigration (CIC 2012).

The Canadian/West-centred CCR

If the meritocratic culture in China has disposed the women with a 'propensity' for training and education, the women's actual choices of training and education programmes are highly regulated by what I call a Canadian and/Western-centred credential and certificate regime (CCR). The CCR is a term used to reference a complex of social practices that make credentials and certificates objective grounds to construct employability and desirability of people from different places and that unduly inflates the value of credentials produced in Canada as well as in some countries in the economic West (Shan 2009a). While the CCR affects everyone, it becomes most evident when examining the women's efforts in trying to navigate the Canadian labour market as newcomers.

Of the 17 women who attended training or formal educational programmes in Canada, two planned to do so prior to immigration. Others did not embark on the journey of re-training and re-education until they found out that their credentials from China, which enabled them to immigrate in the first place, were not typically recognised in Canada, especially not by professional regulatory bodies. There are two major regulated occupations in Canada: regulated professions and apprenticeable trades. Across Canada, there are about 50 regulated professions and more than 100 apprenticeable trades. Together, the regulated occupations account for about 20% of the Canadian workforce (T & CS Canada n.d.). To enter these occupations, immigrants need to apprentice themselves to a licenced practitioner for a varying period of time before they can acquire licences or certificates to practice independently. For regulated professions, they also need to have their foreign trained backgrounds confirmed by either writing exams or attending Canadian training programmes. The systematic and institutionalised devaluation of foreign credentials has 'naturally' designated immigrant newcomers as 'continuous learners', who have to learn to prove themselves in front of professional bodies.

Aside from institutionalised devaluation of foreign credentials, the stories of the women also point to the direction that risk-aversive employers and recruiters often downplay the value of credentials and work experiences from non-traditional immigrant source countries. Such practices constitute what Bourdieu would call an administrative habitus (Bourdieu 1977) that functions outside of consciousness. In other words, an employer's valuation of degrees and credentials forms the 'cultural unconsciousness' (Widick 2003) that shapes the opportunities of immigrants from different places. Such administrative habitus, which rarely receives questioning, constitutes part of the CCR. By 'automatically' rendering foreign credentials less valuable, it also allocates job applicants positions in the hiring queue and thereby participates in the social and economic ordering of workers by racial backgrounds.

Another important social practice that has shaped the women's entrepreneurial investment has to do with the increasingly pervasive desire across industries and sectors for certification of competency and skills. For many professions and occupations, particular kinds of certificates have been made entrance requirements. For instance, Bai[4] started her life in Canada by entering an MA programme in Education in Toronto. However, an MA degree in Canada was not enough for her to land a job. She also took a short-term training programme on lifelong coaching. She said:

> I got a training certificate from [a community training centre]. It's... lifelong coaching certificate. ... Some of the ... community services, require that.

Clearly, the demand for occupation-specific certificates by industries and sectors has become a governing mechanism that regulates the subjectivities and investment activities of individuals. This phenomenon becomes most clear in the IT field. The major IT companies such as Cicco and Microsoft have their headquarters situated in North America. They, however, deliver services and products as well as training and certification programmes worldwide. One of our respondents, let's name her Ling was a computer network engineer in China and in Canada until she got pregnant. To increase her marketability, she wrote a number of tests and obtained certificates of different levels in C language, C ++, Cisco network, Novell network, Unix administration and some other systems too specialised for us as social researchers to know. Most of these certificates are administered by Microsoft in the USA. What make them appealing to Ling are the potential salary returns that may come with these certificates. She said that if she got the highest-level certificate in Cisco route operation, '$100,000 yearly salary is no problem'. Ling was so good at writing these exams that she was once hired by the school where she received training on these certificate exams as an instructor.

Reality check: women's lived life experiences

If Ling's story ends here, she would be fitting most perfectly into the image of a responsible and entrepreneurial immigrant desired in the era of neoliberalism. The reality of her life, however, took a dramatic turn. After getting all the IT certificates, at the time of the interview, Ling had turned herself into a seasonal tax return specialist. She made this niche career move after not only taking a series of tax training programmes offered by a large-tax return company, but also excelling in all the courses taken. While initially puzzled by her choice of a seasonal position after all of her certificate-related learning projects, we learned that Ling made this decision because she needed to take care of her children while her husband worked full time as an IT professional. In this example, it is clear that the women's career 'choices' are deeply gendered. As the primary caregiver in a family, Ling made her career choice that would enable her to fulfil her household and childcare responsibilities first.

Indeed, a closer examination of the women's experiences negotiating careers in Canada shows that the career paths of the women were shaped more than by their career aspiration, but by a web of social relations, such as gender, race and class, that permeate all aspects of our society. For instance, while the women invested in training and education, the majority of them tended to look for short-term educational programmes orienting them towards jobs perceived to be more accessible to immigrants, and immigrant women in particular. For instance, Dan was a chief engineer in China. In Canada, she initially worked in two manufacturing factories. After she was injured on the job, she looked for a new career direction. After some debate with herself, she decided to take a short day care assistant programme in a community centre. She said:

> I decided to study and become a daycare assistant.... My English is not good. Fellow immigrants who are younger and who speak better English than me are having problem landing professional jobs.... I decided to change to something that was suitable for me. I am a patient person. I love children. I am a mom.... I thought ... I would remain younger if I stay with children all the time (laugh). My English was not great. I did not have the courage to study for an ECE diploma in college.... (the training in the community centre) costs $500. It was cheap, and good for me.... I paid it myself. If you go to college, it would be $5,000.

In this case, Dan rationalised her decision by evoking her role as a mother who loves children. She also compared herself with other immigrant women with respect to age and language proficiency. Her choice was also influenced by the low tuition fee in a community centre vis-à-vis an Early Child Education (ECE) programme at the college level. Here, we see clearly how women (re)positioned themselves based on what exists in a gendered and racialised social and economic system that privileges certain groups of people while rendering other groups as less able on the basis of their gender, race, culture, language, work experience, and so forth. In other words, processes of differentiation are integral to the so-called 'free choice' for individuals in the neoliberal labour market.

While re-training and re-education have enabled some women to obtain employment and afforded some certain kind of mobility, they have at the same time acted as a 'sorting' process that inserts immigrant women into a labour market stratified by gender, race, ability and other axes of differentiation. That is, a hierarchical order has been reproduced as the women were articulated to the host labour market through the CCR.

Of note, while negotiating career opportunities in the host labour market, many of the women we interviewed were simultaneously performing their roles within the family. Despite their entrepreneurism, both studies suggest, children's education and spouses' career may easily take precedence over the women's career aspirations. In the case of Yan, who was an engineer in China, she planned to join an accounting programme prior to immigration as she was led to believe that engineering as a profession was closed to immigrants and that Chinese women generally have better opportunity with accounting. After two years on an accounting programme, all she could land was a part-time position as a bakery clerk. At that point, her husband decided to go back to China due to the poor employment prospects for both of them. They decided that she should settle with the bakery job at least for a while:

> My husband told me not to look for accounting jobs. He thought that [a part-time] job suited me the best. It was close to home and I could take care of the kid at the same time. So I have worked there for nearly three years.... When my daughter grows up, I would like to change my job, or go back to school again.

While Yan was certain that she would like to steer herself out of her position as a bakery clerk, she felt that she had to wait until her daughter grew up because her immediate and primary responsibility was to her child.

Lan's story also illustrates the kind of complex relations that professional women need to negotiate. Lan was a paediatrician and medical professor in China. Her husband had similar professional backgrounds. They both worked on a few UNESCO projects in China and worked as visiting scholars in the USA. She came to Canada at the peak of her career to join her husband who decided to immigrate. After immigration, she found a job as a lab researcher and her husband became a lab technician. Neither of them was content with their positions; both were planning to get recertified as physicians in Canada. She said:

> We have invested most money into [getting licensed again], taking tests, buying books, joining training programmes, ... and our spare time has been spent all on this.

Meanwhile, while their credentials and work experience were very similar, their lives in Canada were not. Her husband was able to treat his job as 'a job, and after coming home, study is study'. Lan, as she put it in the interview, was the person who 'sacrificed' after immigration. She described a typical day of her life this way:

> I typically wake up around 7 am ... to cook. I then wake up (my husband and son) around 7:30. They take a shower and have breakfast. Around 8:15, we drive together to school and work.... We get home around 6 pm. My husband and I cook together around 6:30 pm.... By the time we finish dinner, it will be 8 pm. I will then clean up the household while my husband finds some time to read, ... do his homework ... Neither of us could sleep before 11:30. I need to deal with all kinds of things at home and then read. It is extremely exhausting. I need to work.

It is clear that Lan had two jobs on top of her desire to obtain recertification: her paid employment and her domestic duties, whereas her husband was able to devote more time to the recertification process. At the time of the interview, Lan had yet to start the recertification process, and her husband had completed his exams and was trying to secure a residency spot in a hospital setting.

Discussion and conclusion

The ideology of the entrepreneurial self has been mobilised as a mode of governance in the era of neoliberalism. In this paper, I focused on how the 'entrepreneurial self' is produced for the professional Chinese immigrant women who were actively rebuilding their career paths in Canada. The studies show that given their prior education and work experience in China, which led to their belief in meritocracy, and the power of education, the women respondents had little problem adopting the discourse and practice of entrepreneurialism. They showed a great deal of initiative in negotiating their career possibility within a complex institutional nexus of education and training, occupation and employment as well as family and household. Almost all women reached deep into their pockets and invested in further training and education to gain the credentials and certificates that would make them eligible for jobs in fields that they targeted.

Research findings from the studies disrupt the myth of an unencumbered, generic and entrepreneurial worker presupposed within the entrepreneurial culture. The women respondents we interviewed are mothers and wives as well as career women who lived particular material realities. Often, financial exigencies, coupled with gendered expectations within the family may restrain their career aspiration. Professional closure and institutionalised devaluation of their credentials further complicate the picture that they needed to navigate. As a result, majority of the women, including the women who were trained and had worked in traditionally male-dominated professions, such as engineers and lawyers before immigration, ended up, after immigration, in sectors traditionally associated with women and their assumed role as caregivers, such as early childhood education and community workers. This process of feminisation of immigrant women's labour should be noted by policy-makers and those working with immigrant women in the settlement sector.

In closing, I reiterate the argument that the rhetoric of the entrepreneurial self is fundamentally flawed. Here is a Swiss saying by Max Frisch while describing the immigration history in his own country: 'we wanted workers, but human beings came'. The expectation by immigration policy-makers that immigrants should 'hit the ground running' is troublesome. Treating immigrant workers, indeed any worker, solely as economic beings is problematic, as the experiences of the respondents suggest. Not only does it obscure the lived realities of immigrant workers but it also reinforces the existing labour market hierarchy and social order that push immigrants and particularly immigrant women to the lower echelons of the labour market. The notion of the entrepreneurial self is problematic also because it does not in fact facilitate immigrant women's entry into professional jobs where they could make use of the professional experiences and expertise that they bring to the host society. It simply acts as an ideological device that encourages newcomers to participate in life-long learning at their own expense and to be inserted into a precarious labour market. Ultimately, the ideology of the entrepreneurial self simply turns the structural deficit of a neoliberal society, particularly its lack of social support system into individual responsibilities. Based on the findings of the studies, it is suggested that labour market support systems need to be strengthened, in particular with regard to childcare services and financial assistance for training and education. Further, labour market incentives should be provided to encourage job design that would help to retain women within professions. Such measures will help create equitable opportunities not only for immigrants but also for other minoritised and marginalised communities and groups to make fuller use of their potentials in the labour market.

Notes

1. This study entitled 'Learning to be good citizens: Informal learning and the labour market experiences of professional Chinese immigrant women' was funded by the Toronto Metropolis Centre of Excellence for Research on Immigration and Settlement (CERIS) between 2005 and 2006. Dr Roxana Ng was the principal investigator. Dr Guida Man was the co-investigator. Research assistants and community contacts were Dr Willa Liu, Ms Peng, Dr Sandra Tam and Dr Hongxia Shan.
2. The second study entitled 'Professional immigrant women navigating the Canadian labour market: A study in adult learning' was funded by SSHRC [No.410-2006-1437]. Dr Roxana Ng was the principal investigator. Dr Tania Das Gupta, Dr. Guida Man and Dr. Kiran Mirchandani were the co-investigators. Research assistants included Dr Hijin Park, Dr. Willa Liu and Dr. Hongxia Shan.
3. Ten Indian women were interviewed in the study. Only interviews with Chinese women were included in the discussion of this paper.
4. All names used are pseudonyms to ensure anonymity of the research respondents.

References

Adamuti-Trache, M., P. Anisef, P. Sweet, and D. Walters. 2011. "Enriching Foreign Qualifications through Canadian Post-secondary Education: Who Participate and Why?" *Journal of International Migration and Integration*. Accessed September 1, 2012. http://www.springerlink.com/content/e2761q0tj76t2qp2/

Arat-Koc, S. 1999. "Neoliberalism, State Restructuring and Immigration: Changes in Canadian Policies in the 1990s." *Journal of Canadian Studies* 34 (2): 31–56.

Bai, C., and W. Chi. 2011. "Determinants of Undergraduate GPAs in China: College Entrance Examination Scores, High School Achievement and Admission Route." *Munich Personal RePEc Archive*. Accessed September 1, 2012. http://mpra.ub.uni-muenchen.de/32797/

Banerjee, R., and A. Verma. 2012. "Determinants and Effects of Post-migration Education among New Immigrants in Canada." *Journal of International Migration and Integration* 13: 59–82.

Bauder, H. 2008. "The Economic Case for Immigration: Neoliberal and Regulatory Paradigms in Canada's Press." *Studies in Political Economy* 82 (Autumn): 131–152.

Bauder, H., and E. Cameron. 2002. "Cultural Barriers to Labour Market Integration: Immigrants from South Asian and the Former Yugoslavia." RIIM working paper series No. 02–03.

Bhuyan, R., and T. Smith-Carrier. 2012. "Constructions of Migrant Rights in Canada: Is Subnational Citizenship Possible?" *Citizenship Studies* 16 (2): 203–221. doi:10.1080/13621025.2012.667613.

Blackmore, J. 1999. *Troubling Women: Feminism, Leadership and Educational Change*. Buckingham: Open University Press.

Blackmore, J. 2002. "Globalisation and the Restructuring of Higher Education for New Knowledge Economies." *Higher Education Quarterly* 56 (4): 419–441. doi:10.1111/1468-2273.00228.

Bourdieu, P. 1977. *Outline of a theory of practice*, New York: Cambridge University Press.

Boyd, M. 1990. "Immigrant Women: Language, Socioeconomic Inequalities, and Policy Issues." In *Ethnic Demography: Canadian Immigrant, Racial, and Cultural Variations*, edited by S. Halli, F. Trovato, and L. Driedger, 275–296. Ottawa: Carleton University Press.

Burchell, G. 1993. "Liberal Government and Techniques of the Self." *Economy and Society* 22 (3): 267–282. doi:10.1080/03085149300000018.

Chakkalakal, A., and J. Harvey. 2001. *Access for Foreign-trained IT Professionals: An Exploration of Systemic Barriers*. Toronto: Job Start and Skills for Change.

CIC (Citizenship and Immigration Canada) 2007. *Facts and Figures 2007 – Immigration Overview: Permanent and Temporary Residents*. Accessed September 1, 2012. http://www.cic.gc.ca/english/resources/statistics/menu-fact.asp

CIC (Citizenship and Immigration Canada) 2011. *Preliminary Tables-Permanent and Temporary Residents*. Accessed September 1, 2012. http://www.cic.gc.ca/english/resources/statistics/facts2011-preliminary/index.asp

CIC (Citizenship and Immigration Canada) 2012. *News Release – Revised Federal Skilled Worker Program Unveiled*. Accessed September 1, 2012. http://www.cic.gc.ca/english/department/media/releases/2012/2012-08-17.asp

Clarke, J. 2004. "Dissolving the Public Realm? The Logics and Limits of Neo-liberalism." *Journal of Social Policy* 33 (1): 27–48. doi:10.1017/S0047279403007244.

Davis, D. 2007. "Narrating the Mute: Racializing and Racism in a Neoliberal Moment." *Souls: A Critical Journal of Black Politics, Culture, and Society* 9 (4): 346–360.

Dobrowolsky, A. 2008. "Nuancing Neoliberalism: Lessons Learned from a Failed Immigration Experiment." *International Migration and Integration* 14 (2): 197–218.

Gan, H. 2008. "Chinese Education Tradition-The Imperial Examination System in Feudal China." *Journal of Management and Social Sciences* 4 (2): 115–133.

Gouthro, P. 2002. "Education for Sale: At What Cost? Lifelong Learning and the Marketplace." *International Journal of Lifelong Education* 21 (4): 334–346. doi:10.1080/02601370210140995.

Grummell, B., D. Devine, and K. Lynch. 2009. "The Care-less Manager: Gender, Care and New Managerialism in Higher Education." *Gender and Education* 21 (2): 191–208. doi:10.1080/09540250802392273.

Guo, S. 2009. "Difference, Deficiency, and Devaluation: Tracing the Roots of Non/recognition of Foreign Redentials for Immigrant Professionals in Canada." *Canadian Journal for the Study of Adult Education* 22 (1): 37–52.

Guo, S. 2010. "Toward Recognitive Justice: Emerging Trends and Challenges in Transnational Migration and Lifelong Learning." *International Journal of Lifelong Education* 29 (2): 149–167. doi:10.1080/02601371003616533.

Hart, M. U. 1992. *Working and Educating for Life: Feminist and International Perspectives on Adult Education*. London: Routledge.

Harvey, D. 2005. *A Brief History of Neoliberalism*. Oxford: Oxford University Press.

Industry Canada 2010. *The Teaching and Practice of Entrepreneurship within Canadian Higher Education Institutions*. Accessed September 1, 2012. www.ic.gc.ca/sbresearch/sbreports

Jakubowski, L. M. 1997. *Immigration and the Legalization of Racism*. Halifax, NS: Fernwood.

Komulainen, K., P. Naskali, and S. Keskitalo-Foley. 2011. "Internal Entrepreneurship – A Trojan Horse of the Neoliberal Governance of Education? Finnish Pre- and In-service Teachers' Implementation of and Resistance towards Entrepreneurship Education." *Journal for Critical Education Policy* 9 (1): 341–374.

Man, G. 2004. "Gender, Work and Migration: Deskilling Chinese Immigrant Women in Canada." *Women's Studies International Forum* 27 (2): 135–148. doi:10.1016/j.wsif.2004.06.004.

Matejskova, T. 2012. "'But One Needs to Work!': Neoliberal Citizenship, Work-based Immigrant Integration, and Post-socialist Subjectivities in Berlin-Marzahn." *Antipode* 45 (4): 984–1004. doi:10.1111/j.1467-8330.2012.01050.x.

Morley, L. 1999. *Organising Feminisms: The Micropolitics of the Academy*. Basingstoke: Macmillan.

Ng, R. 1988. "Immigrant Women and Institutionalized Racism." In *Changing Patterns, Women in Canada*, edited by S. Burt and L. Code, 184–203. Toronto: M&S.

Ng, R., and H. Shan. 2010. "Lifelong Learning as Ideological Practice: An Analysis from the Perspective of Immigrant Women in Canada." *International Journal of Lifelong Education* 29 (2): 169–184. doi:10.1080/02601371003616574.

Olssen, M., and M. A. Peters. 2005. "Neoliberalism, Higher Education and the Knowledge Economy: From the Free Market to Knowledge Capitalism." *Journal of Education Policy* 20 (3): 313–345. doi:10.1080/02680930500108718.

Ong, A. 2007. "Boundary Crossings: Neoliberalism as a Mobile Technology." *Transaction of the Institute of British Geographers* 32 (1): 3–8. doi:10.1111/j.1475-5661.2007.00234.x.

Peck, J., and A. Tickell. 2002. "Neoliberalizing Space." *Antipode* 34 (3): 380–404. doi:10.1111/1467-8330.00247.

Peters, M. 2001. "Education, Enterprise Culture and Entrepreneurial Self: A Foucaldian Perspective." *Journal of Educational Enquiry* 2 (2): 58–71.

Raghuram, P., and E. Kofman. 2004. "Out of Asia: Skilling, Re-skilling and Deskilling of Female Migrants." *Women's Studies International Forum* 27 (2): 95–100. doi:10.1016/j.wsif.2004.06.001.

Reimers-Hild, C., J. W. King, J. E. Foster, S. M. Fritz, S. S. Waller, and D. W. Wheeler. 2005. "A Framework for the Entrepreneurial Learner of the 21st Century." *Online Journal of Distance Learning Administration* 8 (2). Accessed January 15, 2009. http://www.westga.edu/~distance/ojdla/summer82/hild82.htm

Roberts, D. J., and M. Mahtani. 2010. "Neoliberalizing Race, Racing Neoliberalism: Placing 'Race' in Neoliberal Discourses." *Antipode* 42 (2): 248–257. doi:10.1111/j.1467-8330.2009.00747.x.

Sakamoto, I., M. Chin, and M. Young. 2010. "'Canadian Experience,' Employment Challenges, and Skilled Immigrants: A Close Look through 'Tacit Knowledge.'" *Canadian Social Work Journal* 10 (1): 145–151.

Satzewich, V. 1998. "Introduction." In *Racism and Social Inequality in Canada: Concepts, Controversies and Strategies of Resistance*, edited by V. Satzewich, 1–46. Toronto: Thompson Educational Publishing.

Shan, H. 2009a. "Shaping the Re-training and Re-education Experiences of Immigrant Women: The Credential and Certificate Regime in Canada." *International Journal of Lifelong Education* 28 (3): 353–369. doi:10.1080/02601370902799150.

Shan, H. 2009b. "Practices on the Periphery: Chinese Immigrant Women Negotiating Occupational Niches in Canada." *Canadian Journal for the Study of Adult Education* 21 (2): 1–18.

Shan, H. 2012. "Articulating the Self to the Engineering Market: Chinese Immigrants' Experiences from a Critical Transformative Learning Perspective." In *Immigration and Settlement: Challenges, Experiences and Opportunities in Global and Local Contexts*, edited by H. Bauder, 95–108. Toronto: The Canadian Scholars' Press.

Shan, H. 2013. "Skill as a Relational Construct: The Hiring Practices in the Engineering Profession in Canada." *Work, Employment and Society* 27 (6): 915–931. doi:10.1177/0950017012474710.

Simons, M., and J. Masschelein. 2006. "The Permanent Quality Tribunal in Education and the Limits of Education Policy." *Policy Futures* 4: 294–307.

Slade, B. 2012. "'From High Skill to High School': Illustrating the Process of Deskilling Immigrants through Reader's Theatre and Institutional Ethnography." *Qualitative Inquiry* 18 (5): 401–413. doi:10.1177/1077800412439526.

Smith, D. E. 1987. *The Everyday World as Problematic: A Feminist Sociology*. Toronto: University of Toronto Press.

Smith, D. E. 2005. *Institutional Ethnography: A Sociology for People*. Toronto: AltaMira Press.

Stanley, L. 1997. *Knowing Feminisms: On Academic Borders, Territories and Tribes*. London: Sage.

Theodore, N. 2007. "Closed Borders, Open Markets: Day Laborers' Struggle for Economic Rights." In *Contesting Neoliberalism: Urban Frontiers*, edited by H. Leitner, J. Peck, and E. Sheppard, 250–265. New York: Guilford.

T & CS Canada. n.d. *Regulated Occupations*. Accessed April 1. http://www.tcscanada.net/canada-companies/canada-immigration-regulated.php.

Webb, P. T., K. N. Gulson, and V. O. Pitton. 2014. "The Neo-liberal Education Policies of Epimeleia Heautou: Caring for the Self in School Markets." *Discourse: Studies in the Cultural Politics of Education* 35 (10): 1–14.

Widick, R. 2003. "Flesh and the Free Market (on Taking Bourdieu to the Options Exchange)." *Theory and Society* 32 (5/6): 679–723. doi:10.1023/B:RYSO.0000004950.74462.26.

Wilson, D. 2004. "Toward a Contingent Urban Neoliberalism." *Urban Geography* 25 (8): 771–83. doi:10.2747/0272-3638.25.8.771.

Wilson, D. 2006. *Cities and Race: America's New Black Ghetto*. New York: Routledge.

Xue, L. 2008. *Social Capital and Employment Entry of Recent Immigrants to Canada*. Ottawa: Citizenship and Immigration Canada.

Yu, K., and H. Ertl. 2010. "Equity in Access to Higher Education in China: The Role of Public and Nonpublic Institutions." *Chinese Education and Society* 43 (6): 36–58. doi:10.2753/CED1061-1932430602.

The making of the 'precarious': examining Indian immigrant IT workers in Canada and their transnational networks with body shops in India

Srabani Maitra

Centre for Feminist Research, York University, Toronto, ON, Canada

> Since the 1990s, temporary staffing agencies have been playing a key role in managing and supplying a ready pool of skilled workers to the global IT market. Yet, such agencies often regulate their workforce to maintain flexible, low-cost and accommodating workers. Due to continuing racial and gendered barriers, many immigrant Indian IT professionals living in Canada are increasingly depending on many such India-based staffing agencies (body shops) to get into IT employment globally. Such associations I argue are turning the workers into a self-regulated and precarious workforce subjected to severe regulations and flexible work patterns of the agencies.

Introduction

Since the 1980s, allied practices of market deregulations, transnational flows of capital, freeing of international trade policies and labour market flexibility have led to an increased mobility of labour around the world. Such changing economic conditions coupled with developments in communication, technology and Information Technology (IT) Enabled Services have spawned the global demand for a well-educated, professional and 'skilled workforce' (Li 2008, 11). New opportunities have enabled these workers to circulate around the world in search of 'competitive market prices for their labour' (Li 2008, 20).

The scope for such global mobility has necessitated the proliferation of temporary staffing agencies that serve as crucial channels in facilitating the global circulation of capital, labour and skill (Vertovec 2002). Within the current neoliberal production and labour distribution system, such agencies serve three purposes: manage and coordinate a ready supply of 'just-in-time' workers to meet employer's requirements; 'match' the right worker to the specific needs of the employer; enhance the efficiency of hiring and production by reducing the employer's cost of recruitment (Barrientos 2011, 14). An apposite example is the 'India-based, global labour management system in the IT [Information Technology] industry known as body shopping' (Xiang 2007, 1) that plays a key role in managing and supplying a ready pool of trained, highly professional and skilled labour to the 'extremely volatile global IT market' (Xiang 2007, 1).

However, in order to ensure the steady supply of a compliant, malleable, 'non-confrontational workforce' (Kelly 2001, 7–8) that is permanently on-call (Smith 2009, 11), these recruitment agencies impose stringent regimes of labour control and regulation (Aneesh 2006; Findlay et al. 2013; Gottfried 1991; Kelly 2001, 2002; Upadhya 2009; Xiang 2001, 2002, 2007). Such control is achieved not necessarily through overt coercive means but through implanting within workers hegemonic desires of opportunity and mobility. The production of a 'docile' workforce is in turn used by these agencies as an inducement for prospective employers and for attracting international contracts or collaborations.

Given the above context, the primary concern of this study revolves around India-based IT recruitment agencies (body shops), and how immigrant Indian IT professionals living in Canada are being increasingly drawn to these Indian body shops to get into IT-related employment globally (including North America). Based on the interviews with 15 Indian immigrant IT workers in Canada and 5 IT recruiters in India, I argue that while immigrant Indian workers are able to get employed in the IT field by cultivating transnational networks with agencies in India, such opportunities have often undesirable consequences. Their associations with body shops are increasingly turning the immigrants into a globally circulating and precarious workforce subjected to multiple insecurities of severe regulations and flexible work patterns of the recruitment agencies. The workers are ready to accept such regulatory conditions in order to avoid unemployment and survive in a labour market that is racialised, gendered and lacks 'stability and predictability' (Standing 2011). Furthermore, the availability of contractual/project-based workers through body shops has ramifications for the Canadian labour market as well. First, Canadian employers are able to hire highly skilled and experienced workers at a cheaper rate. Second, the Canadian state and other stakeholders are absolved from addressing the more vexing issues of continuing gender/race/class discriminations in the labour market, and providing tangible economic and social security to its immigrant populations (especially of colour). Rather, the responsibility is squarely put on the immigrants themselves to continually engage in self-management, strategies of networking and self-initiated lifelong learning in order to remain gainfully employed. Those who are unable to do so are made to believe that they 'have only themselves to blame if they do not bother to set about improving their circumstances' (Heelas and Morris 1992, 8).

The rise of temporary recruitment agencies in the global economy and their labour control techniques

Since the 1990s, there has been a rapid growth in various formal temporary staffing agencies in the developing world that supply short-term contractual workers (especially skilled) to advanced industrial societies (Martin 2012). For many years, countries like USA, Germany, Australia and Canada have been attracting highly skilled workers from places like India and China by offering these temporary workers short-term visas (e.g., H1–B in USA) to enable them to work in project-based contracts. The increase in such agencies can be linked to global capitalism and the rise in demand by multinational companies for a flexible labour force for whom the corporation has to make no definite long-term economic or employment-related commitments (Standing 2011). Companies now increasingly seek out temporary migrant workers as they help keep the costs low and curtail the bargaining rights of employees arising out of long-term affiliations with the company. Employees can be paid less, 'experience-rated pay' can be avoided, 'entitlement to enterprise benefits is less… [and also] there is less risk; taking on somebody temporarily means not making a commitment that might be regretted for whatever reasons' (Standing 2011, 32). The presence of these recruitment agencies therefore provides the employers the opportunity to bypass labour laws and yet at the same time have access to skilled but easily disposable workers (Kelly 2001).

Body shop and the management of contractual workers

An important rendition of temporary staffing agencies is body shopping, under which 'small consultancy firms shop for skilled bodies – i.e., recruit software professionals – in India to contract them out for short-term projects' (Aneesh 2006, 39) to various countries around the world. The flexibility within the IT industry was spurred by growth in IT applications and the need for customised software packages that required IT workers to move from one project to the other (Xiang 2007, 6). The industry 'thus needed not only a sufficient supply of skills but a mobile workforce so that it can respond to market fluctuations with minimum time lag' (Xiang 2007, 6). Body shops fulfil such requirements by supplying migrant workers from India to USA, Australia, Canada and other countries in the Middle East to fulfil short-term/contractual IT jobs in those countries. The system is based on highly integrated global networks, where small consulting agencies in India are usually in liaison with other globally located recruitment agencies to place workers in different corporations (Xiang 2007). In the process, 'each agent in the chain [takes] away part of the worker's monthly wage as part of the deal' (Xiang 2007, 5).

Unlike other conventional recruiters or 'head hunters' who only 'introduce' workers to employers thereby serving more as facilitators, body shops 'manage' employees 'on behalf of employers – from sponsoring their temporary work visas to paying their salaries, arranging for accommodation and the like' (Xiang 2007, 4). Thus workers hired by body shops have no direct relationships with the main employer and can be terminated any time. Later he or she can be placed into another project or asked to wait till a new contract comes in (Xiang 2007).

The practice of body shopping is attractive to IT workers as it ensures them an entry into the global economy by allowing what is perceived as unrestricted movement of labour and skills around the world. The scope for 'multiple mobility' that Indian IT workers get while working for body shops is rare for any other class of migrants from the region. Given the cognitive nature of the work, its association with a high level of academic competence and the prospect of working in various parts of the developed world, working for body-shopping agencies is a matter of social prestige for many professionals in India – a way of thinking that persists even after the immigration of some of these professionals. Agencies, therefore, stimulate the hopes of the workers by their projected ability to place them in the West (Aneesh 2006). While such international placements are not without dilemma and often place the migrant worker in a vexed position where they have to constantly negotiate transnational spaces and identities (racial and cultural), the opportunity to be in a western country does induce the self-regulation of the worker's mind and body.

What is crucial to understand within this particular recruiting system is how such agencies buttress neoliberal labour market practices through multiple processes of modulating and managing flexible, low-cost and accommodating yet skilled workers. The process of labour control is apparent at every level, from recruitment to placement to movement from one contract to another. Rather than being overtly coercive, such regulation is enacted, 'not by telling workers to perform a task, nor necessarily by punishing workers for their failure, but by shaping an environment in which there are no alternatives to performing the work as desired' (Aneesh 2006, 110). Control, therefore, is embedded in the work structure itself that prods workers' inclination to self-regulation by repeatedly emphasising the competitive nature of their activity. Each professional becomes a productive terminal in a highly unstable and competitive field of activities where individual success, failure or survival depends on a relational context of staying ahead of the other competitors even while working through a network of collaborations. Anxious to fit into this flexible and competitive work culture of the agencies and the neoliberal market at large, workers thus remain absorbed in constant monitoring and modification of their attitude, appearance and behaviour (Findlay et al. 2013). Such self-regulation is imperative to survive in this new economy; otherwise as Berardi (2009) points out, one will be eliminated and labelled as a failure.

Let us scrutinise how control is entrenched in the work structures of the agencies. As discussed earlier, agencies like body shops need to ensure the flexibility of labour by always maintaining a reserve pool of workers who can serve employer's needs at any moment. This presupposes that workers as well have to be footloose and ever ready to fulfil such labour market demands. They have to be 'transnationally flexible' as well, since they can be asked any moment to go back to India in between bigger projects (Aneesh 2006). The need to remain flexible can be passed on through several ways. For example, agencies constantly harp on the need for the workers to keep learning new skills and remain prepared to join any project on a moment's notice. Flexibility resides here not only in terms of the bundle of skills that workers are able to bring to their work through a constant process of upgrading themselves, but also in the readiness to move and relocate themselves repeatedly in terms of available contracts. It is a hegemonic process where the market itself is projected in such a manner that it seems imperative to the workers to self-regulate their behaviour and work patterns so that they can fit into the competitive, capitalist economy. Such self-regulation entails constant modulation of their skills, knowledge, intelligence, creativity and/or communicational abilities to suit the indeterminate and ever-changing demands of capital and knowledge economy (Berardi 2009). This flexible disposition is however immensely disruptive of the worker's lives and 'exemplifies to a degree the colonisation of the life world for systemic purposes' (Aneesh 2006, 48). The constant need to be in flux takes away from the workers their social lives, happiness and eroticism and leaves them in an impoverished state of existence (Berardi 2009).

Individualisation of workers is another key technique that agencies utilise to control workers. Xiang (2007) shows through his ethnography on body shops in India how agencies portray individual merit and knowledge of the workers as key to success so that even when workers are retrenched, they are made to believe that such set-back is due to their lack of merit or mismatch and not because of the agents or the employers. Such emphasis on merit and skills serves two other purposes. First, it helps the agencies to justify hierarchical differences between employees as 'natural [since] every individual has different merits' (Xiang 2007, 9). Second, it undermines any possibility for collective solidarity/bargaining that might arise within the workers. Negotiations between workers and agents are usually conducted on a one-to-one basis, and workers are prohibited from discussing their salary or contractual terms with other workers under the rubric of maintaining professionalism (Xiang 2007). The end result is the creation of a 'more manageable workforce that is compliant with the needs of their employers' (Kelly 2002, 407). By employing such techniques to maintain an obedient workforce, body shops thus contribute to the bolstering of what Kelly (2001) defines as a 'labour control regime'. While Kelly contends that such a regime is usually operationalised by the concerted networks of a wide range of actors (from national governments to villages, municipalities and so on) involved in a 'complex network of relationships' (Kelly 2001, 20), recruitment agencies often constitute one of the strategic participants in such a regime. They feed on the looming sense of insecurity that workers enter into as soon as they start working for the temporary agencies. Yet, it is this insecurity coupled with desire for economic accumulation and a 'good' life that lead to the 'voluntary yet inevitable submission' (Berardi 2009, 192) of the workers to the exigencies of the body shops.

Research method

The current paper is based on a qualitative study of the experiences of 15 immigrant Indian IT workers (11 men, 4 women) who, unable to get jobs in Canada, utilised transnational networks with body shops to find employment in their own areas of experience. All of these interviewees had university degrees (primarily in Science, Commerce and Engineering) and 4–6 years of experience in their respective areas (e.g., programming, database architecture and business intelligence analysis). They were between the ages of 30–35, married and have lived in Canada for more than three years. All the women and nine of the men had children as well. Interviews were also conducted with three recruiters in Kolkata, the economic epicentre of eastern India and two in New Delhi, the national capital of India. Both New Delhi and Kolkata are amongst the top seven cities selected by the National Association of Software and Service Companies (NASSCOM) for IT development and leadership (NASSCOM and A.T. Kearney 2012–13). The initial contacts with the recruiters were done through two of my Indian interviewees who personally spoke to the agency personnel in order to introduce me and my research to them. Subsequently, snowball sampling was used in identifying 'cases of interest from people who know people who know what cases are information-rich, that is, good examples for study, good interview subjects' (Patton 1990, 182).

I conducted semi-structured (open-ended) face-to-face interviews with the participants, and as semi-structured interviews are much more flexible (Fontana and Frey 2000) such interviews enabled the participants to narrate personal experiences in a variety of ways not necessarily dictated by linear or temporal logic. This allowed for the depth, complexity and contradictory experiences of interviewees to emerge, which structured interviews or questionnaires might have hindered. Finally, thematic analysis was undertaken to identify patterns or themes within the data-set (Braun and Clarke 2006). The themes were then pieced together to prepare a comprehensive picture of the collective experiences of the interviewees (Aronson 1994). In order to maintain privacy and confidentiality, all the names mentioned in this paper are pseudonyms.

Exploring transnational networks: issues of flexibility, vulnerability and regulation

Canadian labour market barriers

My interviews with the Indian immigrants in Canada revealed a concern that now has been documented extensively in a growing body of literature: the multi-faceted labour market barriers experienced by immigrants of colour in the Canadian labour market (Mirchandani et al. 2010). Despite being highly educated with experience in the IT sector, my respondents faced what can be described after Guo (2013) as the 'triple glass effect' (glass gate, glass door and glass ceiling) while trying to translate their skills into appropriate opportunities in Canada. In what became an exhausting and alienating experience, for months and years, they kept applying for jobs and getting rejected. What was even more debilitating was that in most cases there were no definite acknowledgement or replies from the employers or the recruiters about their applications. The pervasive nature of this experience of an insurmountable barrier led many Indian immigrants to perceive their lack of access to the job market due to the racialised nature of the labour market itself which excludes those not seen as 'desirable' in terms of appearance or skin colour (Maitra 2013). In some cases they were either asked to get Canadian work experience, or told that their foreign credentials were not enough and that they need Canadian education or certification. Many others were unemployed even after undergoing retraining in Canada. To sum, the Indian workers encountered the 'glass gate' that denied them an entry into professional communities along with the 'glass door' that blocked their job opportunities by devaluing their credentials (Guo 2013). Such demands for Canadian experience or credentials also become coded euphemisms for hiding the more overt references to race or gender.

Thus, Subhash, a computer professional from India who had to work in a retail store for sustaining his family, as well as people like him, expressed the frustration he felt for remaining confined to the grinding chores of low-level retail work and the looming economic anxieties that seemed to constantly cloud over his life ever since his immigration:

> it was just so frustrating. I could never imagine that something like this would happen to me in Canada and I will have to work in such a low position. It was such a setback. They could give me immigration based on my skills but then they wouldn't hire me because now they find those very skills not good enough. Is this some kind of a joke?

Subhash's experience explicates how immigrants' skills and education are discounted and remain under-utilised (Reitz 2011) in the Canadian labour market. Guo (2009) contends that such de-recognition of foreign skills arises out of three interlocking factors. First, anything different from the Canadian norm is seen as deficient; second, knowledge is racialised in Canada so that it is the education and skills brought by immigrants of colour that is considered 'inferior' and 'incompatible' with the sociocultural 'fabric of traditional Canada' (40); third, the evaluative process is based on 'objectivist ontology' and 'liberal universalism' (48) that maintains a 'one-size-fits-all criterion' for measuring foreign credentials rather than recognising the sociocultural and political context within which knowledge is produced. Together, these three phenomena successfully 'exclude the undesirable [read: racialised immigrants] and perpetuate oppression in Canada' (Guo 2009, 49).

Furthermore, the need for Subhash and many other immigrants of colour to take up low-paying jobs for economic survival, a manifestation of the 'glass floor' effect (De la Rica, Dolado, and Llorens 2005), severely deskills them in a rapidly shifting technological field such as IT and impacts their home and family lives. Summing up these multiple processes affecting immigrants of colour, it can be therefore argued after Galabuzi (2004) that, 'persistent devaluation of racialised human capital, social marginalisation, and racial polarisation in the labour market' turn these racialised groups 'into a reserve army of labour that bears a racial dividend for capital' (198) through the widespread production of structural anxiety, need to somehow survive at the bottom of the capitalist order and the consequent willingness to take up any opportunities when they come.

Transnational networks

Unable to find jobs in the mainstream Canadian labour market, my respondents started to network actively with their own ethnic groups in the IT sector. It was, through their friends and colleagues living both in India and Canada, that the interviewees garnered information about 'body-shopping' agencies that do global placement of IT personnel. After contacting the organisations, they had to go to India to personally meet and liaise with the agencies. The initial process took some time and they had to stay in India for at least a month, in order to meet the recruiters, appear for interviews and understand project details. Once hired, the workers were given some training and subsequently placed in various short-term, contractual projects in India. Consequently most of them were moved to other projects in different parts of the world. Five of them were placed eventually in Canada.

While body shoppers have been employing Indian IT workers globally for many years now on temporary migrant visa, what is unique about my research is the hiring of immigrant IT workers by the agencies. My interview with the organisations revealed that this process proliferated with the global recession in 2008 and the policy changes in H1-B visa that severely hit labour migration to the USA, one of the major destination points for IT professionals from India. One of the Indian recruiters from New Delhi pointed out:

> since the recession in North America we have been contacted by many Green card holders and immigrants from Canada asking us to place them in IT projects. We are successfully placing them in various projects. It works out for us as we do not have to worry about their VISA status, or travel documents when we send them abroad.

This new arrangement, while seemingly favouring both the agencies as well as the immigrants, actually has very different consequences in terms of the relationship between the prospective workers and their recruiters. While the agencies are able to save on the visa-processing formalities of the workers and get profit out of the deal, for the immigrants, these short contracts provide them with a renewed hope to enter their own professional fields in Canada/ North America. Thus, Raju, a software developer, showered praise on the practice of body-shopping for providing him with the global opportunity to utilise his education and skills and thereby releasing him from the drudgeries of unemployment and low income, 'I have been trying for two years and never got an opportunity in Canada. Now at least I am employed in my own field. I have a decent life'.

Leading newspapers in cities like Kolkata and New Delhi now often carry advertisements of organisations that offer to provide training and global placement to qualified IT workers. Such advertisements harp on visions of economic success, a new valorisation of the personal self attached to the ability of doing work relating to problem-solving, complex data processing and the insertion into a global corporate culture and lifestyle based on mobility, excitement and passion for competitive work. Immigrants and Green card holders are now preferred by many body shoppers for both administrative reasons (ease of emplacement in North America primarily) and also as a category of 'good qualified workers' who through their desire for mobility and successful attempts to translate those desires into practice embody the best ideals of work ethics that body-shopping inherently depends on. As one of the recruiters explained:

> if we find that there is a well-qualified person who is already an immigrant or Green card holder, you see he has already been in the foreign country, so he would know the work culture there, so we don't have to worry about training him. He has keen knowledge of how things work in the global corporate culture. We just put him in a project.

The self-regulated worker

Despite the positive adulation of agencies shared by the interviewees, what I also noted was how the workers were subtly regulated to meet agencies' demands for a flexible, self-motivated and committed workforce. Such regulation was achieved in several ways. First, all of the interviewees mentioned that they were clearly told by the recruiters of the need for them to remain flexible. For instance, Amin, an immigrant IT specialist from Toronto, mentioned how initially he had to work in Noida (near New Delhi in India) for seven months in a project for a leading IT company before being sent to the Middle East. He described to me his hiring process in detail:

> when they [body shopping agency] hired me they made it very clear that there is no guarantee where I will be placed for projects. So I was kind of prepared. My only concern was that my wife and son were in Toronto by themselves. But I had no option. I had to get into a good job. First I worked in Noida for 7 months. When I was almost done with my first assignment, the agent informed me of a bigger project in the Middle East for 5 months. I promptly agreed. After the Middle East they sent me to Toronto to work in a project for a Telecom Company. This is how body shopping works.

What becomes evident from Amin's story is how racialised immigrant IT workers' vulnerable position and lack of stable jobs in the Canadian labour market force them to be amenable to the 'contractualisation' of their lives (Standing 2011, 37) within body shops. They prefer accepting the flexible work patterns rather than having to go back to unemployment. Implicit within this preference is the fear arising out of structural problems of unemployment and racial discrimination making them susceptible to the profit motives of body-shopping agencies. Additionally, Amin's story is also symptomatic of the constant sociocultural remaking that workers undertake when moved from one country to the other. Every time when placed in a new country, a new project and a new team, the workers have to manage their attitudes, approach or communicational styles to adapt to the changing environment. As Amin pointed out:

> this work has taught me to control my emotions. I have learnt to be more accommodating. I have to work with different people all the time, sometimes of different race. They are all different. So I try to study them, watch their habits, strengths or weaknesses and accordingly deal with them. Sometimes I have to be extra polite to get my work done and sometimes I have to be curt so that I am not taken for granted. This is all for survival. You have to learn to watch your step here.

What follows from the above is how along with the manipulation of digital data, workers are also required to harness one's dispositional qualities such as emotions, intelligence, social communication and cultural sensitivity.

Recruiters were quite aware of the barriers that Indian IT workers often experience in Canada and clearly took pride in the fact of how through their transnational contacts they were integrating these workers into the global economy. A recruiting agency spokesperson asserted that:

> when they [immigrants] come to us we tell them that we can provide them with global opportunities. They can even get jobs in Canada and America. But they have to prove themselves. They have to work hard as IT is a highly competitive field.

What is interesting to note in the above remark is how recruiters ceaselessly raise hope in the mind of the workers about their potential chance to work and live in the West while being more integrated into productive circuits of capitalist work processes as opposed to remaining peripheral to such circuits. Failure, however, remains the dark underside of this hope, always accompanying it unless the worker relentlessly submits to the various mechanisms of control and productivity demanded of him/her. For Indian immigrants who have already settled in Canada with their families, the arousal of such desires is quite effective in moulding them into 'productive' yet 'docile' workers. Being aware of the fact that their own job-searching techniques might not be effective in Canada to get them employed, they depend on these recruiting agencies and their networks to gain an entry into the global IT field. Moreover, they are aware of the intense competition and the performance-based incentives the work entails; they know that in order to remain employed, they need to be always 'visible' to their employers (Upadhya 2009), actively embodying all the qualities that the corporation or recruiting agencies demand of them.

Therefore, in a bid to escape the immovable status at the lowest end of the Canadian economic and social hierarchy, immigrant workers during the process of body-shopping take it upon themselves to regulate their mind and body to ensure that they belong to the 'desired' category of employees from the perspective of recruiting agencies. Sheila, an Oracle programmer from Toronto, described the various strategies employees adopt to continue working with the agents:

> we have to show our eagerness to learn and upgrade. We often have knowledge-transfer sessions where we are upgraded about new systems and software and even if we know about some of them already we still have to be in those sessions. It shows our willingness to learn. The working hours can be very erratic. We often work on weekends and till late nights. We have constant meetings that can go beyond the specified work hours. We are as if always on call, even during vacations. [Q: can you say no?]. Technically we can but nobody ever says no, it's an unwritten commitment. Who knows what will happen if we say no?

Sheila's experience reveals how control embedded within work structures leads to the self-regulation of the employees, where work effectively transforms the self. Being under the constant insecurity of not knowing whether they will continue to be working with the agents or not, workers remain submissive to the needs of the employers. Production of value under these circumstances always already requires the constant self-production of an individual self-hood that best responds to and internalises all the ideals emanating from the work environment (Gorz 2010). The fear of losing what they have prepares the IT workers to 'do labour as and when required, in conditions largely not of ... [their] own choosing' (Standing 2011, 13).

Additionally, they also lack any team-based solidarity, in fact the cultivation of any long-term relationship – between employees – is seen as nullifying the competitive edge of the individual by placing him or her under non-work-related obligations and emotions of trust/empathy/sensitivity.

These emotions can in turn have a corrosive effect on the ability to stay ahead of the field in a social milieu that recognises and awards only competitive flexibility. The competition and insecurity inherent within the work processes render each worker as concerned only about his/her self-interests. Every contract is different, salaries vary and the 'blurring of boundaries of decision-making and responsibility adds to the precariousness' of the workers (Standing 2011, 37).

Gendered networks

Various contestations over gender are integral to the creation of particular types of desirable worker identities through which the process of body-shopping takes shape. The gendered structure of transnational practices of body-shopping was evident when agencies expressed their scepticism about placing women (especially unmarried, single) to countries outside India during my interviews. Agencies were reluctant to take extra responsibilities for ensuring the security of women. They also mentioned that usually its immigrant men who primarily contact them for jobs rather than immigrant women. For example, one of the recruiters shared the following:

> you know it's a lot of responsibility to place a single, unmarried woman in a foreign project. We have to be extra careful because if something happens their parents will come and question us. We do get female clients but we prefer males.

What is important to note here is how within the global circuits of capitalism, women continue to be seen as weaker, subordinate and in need of protection. This infantilisation of women workers (who must be placed under some form of tutorship) combined with an overt threat perception of women's sexuality (as distractive and disrupting for the smooth functioning of work) lead to the negation of their skills and qualifications and curtail their possibility for economic mobility.

As far as the women interviewees were concerned, gendered work responsibilities were an important consideration when it came to working in contractual projects. For example, Sheila pointed out how difficult it was for her to go to Germany to work as she had a small baby. Since her husband was working in Canada, she had to ask her mother to accompany her. Maya, a programmer, similar to others, had to leave behind her home and family in Canada to work in a project in India for seven months. While working in India loneliness pervaded her life and she would often come home and cry. Yet, in the morning while leaving for her office she would put on a visage of a happy, competent self as if satisfied with her professional achievements. This is what I call a masking effect where work entails the appropriation of multiple personas to suit professional requirements.

Razia was the only one who never had to travel alone as she and her husband had similar technical skills and were always placed together in the same project. While all the women mentioned how agencies try to place spouses together in the same country, what they were mainly sceptical about was the masculinised work environment of the IT industry (Butterwick, Jubas, and Liptrot 2008). Female participants indicated that they had to learn how to speak up and emphasise their work during team meetings as male colleagues often tried to dominate. Moreover, women complained how long working hours disrupted their family lives. Since the women were primarily responsible for housework and childcare, most of them often found it difficult to keep up with the high pace of the industry. Thus they would constantly try to upgrade themselves and show more willingness to accommodate in order to overcome their perceived feminine 'inefficiency'. But that too had its repercussions. Sheila mentioned how often she would come home and shout at her husband and child for simple reasons. By realising how her frustration at workplace is turning into anger at home, she joined a meditation course to de-stress her mind and body. She thus mentioned, 'I realised I couldn't leave my job. So I thought let me at least take care of my mind. What else can I do?' Along with formal training, women thus engaged in several self-directed learning practices to survive the 'IT work culture' (Butterwick, Jubas, and Liptrot 2008, 116).

Concluding remarks: implications for lifelong learning

In this chapter I discussed how transnational networks with India-based body-shopping agencies are assisting Indian immigrant IT workers in Canada to get employment in their own fields. Faced with various systemic and racialised barriers such as the 'triple glass effect' in the Canadian labour market, these workers strategically build their own networks to enter their respective fields rather than working in low-end, contingent sectors. Yet, at the same time, to access such opportunities immigrants are learning to become more adaptable and flexible to suit the demands of the staffing agencies. Along with their skills in digitised work they are now also expected by the agencies to imbibe a range of social, cultural, emotional and communicative skills necessary to quickly adapt from one site of work to the next over a very short period of time. Such mobilisation of the total entity of the individual becomes emblematic of what Berardi (2009) calls the 'soul' of the individual that is now put to work. Fear, insecurity, distance from the close ones permeate their lives while they struggle to hold on to their temporary employment contracts in a fiercely competitive neoliberal workspace. They are thus turning into a precarious workforce.

Both the Canadian state and the Indian recruiting agencies are complicit in the production of this precarious soul. While the state and its allied labour market do not adequately address the systemic barriers experienced by immigrants of colour, they, however, do not shy away from employing the same workers under low-paid contracts when supplied by Indian body shops. Similar to the migrant workers hired through temporary worker programme (Foster 2012), these immigrant employees can also be paid low wages, less benefits and can be retrenched easily during downturns. What is important to highlight here is the inherent contradiction in this growing workforce. While the Indian workers' professional skills qualify them for entry into the high end, cognitive global labour force, their racialised identities as immigrants of colour undercut this privilege by relegating them to a position of flexible, cheap and vulnerable workers.

The Indian recruiters, on the other hand, aware of the job insecurity and vulnerability experienced by these workers in Canada subtly control and regulate them to their own advantage and profit. They manage and govern the immigrants to fulfil the labour needs of the globalised economy that 'require a committed, educated and multiskilled workforce, able to learn new abilities continuously and take up new functions as the market dictates' (Martin 1994, 152).

What I further want to highlight in this paper is how the responsibility for employment-related learning and labour market incorporation is being downloaded on the immigrants themselves. For instance, when faced with racial barriers and marginalisation in the Canadian labour market, the Indian immigrants had to take initiatives to identify networking opportunities, develop interpersonal skills, undertake IT-related training and come up with individual strategies to enter the labour market through the body shops.

In the absence of proper resources and adequate guidance, they were thus expected to depend on their own abilities to maximise their latent potentialities and become self-sufficient and enterprising worker subjects (Fenwick 2002), suitable for the neoliberal labour market. In Canada, this entrepreneurialism is promoted as an effective response to the problem of work (Shragge 1997) so that people expecting to penetrate the labour market are made to depend on their own initiatives and abilities rather than on any kind of cushioning provided by the state (Fenwick 2002). Such emphasis on entrepreneurialism 'obscures the reality of systemic racism and discrimination' (Goldberg 2007, 33) and is a manifestation of the distributive social justice in lifelong learning that 'seemingly values all individuals equally' and 'assumes that lifelong learners are all the *same* with the *same* learning needs, and therefore treating them as the *same* will erase issues of inequity and injustice' (Guo 2010, 163). The discourse of lifelong learning then becomes a tool of governing individuals to accept certain normative discourses about the neoliberal values of productivity, competitiveness and self-regulation. I therefore join Guo in advocating for a transnational lifelong learning that would emphasise 'recognitive justice' and 'pluralist citizenship'. This framework, Guo (2010) suggests, would reject:

> the deficit model of lifelong learning that seeks to assimilate migrants to the dominant social, cultural and educational norms of the host society. Alternatively, it proposes to build an inclusive education that acknowledges and affirms cultural difference and diversity as positive and desirable assets. (164–165)

References

Aneesh, A. 2006. *Virtual Migration: The Programming of Globalisation*. Durham and London: Duke University Press.

Aronson, J. 1994. "A Pragmatic View of Thematic Analysis." *The Qualitative Report* 2 (1). Accessed April 10, 2013. http://www.nova.edu/ssss/QR/BackIssues/QR2-1/aronson.html.

Barrientos, S. 2011. *Labour Chains: Analysing the Role of Labour Contractors in Global Production Networks*. Brooks World Poverty Institute Working Paper 15. Manchester: University of Manchester.

Berardi, F. 2009. *The Soul at Work: From Alienation to Autonomy*. Los Angeles: Semiotext(e).

Braun, V., and V. Clarke. 2006. "Using Thematic Analysis in Psychology." *Qualitative Research in Psychology* 3 (2): 77–101. doi:10.1191/1478088706qp063oa.

Butterwick, S., K. Jubas, and J. Liptrot. 2008. "Lessons of Gender Politics from the Centre and the Fringes of the Knowledge-based Society." In *The Future of Lifelong Learning and Work: Critical Perspectives*, edited by D. W. Livingstone, K. Mirchandani, and P. H. Sawchuk, 107–18. Rotterdam: Sense.

De la Rica, S., J. Dolado, and V. Llorens. 2005. *Ceiling and Floors: Gender Wage Gaps by Education in Spain*. Discussion Paper No. 1483. Bonn: The Institute for the Study of Labour, IZA.

Fenwick, T. 2002. "Transgressive Desires: New Enterprising Selves in the New Capitalism." *Work, Employment and Society* 16 (4): 703–723. doi:10.1177/095001702 321587433.

Findlay, A., D. McCollum, S. Shubin, E. Apsite, and Z. Krisjane. 2013. "The Role of Recruitment Agencies in Imagining and Producing the 'Good' Migrant." *Social & Cultural Geography* 14 (2): 145–167. doi:10.1080/14649365.2012.737008.

Fontana, A., and J. Frey. 2000. "The Interview: From Structured Questions to Negotiated Text." In *Handbook of Qualitative Research*, edited by N. Denzin and Y. Lincoln, 645–672. London: Sage.

Foster, J. 2012. "Making Temporary Permanent: The Silent Transformation of the Temporary Foreign Worker Program." *Just Labour: A Canadian Journal of Work and Society* 19: 22–46.

Galabuzi, G.-E. 2004. "Racialising the Division of Labour: Neoliberal Restructuring and the Economic Segregation of Canada's Racialised Groups." In *Challenging the Market: The Struggle to Regulate Work and Income*, edited by J. Stanford and L. F. Vosko, 175–204. Montréal: McGill-Queen's University Press.

Goldberg, M. P. 2007. "How Current Globalisation Discourses Shape Access: Professions and Trade Policy in Ontario." *Canadian Issues: Foreign Credential Recognition* Spring: 31–35.

Gorz, A. 2010. *The Immaterial: Knowledge, Value and Capital*. London: Seagull Books.

Gottfried, H. 1991. "Mechanisms of Control in the Temporary Help Service Industry." *Sociological Forum* 6 (4): 699–713. doi:10.1007/BF01114408.

Guo, S. 2009. "Difference, Deficiency, and Devaluation: Tracing the Roots of Non/recognition of Foreign Credentials for Immigrant Professionals in Canada." *Canadian Journal for the Study of Adult Education* 22 (1): 37–52.

Guo, S. 2010. "Toward Recognitive Justice: Emerging Trends and Challenges in Transnational Migration and Lifelong Learning." *International Journal of Lifelong Education* 29 (2): 149–167. doi:10.1080/02601371003616533.

Guo, S. 2013. "Economic Integration of Recent Chinese Immigrants in Canada's Second-tier Cities: The Triple Glass Effect and Immigrants' Downward Social Mobility." *Canadian Ethnic Studies* 45 (3): 95–115. doi:10.1353/ces.2013.0047.

Heelas, P., and P. Morris. 1992. "Enterprise Culture: Its Values and Value." In *The Values of the Enterprise Culture: The Moral Debate*, edited by P. Heelas and P. Morris, 1–26. London: Routledge.

Kelly, P. F. 2001. "The Political Economy of Local Labour Control in the Philippines." *Economic Geography* 77 (1): 1–22. doi:10.2307/3594084.

Kelly, P. F. 2002. "Spaces of Labour Control: Comparative Perspectives from Southeast Asia." *Transactions, Institute of British Geographers* 27 (4): 395–411. doi:10.1111/1475-5661.00062.

Li, P. S. 2008. "World Migration in the Age of Globalisation: Policy Implications and Challenges." *New Zealand Population Review* 33/34: 1–22.

Maitra, S. 2013. "Points of Entry: South Asian Immigrant Women's Entry into Enclave Entrepreneurship in Toronto." *South Asian Diaspora* 5 (1): 123–137. doi:10.1080/19438192.2013.721065.

Martin, E. 1994. *Flexible Bodies: Tracking Immunity in American Culture-from the Days of Polio to the Age of AIDS*. Boston: Beacon Press.

Martin, P. 2012. "High-skilled Migrants: S&E Workers in the United States." *American Behavioural Scientist* 56 (8): 1058–1079. doi:10.1177/0002764212441786.

Mirchandani, K., R. Ng, N. Coloma-Moya, S. Maitra, T. Rawlings, H. Shan, K. Siddiqui, and B. Slade. 2010. "Transitioning into Precarious Work: Immigrants' Learning and Resistance." In *Challenging Transitions in Learning and Work: Reflections on Policy and Practice*, edited by P. Sawchuk and A. Taylor, 231–242. Rotterdam: Sense.

The National Association of Software and Services Companies (NASSCOM), and A.T. Kearney. 2012–13. *Location Road Map for IT-BPO Growth: Assessment of 50 Leading Cities*. Accessed March 10, 2013. http://www.nasscom.org/sites/default/files/researchreports/Executive_Summary_5.pdf.

Patton, M. Q. 1990. *Qualitative Evaluation and Research Methods*. Newbury Park and London: Sage.

Reitz, J. G. 2011. "Canada: New Initiatives and Approaches to Immigration and Nation-building." Paper presented at Immigration Policy in an era of Globalisation, Dallas, May 18–20, 1–47. Accessed March 12, 2013. http://pscourses.ucsd.edu/ps150a/resources/Controlling-Immigration–Chap-3–Canada.pdf.

Shragge, E. 1997. *Workfare: Ideology for a New Underclass*. Canada: Garamond.

Smith, J. 2009. *Preface to the Soul at Work: From Alienation to Autonomy by F. Berardi*. Los Angeles: Semiotext(e).

Standing, G. 2011. *The Precariat: The New Dangerous Class*. New York: Bloomsbury Academic.

Upadhya, C. 2009. "Controlling Offshore Knowledge Workers: Power and Agency in India's Software Outsourcing Industry." *New Technology, Work and Employment* 24 (1): 2–18. doi:10.1111/j.1468-005X.2008.00215.x.

Vertovec, S. 2002. *Transnational Networks and Skilled Labour Migration*. Ladenburg: Ladenburger Diskurs "Migration" Gottlieb Daimler- und Karl Benz-Stiftung.

Xiang, B. 2001. "Structuration of Indian Information Technology Professionals' Migration to Australia: An Ethnographic Study." *International Migration* 39 (5): 73–90. doi:10.1111/1468-2435.00172.

Xiang, B. 2002. "Ethnic Transnational Middle Classes in Formation: A Case Study of Indian Information Technology Professionals." Paper presented at the 52nd Annual Conference of Political Studies Association (UK), Making Politics Count, University of Aberdeen, April 5–7.

Xiang, B. 2007. *Global "Body Shopping": An Indian Labour System in the Information Technology Industry*. Princeton: Princeton University Press.

Becoming transnational: exploring multiple identities of students in a Mandarin–English bilingual programme in Canada

Yan Zhang and Yan Guo

Werklund School of Education, University of Calgary, Calgary, Canada

> Guided by post-structural perspectives of identities as processes of becoming and transculturation and transnationalism, this study explores how multilingual students in a Mandarin–English bilingual programme form their sense of identities in a dynamic process. Multiple forms of data are collected, including observations, interviews and documents. The findings indicate that multilingual students are mobile, namely, they move across linguistic, cultural and ethnic spaces of interaction. In addition, they challenge the dominant discourse of any fixed and hyphenated identity and take up transcultural and transnational identities that allow their comfortable circulation among different worlds. This study calls for a need to unfold children's multiple and mobile identities and explores new possibilities for life.

Introduction

Foreign-born and Canadian-born children and youth from immigrant families have a numerically strong presence in Canadian society. In 2006, such children represented about 20% of all young Canadians under the age of 18 and are expected to reach 25% by 2016 (Canadian Council on Social Development 2006). Many of these children are multilingual. More than 200 languages were reported in the 2011 Census as a home language or mother tongue (Statistics Canada 2012). The dominant discourse tends to present immigrant children as a problematic group stuck 'between two cultures' (Gardner 2012, 891). In the study of globalisation and transnational migration, adult immigrants' experiences and perspectives are well studied (Satzewich and Wong 2006). Little attention has been paid to immigrant children (see Hoerder, Hébert, and Schmitt 2006, for an exception). This study explores how immigrant children negotiate their identities in transnational contexts.

This study answers the call of Hébert, Guo, and Pellerin (2008) to explore the realities of multilingual students' construction of multiple identifications through multiple languages and literacies. It aims to explore the process of how a group of multilingual children in a Mandarin–English bilingual programme become transcultural and transnational in their multiple literacy practices and identity negotiation. Two research questions guided this study:

(1) How do multilingual children engage in transcultural and transnational literacy practices?
(2) How do they negotiate their complex transnational identities among these literacy practices?

Theoretical frameworks and prior research

The study draws on two theoretical frameworks: (1) post-structural perspectives of identities as processes of becoming (Andreotti 2008; Deleuze 1990; Deleuze and Guattari 1987; Kramsch 2009; Semetsky 2006) and (2) transculturation (e.g., Hébert, Wilkinson, and Ali 2008) and transnationalism (e.g., Vertovec 1999, 2009). We will take up each in turn.

Post-structural understandings of identities

Most previous studies on immigrant children's identities have viewed identity as an essential part of self associated with dimensions of culture, ethnicity, nationality, gender, religions and race (Hébert, Wilkinson, and Ali 2008; Michael-Luna 2008). Post-structural scholars view identity as processes of becoming (Deleuze 1990; Deleuze and Guattari 1987; Semetsky 2006). This means identity is provisional and relational (Andreotti 2008; Kramsch 2009). The provisionality of identities can be understood in both symbolic and historical dimensions (Kramsch 2009). First, post-structuralists suggest that the self is formed through the use of language and other symbolic systems. Embedded in webs of social relations that involve multiple symbolic exchanges, individuals' subjectivities always carry potentials for change (Hébert 2001; Kramsch 2009). For example, students can shift their senses of themselves as language learners, painters, computer game players, text message writers, story makers and online chatters as they shift time and space in their social interactions, actual or virtual. Second, post-structuralists believe that subjects strive to see themselves and others as embodying their full range of historical possibilities – 'hearing and seeing not only what they say and do, but what they could have said and done in the past, and what they could say and do in the future given the appropriate circumstances' (Kramsch 2009, 18). One could say that becoming a subject means becoming aware of the gap between the words that people utter and the many meanings these words could have, as well as between who one is and who one could be. The historical possibilities and potentiality suggest the provisionality of subjectivity (Andreotti 2008).

Identities are relational, which means an individual is formed not only through interpersonal relationships with others, but also through intrapersonal changes (Kramsch 2009), as identity involves the conscious mind and unconscious body's memories, fantasies, identifications and projections of the individual, all of which are always products of our socialisation in a given culture (Kramsch 2009; Weedon 1987). In examining immigrant youth's perceptions of identifications in an increasingly globalised society, Hébert, Wilkinson, and Ali (2008) have found that the immigrant youth are mobile in imagining themselves as others – as elsewhere in another place or time. They are familiar with and aware of the journeys of both their parents and themselves across cultural and other spaces of interaction. Being aware of change, they can either redefine identifications beyond and across cultural, linguistic, religious, ethnic and racial boundaries or disregard them. These actions and experiences of imagination and awareness are relational. These relationships, in turn, can be situated within a framework consisting of continua of mobilities of mind, body and boundaries. According to Hébert, Wilkinson, and Ali (2008), mobility of mind allows for mobile identities and shifting experiences of belonging between different references of identification. Mobility of bodies refers to migration and frequent movement across places and different spaces of interaction. Mobility of boundaries recognises shifting territorial, political, cultural, economic, social and individual boundaries.

Most previous studies on identities drawn from Deleuzian post-structural perspectives were conducted in French immersion programmes in Canada and are in their very early stages, compared to research on literacy (Dufresne 2009). Adopting post-structural perspectives of treating identities as processes of becoming, we find this is insufficient as it does not accommodate the dynamic interactions between transnational and transcultural communities envisioned by students in the Mandarin–English bilingual programme in this study. It is important to expand post-structural understandings of identities by including transnational and transcultural issues. All these strands draw more attention towards relationships, linkages and flows. These perspectives are woven together to explore the on-going and open-ended process of multilingual children's mobile literacy practices and identity formation.

Transculturation and transnationalism

Transculturation refers to 'the process of individuals and societies changing themselves by integrating diverse cultural life-ways into dynamic new ones' (Hoerder, Hébert, and Schmitt 2006, 13). During the process of transculturation, cultures are fluid. Two or more different cultures interact and envisage the formation of new cultures in which some existing cultural features are combined, while some are lost and new features are generated (Murray 2010). 'More a perspective than a fixed concept, transculturation permits re-readings of homogenised histories that construct belongings as fixed and that essentialised cultural, ethnic, national, gendered, religious, racial and/or generational dimensions' (Hébert, Wilkinson, and Ali 2008, 51–52). It is based on the breaking down of boundaries (Cuccioletta 2002) and reconceptualises difference and diversity as negotiable, intersectorial, strategic and mobile.

Transnationalism refers to 'the phenomenon of immigrants maintaining connections to their country of origin and using a dual frame of reference to evaluate their experiences and outcomes in the country in which they have settled' (Louie 2006, 363). From a more dynamic perspective, Gardner (2012) believes that *transnationalism* 'draws attention away from the binaries of "sending" and "receiving" contexts, and towards relationships, linkages and flows' (894). Similarly, transnationalism refers to 'multiple ties and interactions linking people or institutions across the borders of nation-states' (Vertovec 1999, 447), and it is 'various kinds of global or cross-border connections' (Vertovec 2001, 573).

Gardner (2012) points out that a useful way of theorising transnational worlds is via the concept of 'social fields'. With this concept, attention is paid primarily to the relationships between people and places that configure the network, rather than geographical movement being the main focus of enquiry. Accordingly, 'attention to children's "places" is thus necessarily multi-faceted' (Gardner and Mand 2012, 978). Therefore, places can be analysed as physical locations. At the same time, places are experienced by children in terms of the social relationships and social practices that take place within them. Gardner and Mand (2012) draw attention to the ways in which British-born Bangladeshi children are mobile across places. By moving across geographical spaces, they also move socially and culturally. Their journeys lead to new social roles and statuses as well as physical and emotional experiences. Meanwhile, children are mobile across time, as they 'grow older and move up (and down) social hierarchies which are realigned according to geography' (969–970).

Li (2011) explores the experiences of three Chinese university youth in Britain, including how they show their creativity and criticality in multilingual practices, how they construct their identity positions in wider social spaces. Being comfortable with their linguistic identity as multilinguals, these youth have much enjoyment with a range of highly creative use of their linguistic resources. Meanwhile, they seek out opportunities to make use of their multilingual resources for personal and social gain, such as opening up their spaces and networks. In addition, all participants have a broad and global outlook, not strongly attached to China or Britain. They realise that they are living in a world which transcends national boundaries. They love mobility and want to live in a transnational and multilingual space.

Most studies on transnational identities focus on university students, youth and adult immigrants (Hoerder, Hébert, and Schmitt 2006; Li 2011; Wong and Satzewich 2006). To address this gap, this study focuses on immigrant children and explores how they negotiate their identities in transnational contexts.

Research methodology
Research context
The research was conducted in a Mandarin–English bilingual programme in a western city of Canada. Established in 1998, this programme is multi-functional, serving students from various linguistic backgrounds. Most children in this programme speak English and Mandarin at home, school and community. Some of them also speak Cantonese, Vietnamese, Korean and others. This programme offers the same curriculum as any public school in Alberta. English and Mandarin are used as the medium of instruction, each taking 50% of the instruction time. For half of the day, one class of students are instructed by a native English-speaking teacher in English Language Arts, Social Studies and Health in English. For the other half of the school day, these students are instructed by a native Mandarin-speaking teacher in Mandarin Language Arts, Math and Science mainly in Mandarin.

Research participants
Eight Grade 5 students as well as their parents, their English and Chinese teachers and the programme coordinator of this Mandarin–English bilingual programme participated in this study. The eight participant students have very different family linguistic backgrounds. They adopted whatever languages they were comfortable with for different occasions, or whatever languages could serve them best.

This paper reports the experiences of two student participants from the large study. One participant, Cindy[1], a 10-year-old girl, born and raised in Canada, speaks English most of the time at home. Cindy sometimes speaks Cantonese or Mandarin with her grandparents who were originally from Guangdong Province of China. Cindy was also exposed to Vietnamese because her father, who was born in Vietnam, immigrated to Canada when he was 12, speaks Cantonese, Vietnamese and English. Cindy's mother, born in Brunei, immigrated to Canada when she was 10. She speaks English and a little Cantonese. Cindy's mother is a housewife and her father is a mechanic. Another participant, Linda, a nine-year-old girl, born in China, came to Canada with her parents as immigrants when she was in Grade 1. She speaks Mandarin mostly with her parents at home and stays in constant close communication in Mandarin with her relatives in China. Linda's parents were unemployed. Her mother was enrolled in an English as a Second Language class and her father was in a computer certificate programme in a local college.

Data collection

Multiple forms of data were collected, including observations, interviews and documents. The fieldwork observation entailed three to four days' classroom visit per week during the period from March 2011 to January 2012. The observation started with a panoramic understanding of what were happening and what were the routine literacy events in the classroom. The observation focused more on the literacy events that were related to identity issues, such as the identity topics 'all about me' or 'what it means to be Canadian'. Field notes were taken and transcribed afterwards.

The semi-structured interviews were conducted with the coordinator of the programme to understand the policy issues, educational goals, curriculum implementation and availability of resources. The interview with the two teachers of the class focused on their educational and teaching experiences, beliefs regarding students' literacy development, views on the language of instruction and goals of students' identities. The interview with the participant parents focused on their cultural beliefs about children's literacy and identity development, their views on this programme and their children's literacy practices at home. In addition, as the research went on, we conducted many additional conversations with the participant students, teachers and parents, to contextualise the situations, and to clarify the uncertainties from data analysis.

We also used a wider repertoire of research techniques. Documents were collected for the present study, including students' folders at school, such as English writing journals, Chinese homework notebooks, notebooks for science learning, and so on. With parents' support, we also collected children's photographs, journals, drawings and artefacts made at home. All these stories, pictures and artworks can help to discover children's imaginings (Young and Ansell 2006; Zeitlyn and Mand 2012).

Data analysis

Deleuze and Guattari (1987) use the rhizome to articulate their anti-hierarchical philosophical stance in attempt to derail modernist, linear thinking. As graphically represented in Figure 1, *rhizome* is a 'metaphor for multi-directional growth and diverse productivity' (Semetsky 2008, xiii). It describes an open system of multiple interactions and connections on various disparate planes. Rhizomes can be used to describe theory and research that allow for multiple, non-hierarchical entry and exit points in data representation and interpretation (Deleuze and Guattari 1987).

Rhizoanalysis is adopted to explore children's transcultural and transnational experiences in this study (Deleuze and Guattari 1987). It views data as fluid and in flux with no beginnings or ends but wholly constituted by middles and muddles (Semetsky 2006, x). As an inductive approach, rhizoanalysis 'does not apply pre-established categories. It resists temptations to interpret

Figure 1. A representation of the rhizome.

and ascribe meaning; rather looking for what emerges through the intensive and immanent reading of data' (Masny 2009, 7). It entails mapping and creating rather than tracing and representing (Deleuze and Guattari 1987).

Rhizoanalysis keeps the way open by asking what connections may be happening between multiplicities. Grosz (1994) uses 'provisional linkages – to represent the non-linearity, fragmented and processual nature of these connections' (167). Borrowing from Grosz, we were looking for the rhizomatic linkages between various data. For instance, when we were reading some writings of a participant, we focused more on asking what connections could be made with other events regarding this participant, his or her families, his or her teachers, and so on. These provisional linkages were read as assemblages, 'in that they work within and across the discourses to allow plausible readings' (Honan 2007, 537).

Findings and discussion

The findings indicate that the multilingual children negotiated their multiple identifications in transnational and translingual spaces by incorporating different aspects of varying cultures through the process of transculturation. They took transcultural and transnational identities that allowed for the comfortable circulation among different worlds, exemplified by the two cases of Cindy and Linda.

Taking up new belongings in transcultural modes: Cindy's sketch book

In our observations, we found that Cindy seldom participated in the class discussion, whether in her Chinese or English class. Mr Wang, her Chinese teacher, thought Cindy's silence was due to the lower proficiency of her Chinese language. Communicating with Mrs Sprau, he learned that Cindy did not speak much in the English class, in spite of the fact that Cindy's English reading and writing were almost the best in the class. Regarding Cindy's silence, Mrs Sprau believed it was a personality issue. Mr Wang thought

Cindy was pursuing perfection and would speak up when she was ready. However, was Cindy always silent?

Cindy had a sketch book at home where she drew pictures and pasted stickers or candy wrappers she collected. Her grandfather bought the sketch book for her when he visited Japan. The cover page, as Figure 2 shows, is one of the figures from *Harajuku Lovers*, with a traditional Chinese character, 愛 (love) which has a radical part of 心 (heart) in the middle.

Harajuku Lovers is a brand for different products, such as fragrances, bags and watches, created by Gwen Stefani, an American singer and fashion designer, who was inspired by Japanese culture and fashion. Gwen Stefani has four Japanese dancers, an entourage called *Harajuku Girls*, namely Love, Angel, Music and Baby. Each dancer, plus Gwen Stefani, represents a different kind of woman in her dresses. For instance, Love represents a caring person with the symbol of love all over her hair and sleeves. Baby represents a sweet and innocent girl in a pink dress.

These girls held an undeniable attraction for Cindy. In Cindy's eyes, the images and clothing of the *Harajuku Lovers* were cute. They were both symbolic and real. She loved them, collected many stickers and drew the portraits of each person (see Figure 3).

In addition, she drew the girls in different forms and styles. As Figure 4 shows, the girls enjoyed the blue sky and beautiful flowers in the park, with fish in the water and butterflies flying around; in the fitness centre, the girls did body building with their slogan 'looking this cute takes hard work'; the girls were passionate about fashion; they were playing the roles of snow bunnies; they swam as mermaids; and they were role-playing as cupid girls.

Cindy did this sketch diary during her summer break. To her, the summer break was boring because she had to stay at home for a long time. Although Cindy had been expecting to travel to Disneyland or other interesting places, she had to wait for a few years until her little brother became older, according to Cindy's mother. Cindy described all the places she liked to go in her sketch

Figure 2. Cover page of Cindy's sketch book.

Figure 3. Stickers and portraits of the girls.

diary. These pictures could be Cindy's virtual tours to escape the boredom of summer. Cindy's mobile minds of girls' enjoyment possibly allowed for the experiences of enjoyment for herself.

Not only imaging these interesting moments, Cindy also imagined *Harajuku Girls* as cooks to instruct how to make a dish called Banh Xiao (xeo), literally a sizzling cake, which is a Vietnamese savoury fried pancake. The recipe was carefully designed, including utensils, ingredients and step-by-step written instructions with pictures (Figure 5). Cindy explained in our conversation:

> When I was younger, I like cooking. And I like writing down all the stuff my dad does to cook. I like that kind of food.

How did Cindy's childhood memory of her father's cooking, her real meal of Banh Xiao, her love to Harajuku girls, her learning of writing, her enjoyment of drawing all come together for the creation of this recipe?

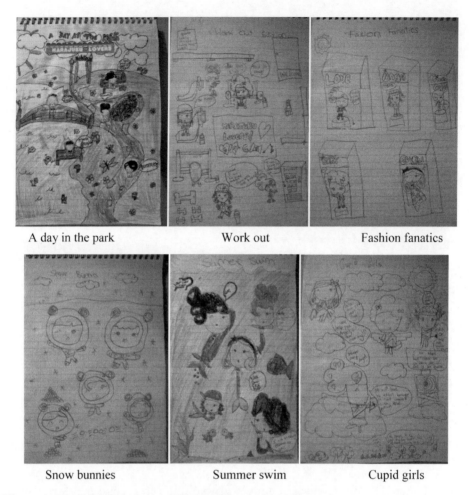

Figure 4. Harajuku Lovers in different forms and styles.

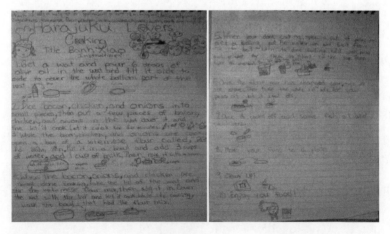

Figure 5. Harajuku Lovers' cooking vignette.

Cindy had other fun with *Harajuku Lovers*. For instance, she mixed the girl figures with other animated characters from Japanese culture, such as *Kuromi* and *Cinnamoroll*[2]. Cindy obtained some stickers of Kuromi and Cinnamoroll from her aunt. She put them together with Harajuku girls and some other stickers obtained from the Summer Festival[3], making two Summer Festival collages, as Figure 6 shows.

On the first collage, Cindy posted two stickers of 'Howdy!' and 'Ya-Hoo!', the popular slogans shouted by people to cheer for rodeos during the Summer Festival. Below the sticker of 'Ya-Hoo!' Cindy posted Kuromi, which looked like a cheerleader in this place. Cinnamoroll was riding a horse nearby. Harajuku girls also entertained themselves in the Summer Festival. One girl said, 'At Summer Festival, I got to go on a fire truck.' The second girl said, 'I saw horses'. Another girl added, 'We took many pictures'.

On the second collage, which Cindy named Kuromi + Cinnamoroll + The Harajuku, she included various places in the Summer Festival where children had fun. For instance, around the games area, one Kuromi was looking for her daughter. Close to the sugar shack, another Kuromi was thinking hard about what to choose after seeing one Harajuku girl eating the 'yummy' cotton sugar. Not far away, Cinnamoroll enjoyed the pony rides with 'weo'. In the spinning teacups, a group of Kuromis and Cinnamorolls shouted happily 'ahh, yeah and whoa', while one Harajuku girl was watching and worrying that 'She looks dizzy'. Near the sign 'more ride', another Harajuku girl waited anxiously with 'is it my turn yet?'

What complexity can we see from these multimodal collages? What transcultural and transnational spaces did Cindy make for her life situations in her writings and drawings at home despite being inaudible in both English and

Figure 6. Summer Festival collages.

Chinese classes? She loved the brand figures of Japanese girls launched by an American singer; she loved Japanese cartoon characters. These elements of popular culture have to do with how people relate to style, community, pleasure and images (Pennycook 2005). Cindy might have enjoyed the cool clothing of these figures and the exciting music by the singers; she might have shared her feelings with her peers and families; she might have imagined herself to be as cute, lovely, pleasant and smart as these figures.

All these images from popular cultures 'move across space, borders, communities, nations and become localised, indigenised, recreated in the local' (Pennycook 2005, 33). Within a local/global continuum, Cindy located her 'everyday experiences and relationships within transnational space, thereby transnationalising the local and localising the transnational' (Golbert 2001, 713). Being comfortable with the multiplicity, Cindy mingled all these elements together, such as brand figures, lovable characters, stickers from different people and places, her personal experiences of the Summer Festival, her school learning about story writing, her beloved drawings, her love of Vietnamese food, her love of playing, fashion, working outs, swimming, snow bunnies and cupid bows, and possibly other sources.

According to Vertovec (2001), the transnational flow of images, practices, discourses and perspectives can have a profound effect on people's identities. How would we understand the complexity of the unpredictable connections she made among American popular music, Japanese dancers and cartoon characters, the Canadian Summer Festival, Vietnamese food and Chinese love with a heart? How would we understand the richness of the rhizomatic linkage she made? Did Cindy take up new belongings in these transcultural and transnational modes, while moving across and beyond linguistic, cultural and ethnic spaces of interaction and boundaries (Hébert, Wilkinson, and Ali 2008)?

Challenging fixed and hyphenated identity: 'I am a living person'

As previously explained, Linda was born in China and immigrated to Canada with her parents when she was in Grade 1. She had been in Canada for three years by the early stage of the research (March 2011). At that time, Linda was working on a Chinese project 'About me'. She proudly claimed that she was a Chinese. When she described her half year's public schooling experience in China, she said that one thing that impressed her most was the school's flag-raising ceremony every Monday. At the ceremony, all the students swore to the Chinese national flag that they would be Chinese forever. Linda loved China so profoundly that she felt pity for her younger brother who was unfortunate to be born in Canada, because he had no choice but to be a Canadian. She even despised her parents when they considered applying for Canadian citizenship. With such affection to China at that time, Linda considered China to be her only country, as shown in Figure 7:

Figure 7. One slide in Linda's PowerPoint 'About me'.

Translation: My country
My nationality is Chinese. Our family immigrated to Canada in 2008.
I lived in Shanghai when I was in China. Shanghai is a bustling modern city with a large population and busy streets. I like to go to Waitan (the River Bund) and Jinjiang Amusement Park where people can do many fun things, such as riding the Ferris wheel and bungee jumping. There are so many people in Shanghai, like hordes of ants moving if you look from the Oriental Pearl TV Tower. Shanghai's weather is very hot. The maximum can reach forty degrees. One needs to eat popsicles every day in the summer. If you do not eat popsicles, you could get a heatstroke. When I was in Shanghai, I can eat four popsicles at one time in the summer!!!

Mr Wang, the Chinese teacher, assigned a project 'About me'. He suggested that students write about their names, families, countries, schools, classmates and hobbies. This project provided Linda with an opportunity to share her fond memories about China. In this PowerPoint slide, Linda described her favourite places in Shanghai and the activities she enjoyed in China. She also demonstrated a sense of pride about living in Shanghai, the largest city in China. Positioning herself as a Chinese, she might want to remove herself from Canada, a cold country with fewer people, an 'othering' environment where she still felt out of place at that time. Through this narrative, she may possibly find happiness, 'for her safe and homely' (Cole 2012, 40). She might feel a sense of intimacy, safety and warmth as experienced at home in Shanghai.

Several months later, around Remembrance Day of Canada (November 2011), the school and teachers conducted some educative activities for students in memory of veterans. For instance, the school held one assembly, where students had a moment of silence and listened to the war poem *Flanders Field*, read by two students, respectively in English and Chinese. In Linda's English class, the teacher played one movie about Remembrance Day and asked students to do more online reading about veterans. The English teacher then asked students to write their reflections about Remembrance Day. Most students expressed their appreciation that the soldiers fought for their freedom. The following vignette is part of my conversation with Linda about her composition on Remembrance Day:

> It's more peace in Canada than most of the other countries. (From Linda's writing on Remembrance Day)
> R: In which countries do you think there is less peace?
> L: China.
> R: But there are no wars currently in China.
> L: But I was not well respected in China. When I went back to Shanghai this summer, I accidently stepped on someone's luggage. She was angry and blamed me, 'Are you blind?'

Linda's understanding of peace was different from what we had expected. In various school activities, such as movie watching or assembly attendance, students had been encouraged to relate the peace to the real war issues. Linda, however, connected peace to respect. She explained how she was not well respected in China. Linda also expressed her concerns about many other issues in China as our conversation went on:

> L: There are many criminals in China. Even in our neighborhood, you can see posted photos of criminals wanted by the police. I was scared to death. In addition, there are many traffic problems in China. Last time when I was in China, I was almost hit by a car when I crossed the street (The drivers in China seldom respect the rules that pedestrians should walk first). By the way, the environment in China is so bad and the people are not nice.

Linda dwelled on her negative experiences in China when she went back for a visit in the summer. In addition, her parents explained in the interview that they sometimes discussed the social and environmental issues in China at home. The parents wanted Linda to know the facts and learn how to protect herself. Overall, how had Linda's school education about peace, her own experiences in China and her parents' discussions at home influenced her understandings of peace. What other investments had taken place regarding her understanding of peace? How did these experiences lead her to reconsider where she most belonged?

Around Remembrance Day, Linda's English teacher also assigned another writing task, describing the autumn with five senses. Linda wrote:

> Autumn felt quiet and peaceful. In autumn, leaves are falling. When the leaves fall, it looks soooooooooo beautiful ... there is a leaf on the Canada flag. I think the person that created it must think that the leaf represents Canada. (From Linda's writing journal)

The following is part of my conversation with her about her writing:

> R: Why did you write like this?
> L: Leaves don't fight. Neither does Canada.
> R: Where do you think there is a fight?
> L: China. All is centered on the Communist Party. We can see it from its national flag. Tyranny.
> R: What made you think so?
> L: I do not know, possibly because I read some stories in the Bible?
> R: But there is not anything about the Communist Party in the Bible.
> L: Yes, but there is something about peace in the Bible.
> R: Why did you read the Bible?
> L: One person recently came to my home and recommended us reading the Bible. So my mom began to read it. One thing she learned from the Bible was that a person was considered to be stupid if he talked too much. After my mom told me this, I talked less.

From this vignette, there was a connection between autumn leaves and the maple leaf on the Canadian national flag. In Linda's mind, since the autumn leaves could not fight, neither could the maple leaf on the Canada flag and nor could the country of Canada. She believed Canada was a peaceful country, where she could feel peace. Fight, however, was connected to the Chinese national flag. On the Chinese national flag, one big star representing the Chinese Communist Party is surrounded by four little ones, which implies the Chinese Communist Party is respected by all the people in the country. How could this image on the flag associates Linda to the fight, and to the tyranny? Could it be related to the family discussions about social and other problems in China? Could it be related to her negative experiences in China? In the final part of this vignette, Linda mentioned the Bible. What Bible stories had she ever heard about? How were the Bible stories related to peace and tyranny issues? How did the Bible stories influence her understanding about peace? How did the Bible influence her character becoming where she learned to talk less? How did these many life experiences connect to be the power of transformation?

> R: Then what do you think about yourself, a Chinese, a Canadian or a Chinese Canadian?
> L: (Thinking) ... I am a living person.

At this moment, regarding my same question about her nationality, Linda, a nine-year-old girl, did not choose to be a Chinese, nor a Canadian or a Chinese Canadian. Instead, she replied with a different answer, *a living person*. In about eight months, what contributed to her change from being a proud Chinese to *a living person*? Did her negative experience of her visit to Shanghai affect her romanticised image of China in her memory? Did her parents' discussions about the social and environmental issues in China influence her uncertainty of being Chinese? Did her response 'a living person' question the fixed identity that we imposed on her? Was this answer of 'a living person' a deterritorialisation of the dualistic being a Chinese or a Canadian, or even a compromise with combining Chinese and Canadian? What changes have taken place in her original thoughts about being a Chinese? How had she been transformed and become Other in the process?

Linda's response of 'I am a living person' made us reflect that the categories of a Chinese, a Canadian or a Chinese Canadian which framed our original interview questions are perhaps too rigid. In asking the question, 'Are you Chinese or Canadian?' we assumed that there would be a choice of being either Chinese or Canadian. Rather than making a binary distinction between Chinese and Canadian, Linda refused to choose between particular signifiers, thus rejecting state boundaries or adult discourses of ethnic belonging insisted on her (Gardner 2012). Her making of places of belonging 'involves the creation of different social sites of belonging connected with the various spheres of life' (Fog Olwig 2003, 17) that she encounters in her everyday lives. As Gardner (2012) put it, 'if children are straddling places and identities, their place-making and perceptions will, therefore, be quite different from conventional models of "integration" in which one's national place is separated from "place of origin"' (902).

Therefore, limiting children's identity choices among certain nationality categories might obscure the opportunities to envisage multilingual children's lives on a series of multiple planes, and therefore restrict the possibilities for multiple identities (Fog Olwig 2003). Mahtani (2002) questions viewing ethnicity as the primary marker of identity in her research on how 'mixed race' women in Canada contemplate their relationship to national identity. The focus on ethnicity 'emphasises the past, putting a person's identity by her parents' origins, rather than by her own current set of ethnic allegiances' (Mahtani 2002, 76). Meanwhile, Mahtani examines the problematic nature of the hyphen (in Italian–Canadian, Japanese–Canadian or Chinese–Canadian, for instance) and the role it plays in articulating ethnic differences in Canada. As Mahtani argues, multicultural policy advocates that immigrants in Canada should link their ethnic identity and Canada with a hyphen. These hyphens of multiculturalism 'produces spaces of distance, in which ethnicity is positioned outside Canadianness – as an addition to it, but also as an exclusion from it' (Mahtani 2002, 78).

Linda performed different identities depending on her different situations as she grew up. As Linda enjoyed being a living person, she chose what was good for her. Linda's response indicates that her identity is always in a process of becoming. Identities are temporary, seeming contradictory and shifting continuously with fluidity. Adopting the theorisation of Andreotti (V. Andreotti, personal communication), she proposes that we treat identity as a verb rather than a noun, a movement that flows. All these imply a continuous redefining of various subjectivities (Deleuze and Guattari 1987). As Semetsky (2003, 213) put it, 'subjectivity, when understood as a process of becoming, differs from the traditional notion of a self looked at, and rationally appealed to, from the top-down approach of the macro perspective of theory. Instead, Deleuze recognises the so called micropolitical dimension of culture as a contextual, experiential and circumstantial site where subjects are situated and produced'. In Linda's case, there is no central power from top down to determine and essentialise her identity with culture and ethnicity. Rather, 'identity is often complex: feelings change over time and between places, and can be a mixture of the positive and the negative' (Gardner 2012, 901). 'If, on a visit to the "homeland", for example, they (children) feel a strong sense of belonging, they are more likely to pursue their links with the place and people than if they feel alienated, or that they do not belong' (Gardner 2012, 901). In this respect, how could Linda's visit to China influence her thinking of belonging? How could her life experiences in Canada, as well as her other life experiences, past, present and future, real and imagined, continue to influence her thinking of belonging?

Conclusion and implications

The findings of the study show that the proliferation of cultural flows, modes of belonging and new practices of citizenship mobilise minds and bodies with identifications beyond nation-states (Hébert, Wilkinson, and Ali 2008). These multilingual children went beyond the country of their origin and the country in which they had settled down. Their identities are not tied to one place and one community. Moving beyond being stuck between two cultures, these children 'switch identities in different contexts' (Ackroy and Pilkington 1999, 445). In so doing, they challenged the dominant discourse of any fixed and hyphenated identity, Chinese–Canadian or Canadian–Chinese (Mahtani 2002). The children prepared themselves for a cross-border life and a global consciousness (Wihtol de Wenden 1995). Therefore, there is a need to move beyond fixed and essentialised identities and 'stable spatial and temporal coordinates' (Bogue 2008, 3). As these students are mobile to imagine oneself as another, to take up new belongings and to move across cultural, linguistic, ethnic, racial spaces of interaction and boundaries (Hébert, Wilkinson, and Ali 2008), it is important that educators unfold children's multiple and mobile identities and explore new possibilities for life.

While the transcultural flows of images, practices and discourses contribute to students' identities, these factors may change over spatiotemporal contexts (Mahtani 2002; Parker and Song 2001; Root 1996). As Appadurai (2001) notes, 'we are functioning in a world fundamentally characterised by objects in motion. These objects include ideas and ideologies, people and goods, images and messages, technologies and techniques. This is a world of flows' (5). Therefore, students can no longer be understood as located in a bounded time and space in and around their classrooms but rather as participants in a much broader set of transcultural practices across home, community and school. It is important for teachers to be 'open to unexpectedness' (Canagarajah 2013, 41) and develop positive attitudes to unpredictability of students' transnational identities.

Pennycook (2005) puts forward the need for a pedagogy of flow when he discusses how global Englishes become a shifting means of transcultural identity formation, focusing on the global culture of hip hop in parts of East and South-East Asia. With a pedagogy of flow, Pennycook argues not only the importance of taking into account the movement of transcultural forms but also of the local take-up of such forms. To teach with the flow, according to Pennycook, suggests not only incorporating students' transcultural texts into curriculum but also opening up possible knowledge, identity and desire and engaging with multiple ways of speaking, being and learning, with multi-layered modes of identity at global, regional, national and local levels.

Notes

1. All participant names in this paper are pseudonyms.
2. These are two characters from Sanrio, a Japanese company specialised in creating cartoon characters. Kuromi is a white rabbit, wearing a black jester's hat with a pink skull on the front and a black tail. Cinnamoroll is a white puppy with long ears that enable him to fly. He has blue eyes, and a plump and curly tail that resembles a Cinnamoroll.
3. The Ridgeville Summer Festival is an annual exhibition and festival held every July in Ridgeville. The 10-day event attracts over one million visitors per year and features a parade, midway, stage shows, concerts, agricultural competitions and many exhibits.

References

Ackroy, J., and A. Pilkington. 1999. "Childhood and the Construction of Ethnic Identities in a Global Age." *Childhood* 6 (4): 443–454. doi:10.1177/0907568299006004004.

Andreotti, V. 2008. "Draft Model of 'Stages' Emerging from OSDE/TOE Research [video]." Accessed September 1, 2012. http://www.youtube.com/watch?v=Nr6pEpeh4PI&feature=related.

Appadurai, A. 2001. "Grassroots Globalization and the Research Imagination." In *Globalization*, edited by A. Appadurai, 1–21. Durham, NC: Duke University Press.

Bogue, R. 2008. "Search, Swim and See: Deleuze's Apprenticeship in Signs and Pedagogy." In *Nomadic Education: Variations on a Theme by Deleuze and Guattari*, edited by I. Semetsky, 1–16. Rotterdam: Sense.

Canadian Council on Social Development. 2006. *The Progress of Canada's Children and Youth*. http://www.ccsd.ca/pccy/2006/pdf/pccy_2006.pdf.

Canagarajah, S. 2013. *Translingual Practice: Global Englishes and Cosmopolitan Relations*. London: Routledge.

Cole, D. R. 2012. "Latino Families Becoming-literate in Australia: Deleuze, Literacy and the Politics of Immigration." *Discourse: Studies in the Cultural Politics of Education* 33 (1): 33–46. doi:10.1080/01596306.2012.632160.

Cuccioletta, D. 2002. "Multiculturalism or Transculturalism: Towards a Cosmopolitan Citizenship." *London Journal of Canadian Studies* 17: 1–11.

Deleuze, G. 1990. *The Logic of Sense*. Translated by M. Lister with C. Stivale. New York: Columbia University Press.

Deleuze, G., and F. Guattari. 1987. *A Thousand Plateaus: Capitalism and Schizophrenia Part II*. Translated by B. Massumi. London: Athlone Press.

Dufresne, T. 2009. "When Worlds Collide: Readings of Self through a Lens of Difference." In *Multiple Literacies Theory: A Deleuzian Perspective*, edited by D. Masny and D. R. Cole, 105–118. Rotterdam: Sense.

Fog Olwig, K. 2003. "Children's Places of Belonging in Immigrant Families of Caribbean Background." In *Children's Places: Cross-cultural Perspectives*, edited by K. Fog Olwig and E. Gulløv, 271–325. London: Routledge.

Gardner, K. 2012. "Transnational Migration and the Study of Children: An Introduction." *Journal of Ethnic and Migration Studies* 38 (6): 889–912. doi:10.1080/1369183X.2012.677170.

Gardner, K., and K. Mand. 2012. "'My Away Is Here': Place, Emplacement and Mobility amongst British Bengali Children." *Journal of Ethnic and Migration Studies* 38 (6): 969–986. doi:10.1080/1369183X.2012.677177.

Golbert, R. 2001. "Transnational Orientations from Home: Constructions of Israel and Transnational Space among Ukrainian Jewish Youth." *Journal of Ethnic and Migration Studies* 27 (4): 713–731. doi:10.1080/13691830120090467.

Grosz, E. 1994. *Volatile Bodies: Towards a Corporeal Feminism*. Bloomington: Indiana University Press.

Hébert, Y. 2001. "Identity, Diversity, and Education: A Critical Review of the Literature." *Canadian Ethnic Studies* 33 (3): 155–177.

Hébert, Y., Y. Guo, and M. Pellerin. 2008. "New Horizons for Research on Bilingualism and Plurilingualism: A Focus on Languages of Immigration in Canada." *Encounters on Education* 9: 57–74.

Hébert, Y., L. Wilkinson, and M. Ali. 2008. "Second Generation Youth in Canada, Their Mobilities and Identification: Relevance to Citizenship Education." *Brock Journal of Education* 17 (1): 50–70.

Hoerder, D., Y. Hébert, and I. Schmitt, eds. 2006. *Negotiating Transcultural Lives: Belongings and Social Capital among Youth in Comparative Perspective*. Toronto: University of Toronto Press.

Honan, E. 2007. "Writing a Rhizome: An (im)plausible Methodology." *International Journal of Qualitative Studies in Education* 20 (5): 531–546. doi:10.1080/09518390600923735.

Kramsch, C. 2009. *The Multilingual Subject*. New York: Oxford University Press.

Li, W. 2011. "Moment Analysis and Translanguaging Space: Discursive Construction of Identities by Multilingual Chinese Youth in Britain." *Journal of Pragmatics* 43 (5): 1222–1235. doi:10.1016/j.pragma.2010.07.035.

Louie, V. 2006. "Growing Up Ethnic in Transnational Worlds: Identities among Second-generation Chinese and Dominicans." *Identities: Global Studies in Culture and Power* 13 (3): 363–394.

Mahtani, M. 2002. "Interrogating the Hyphen-nation: Canadian Multicultural Policy and 'Mixed Race' Identities, Social Identities." *Journal for the Study of Race, Nation and Culture* 8 (1): 67–90.

Masny, D. 2009. "Bridging Access, Equity, and Quality: The Case for Multiple Literacies." Paper presented at Bridging Divides: The National Conference for Teachers of English and Literacy, Wrest Point Conference Centre, Hobart, Tasmania, July 9–12. http://www.englishliteracyconference.com.au/files/documents/hobart/conferencePapers/refereed/MasnyDiana.pdf.

Michael-Luna, S. 2008. "Todos Somos Blancos/We Are All White: Constructing Racial Identities through Texts." *Journal of Language, Identity & Education* 7 (3): 272–293. doi:10.1080/15348450802237913.

Murray, D. 2010. "Female North African–French Students in France: Narratives of Educational Experiences." PhD diss., University of Nevada.

Parker, D., and M. Song. 2001. "Introduction: Rethinking 'Mixed Race.'" In *Rethinking 'Mixed Race'*, edited by D. Parker and M. Song, 1–22. London: Pluto Press.

Pennycook, A. 2005. "Teaching with the Flow: Fixity and Fluidity in Education." *Asia Pacific Journal of Education* 25 (1): 29–43. doi:10.1080/02188790500032491.

Root, M. 1996. *The Multiracial Experience*. London: Sage.

Satzewich, V., and L. Wong, eds. 2006. *Transnational Identities and Practices in Canada*. Vancouver, WA: UBC Press.

Semetsky, I. 2003. "The Problematics of Human Subjectivity: Gilles Deleuze and the Deweyan Legacy." *Studies in Philosophy and Education* 22 (3–4): 211–225. doi:10.1023/A:1022877506539.

Semetsky, I. 2006. *Deleuze, Education and Becoming*. Rotterdam: Sense.

Semetsky, I. ed. 2008. *Nomadic Education: Variations on a Theme by Deleuze and Guattari*. Rotterdam: Sense.

Statistics Canada. 2012. *2011 Census of Population: Linguistic Characteristics of Canadians*. http://www.statcan.gc.ca/daily-quotidien/12.

Vertovec, S. 1999. "Conceiving and Researching Transnationalism." *Ethnic and Racial Studies* 22 (2): 447–462. doi:10.1080/014198799329558.

Vertovec, S. 2001. "Transnationalism and Identity." *Journal of Ethnic and Migration Studies* 27 (4): 573–582. doi:10.1080/13691830120090386.

Vertovec, S. 2009. *Transnationalism*. London: Routledge.

Weedon, C. 1987. *Feminist Practice and Poststructuralist Theory*. Oxford: Basil Blackwell.

Wihtol de Wenden, C. 1995. "Generational Change and in French Suburbs." *New Community* 21 (1): 69–78.

Wong, L., and V. Satzewich. 2006. "Introduction: The Meaning and Significance of Transnationalism." In *Transnational Identities and Practices in Canada*, edited by V. Satzewich and L. Wong, 1–15. Vancouver, WA: UBC Press.

Young, L., and N. Ansell. 2006. "Understanding Migration: Placing Children's Understanding of 'Moving House' in South Africa." *Goeform* 37 (2): 256–272. doi:10.1016/j.geoforum.2005.02.004.

Zeitlyn, B., and K. Mand. 2012. "Researching Transnational Childhoods." *Journal of Ethnic and Migration Studies* 38 (6): 987–1006. doi:10.1080/1369183X.2012.677179.

Language, institutional identity and integration: lived experiences of ESL teachers in Australia

Sepideh Fotovatian

Faculty of Education, Simon Fraser University, Vancouver, BC, Canada

> Globalisation and increased patterns of immigration have turned workplace interactions to arenas for intercultural communication entailing negotiation of identity, membership and 'social capital'. For many newcomer immigrants, this happens in an additional language and culture – English. This paper presents interaction experiences of four non-native English language teachers with other institutional members. It uses a sociocultural perspective of second language to map their approaches to negotiations of professional and institutional identities in and through these interactions. Their discussions highlight the role of language, cultural practices and the emic sociopolitical factors embedded within institutional interactions in individuals' identity negotiation and integration.

Introduction

> I am a creeping creature, creeping into my office and creeping back home.
>
> (Ratna, focus group)

Identifying best practices that improve employment prospects or success for immigrants is a challenging issue – for immigrant advocates, policy-makers and researchers. Assumptions exist that people with high human capital have the right skills or education to integrate into the labour market. Sadly, however, many of these highly educated or highly skilled professional immigrants struggle to integrate their knowledge or abilities in the post-immigration contexts, and find themselves either unemployed or involved in 'survival jobs' or 'transitional jobs' which are well below their expectations and skill levels (Cervatiuc 2009; DeVault and McCoy 2005). Particularly, the hiring trends in the Teaching English as a Second Language (TESOL) field, despite growing scholarly recognition of bilingual, multilingual and non-native English teachers' multi-competence (Cook 1999), suggest the field is still dominated by a native speaker ideology favouring native speaker English teachers (Canagarajah 2006).

In the era of transnational mobility, workplace language interactions are arenas for negotiation of social capital. Bourdieu and Wacquant (1992) stress the significance of engagement in informal institutional interactions in building professional networks and in negotiating social capital defined as 'the sum of the resources, actual or virtual, that accrues to an individual or a group by virtue of processing a durable network of more or less institutionalised relationships of mutual acquaintance and recognition' (119). However, everyday institutional interactions involve power and identity negotiations. Some minority groups may feel reprimanded and devalued for the language, social and cultural capitals they bring to the new contexts.

For newcomer immigrants, regardless of their field or level of expertise, engagement in workplace encounters entails building social capital in an additional language and culture. Language proficiency and sociocultural pragmatics of communication have often been underlined in literature as troubling for newcomer immigrants in their processes of transitioning to employment in their target countries (Cervatiuc 2009; Kerekes 2007). Identities are discursively negotiated in language interactions and the ties between language, identity and legitimacy are frequently highlighted in current research (Norton 2003, 2006). Despite reaching a language proficiency level that makes them eligible to teach English, non-native English language teachers have been reported to lack the confidence to engage in informal social interactions, particularly with their native English-speaking colleagues (Fotovatian 2010; Sawir 2005). In particular, the informal and interpersonal dimension of communication – how to establish networks within their second language community and how to develop their professional and social identity – is reported to be challenging for newcomer English as a Second Language (ESL) teachers (Fotovatian 2010).

Transnational mobility has also turned universities to 'global educational contact zones' (Kenway and Bullen 2003) where people from different countries communicate with each other to negotiate space and identity. Within this context, Kenway and Bullen (2003) compare international student experiences of adaptation, interaction and integration in several major universities in Canada and Australia and conclude:

> international students' perceptions and experiences of the global university contact zone are as heterogeneous as the cohort of students we interviewed. Understanding the globalised university as a contact zone is one step towards recognising the complexity of these students' experiences. (17)

In the guise of globalised educational institutions, particularly the university in this study, which is regarded as the most internationalised university in

Australia, provides what would seem like obvious sites for multicultural workplace interaction where English is recognised not only as the medium of instruction but also as the medium for social interaction among diverse students and staff.

To capture and reflect individuals' lived experiences of interaction, identity negotiation and integration, this paper uses the reflections of four newcomer international doctoral students in Australia who had worked as English language teachers in their own countries for several years prior to making their way to Australia for further study and ultimately seeking permanent migration. The focus of the paper is on providing a synopsis of the processes of the participants' engagement in social interactions, building networks, taking agentive actions in and through daily interactions to negotiate membership and professional identity.

Background literature

Globalisation, immigration flows and increasingly competitive labour markets in immigrant host countries (e.g., Canada, the USA, Australia and New Zealand) have posed new challenges for those working in new contexts, with differences emphasised across language, culture and space. Despite their educational and professional backgrounds, recent immigrant cohorts and post-secondary international students experience serious challenges upon entering their fields of practice (Guo, 2010; Guo and Chase 2011; Shan and Guo 2013). Increased trends of mobility have also meant challenges for host institutions in utilising the skills and experiences of internationally educated professionals. Despite recent eminent scholarly research, equitable integration of internationally educated professionals within 'Western' institutions still seems out of reach. As noted by Shan and Guo (2013), 'immigrants' professional-related learning has been increasingly organised by institutions that privilege the dominant culture as well as credentials gained in the host societies' (38). Relating integration challenges faced by internationally educated immigrants to the politics of difference within Canadian institutions, Guo (2013) argues a 'triple glass effect' consisting of a glass gate blocking entrance to professional jobs, a glass door denying access to high-waged firms and a glass ceiling to the potential promotion of immigrants to managerial positions hinders immigrants' meaningful integration in Canadian institutions

Similarly, in Australian contexts, sense of displacement experienced by international students can intensify by dichotomising institutional labels (i.e., 'international' vs 'local' categories), a divided community and the politics of difference that seem to have overshadowed efforts towards internationalisation of higher education in Australia (Fotovatian 2012a; Ryan and Viete 2009). Minority groups are reported to experience devaluation of knowledge and skills and oppression (Ryan and Viete 2009) that often adds to the challenges of transitioning to a new institution and the associated 'multiple simultaneous identity transitions' (Fotovatian and Miller 2013). Particularly, in the field of TESOL, foreign educated ESL teachers in Australia are reported to experience additional challenges to enter this professional field shadowed by employers' preference to hire native speakers (Fotovatian 2010). Discrimination seems to be institutionalised in this field in Australia (Pennycook 2004). 'Linguicism' (racism based on language, Phillipson 2002) and 'accenticism' (racism triggered by accented English, Fotovatian 2012a, 2012b) are heuristic in this context. Similarly, in Canadian contexts, Guo (2009) relates integration challenges faced by internationally educated immigrants in the process of integration into the Canadian labour market to the politics of difference within Canadian institutions, asserting:

> Many immigrant professionals experience devaluation and denigration of their prior learning and work experience after arriving in Canada. The roots of non-recognition can be traced to the following. First, epistemological misperceptions of difference and knowledge lead to a belief that the knowledge of immigrant professionals, particularly those from Third World countries, is deficient, incompatible and inferior, hence invalid. Second, an ontological commitment to positivistic and universal measurement exacerbates the complexity of this process. The juxtaposition of the misconceptions of difference and knowledge with positivism and liberal universalism forms a new head tax to exclude the undesirable and perpetuate oppression in Canada. (37)

Identity is increasingly used as a lens in understanding immigrants' interaction needs and experiences (Norton 2003). Newcomer institutional members dynamically negotiate legitimacy in and through day-to-day social and professional interactions with their institutions. They are able to negotiate their 'institutional identities' [i.e., identities legitimised through membership in an institution and dynamically constructed, negotiated and renegotiated in and through interactions with other institutional members (Fotovatian 2012b)] and claim social and professional representations associated with legitimate membership in the institution.

Institutions as 'social containers' also play a role in providing their members with chances for interacting, networking and knowledge dissemination (Wenger 2000). Engagement in institutional discourses determines if and how the newcomer members emerge to powerful and successful positions in today's 'highly contested personal and professional spaces [where] institutional attitudes are … matters of … person-to-person interaction' (Cadman 2005, 72).

In this study, second language interactions are perceived as avenues for construction, negotiation and (re)negotiation of new social and institutional identities. For the participants – all international graduate students with diverse language and cultural backgrounds – participation in daily departmental interactions was a crucial channel for developing not only the language, culture and values of the target community, but also knowledge of the institutional practices and norms, 'ruling relations' and new levels of institutional literacy (Smith 2001). This study reflects the participants' reservations, goals, investments and 'agentive actions', instances of making decisions for participation or non-participation. The ethnographic analysis of institutional interactions can contribute to the understanding of diverse approaches to integration, on the one hand, and institutional best practices for encouraging inclusion and integration, on the other.

The study

Bouma's (2000) standpoint that a qualitative ethnographic approach is needed when research is designed to 'describe in detail what is happening in a group, in a conversation or in a community, who spoke to whom, with what messages, with what feelings, with what effect' was used (171). These nuanced details are particularly important for understanding the ties between the background institutional contextual veracities (e.g., power relationships, hegemonic hierarchies of languages and cultures in this study) and the onstage interaction experiences (discourses in use, identities at play, communication strategies deployed, etc.).

A case study was selected since as described by Gall, Gall, and Borg's (2007) case study design has the capacity for 'the in-depth study of instances of a phenomenon in its natural context and from the perspective of the participants involved in the phenomenon' (436). In second language educational studies, Duff (2003) associates case study design with the interpretive qualitative research associated with recurring principles as 'boundedness, in-depth study, multiple perspectives, particularity, contextualization' and interpretation (23). A case study design in research related to language and identity also has the potential to look at language in a sociocultural matrix, to reveal the contextual features in their local settings, to incorporate an emic perspective and to reflect the voices of participants as people and the researcher as the composer.

The data in this study were part of a qualitative longitudinal multiple case study funded by Monash University in Australia. This study was conducted under the stringent ethical clearance procedures of Monash University's ethics requirements. The study comprised data collected from two recorded focus groups, researcher observation notes of participants informal staffroom interactions and narrations of the critical incidents collected from the participants' via electronic communications with the researcher.

Throughout data analysis, I was particularly interested in the ties between the macro-level language practices and sociocultural and socio-political factors governing institutional interactions and the micro-level experiences of engagement or disengagement of the participants in interactions and their strategies for identity negotiation. I first started with theme analysis of the transcribed data recorded from focus groups and then once I identified a potential factor that could influence the individual's decisions and actions, in my judgement,

I delved deeper to their narratives to find the trajectories and epistemological rationales behind the diversity I was observing among the participants in interpreting and engaging with the dominant culture.

The participants were four non-native mid-aged English language teachers who all had enrolled in a Ph.D. research programme in education at an Australian university as international students. Pursuing further study in Australia is a common pathway to immigration for applicants holding higher education degrees. The four participants were looking for opportunities to find networks and local work experience that could assist them in the process of applying for permanent residency and settlement.

I had an emic position in this research as I, too, was working towards my Ph.D. along with my informants. This emic position was instrumental in placing me in a position to purposefully select informants who were most willing to share their stories and reflect on their daily experiences, and who found me a fellow insider, trustworthy for listening to their deep reflections. Being an insider to the institution, I was also able to closely observe the site and add my daily observations and field notes all throughout the three years. I had a deeper sense of the data that helped me generate more meaningful questions in the focus groups.

This study focuses on the participants' engagement in and reflections of the day-to-day processes of settlement, professional recognition, establishing social networks and 'institutional identity' negotiation (Fotovatian 2012b). For the participants in this study, institutional identity was negotiated through day-to-day interactions (formal and informal, verbal, non-verbal or electronic) with other members in their field (TESOL) whether at the university, studying for a Ph.D. degree in TESOL or seeking employment related to their field of interest. As previously argued (Fotovatian 2012b), institutions impose part of an institutional identity on new immigrants by assigning roles and titles to its members which are dynamically negotiated through daily interactions. In the case of the four participants in this study, the label of 'non-native' English teacher was pre-assigned to the participants by their native peers. The diverse agentive actions and counter strategies the participant used to negotiate legitimacy within their institution was at the locus of this study. The main guiding research question in this study was:

> How did the participants (four newcomer non-native English teachers) reproduce the dominant language, social and cultural norms engineering their professional integration, engage in institutional interactions, and negotiate their institutional identities?

Participants' agentive actions for identity negotiation

Upon arrival and alongside their study, the four participants were looking for opportunities to work in a field related to the main field of study (Teaching

English to the Speakers of Other Languages – TESOL). In their home countries, they were all working as English language teachers. Chen (pseudo names are used), a 36-year-old Chinese woman, had been teaching English for seven years at a college in China. She had moved to Melbourne with her 14-year-old son, leaving her husband in China to work and support the family until Chen could secure a stable income in Australia. Ratna, a single 39-year-old Indonesian woman, had lectured for six years at a university. The third participant Aini, a 38-year-old Malaysian woman had taught at a secondary school in Malaysia for five years before moving with her husband and their two children to Australia. The fourth participant Shamim was from Bangladesh. He is a single 34-year-old male who had for the previous five years taught at a high school in Bangladesh. Chen, Ranta, Aini and Shamim had lived in Melbourne for 4, 2, 4 and 3 months, respectively, at the beginning of the study. All four participants simultaneously attended doctoral programme that was being offered at one university in Australia hoping the experience would facilitate their institutional recognition and settlement in Australia.

Despite similarities among the participants in their career goals and field of doctoral study or length of stay in Australia, each participant applied diverse 'agentive actions' (Kettle 2005) for integration. Chen, for example, invested in establishing and maintaining institutional networks through participation in institutional interactions and volunteering to convene social events in her department. She explained:

> I tried to be more involved by participating in many events. Like participating the Faculty's social events last year and convening them this year. Although convening the Faculty's research community was demanding a lot of time and energy but I accepted. Because this way, I know many people and they know me. (Chen, focus group)

Chen was agently negotiating membership and identity in the community by volunteering and engaging in activities. Aini, too, talked about investment in institutional interactions to negotiate membership and identity:

> I am involved in two writing groups and we are very active. Writing groups are very empowering in establishing our identity. We feel we belong here and there are local students there too and they are also like us and we can give them feedback too. The PhD student identity is very strong there. (Aini, focus group)

For Shamim, constructing a professional identity did not happen through interaction with institutional members (i.e., academics and peers in his field). He invested in negotiating legitimacy through producing writing pieces, possibly publications. He mentioned that at times he had felt lonely in his journey, yet he had preserved his time for reading and writing his thesis in isolation and did not invest in institutional interaction and networking. He commented:

> Not much networking I do. I have been in the writing up. So, I have been busy with myself. I don't think that pushing myself to different groups with different interests would be beneficial for me at this time. But lately, I was thinking that I have been lonely in my journey. I feel left behind. But at the moment, I think my writing is better than speaking because of my accent. When I talk to local people, they say 'parden?, parden?' (Shamim, focus group)

The role of agency and intentionality in participation, learning and integration has been emphasised in recent research (Pavlenko and Lantolf 2000; Norton and Toohey 2002; Solé 2007). What the above data is adding to the body of literature is the role of language and accent in appropriating strategies for participation and identity negotiation. Shamim, concerned with his accented English, avoided oral interaction within his institution and instead tried to negotiate legitimacy through other channels. Politics of difference exercised in language interactions, particularly 'accenticism' (i.e., racism based on accented English, Fotovatian 2012a, 2012b), seem to play a role in navigating him away from open engagement in institutional interactions even at the cost of marginalisation.

Despite choosing diverse pathways, the participants actively took agentive actions to negotiate professional identity in their new institution. The role of the immediate institution in integration and empowering identities is highlighted in the data. Language practices, hegemonies and ideologies influence non-native members' legitimacy negotiations.

Integration in the broader community

It is worthy to mention that newcomers' meaningful and full integration in the host society is often referred to as a more idealistic end rather than a realistic one, challenged by issues like identity loss (Li 2003). The four participants in this study faced challenges in negotiating chances for interaction with the local community and integrating into the broader society. Aini reflected on her experience of interactions with her neighbours:

> Aini: I live in a unit, there are 12 units. There are people from Nigeria I think, Chinese also and the owner is Australian. What I experience is my neighbours seem very busy, very busy. I wanted to say hello to them, but the Australian lady seems so far from me. She is always busy. It is very different from what I expected.
>
> Shamim: Do you think it is because they are always busy? But you are busy, too but still you go and say hello! (Aini and Shamim, lunch-time conversations)

Aini mentioned that these encounters were far from what she had imagined prior to immigration. Her 'imagined community' (Norton 2003) was distanced from the neighbourhood community in her real-life experience. Shamim, a part-time employee at a local bakery reflected on his few chances of interaction with the local community at his 'survival job' workplace, 'I work in a bakery. And most workers were Indians and Indonesians, only very few local workers. And it was very friendly you know. But I had contact only with non-locals'. He highlighted the fact that most 'entry level' or survival jobs in Melbourne are taken by immigrants, and there is little chance for him for interactions with the local community. Shamim perceived himself behind a 'glass door' holding immigrants like himself engaged in survival jobs, distanced from the local community.

Ratna and Aini reflected on educational experiences and the social class relating to intercultural communication. Their belief was that the language used 'on the streets' was difficult to understand for a newcomer due to colloquial, heavily peppered Australian slang and inflection:

Ratna: But you know, I think what I am experiencing is different. I have no problem understanding people here. I mean local staffs here, but outside, I mean in the streets, I can't understand local people at all, not in the university.

Aini: Yes, non-academics, their language is very different, also very heavy Australian accents.

Ratna: Yes, I just can't understand them.

Aini: Yes, and they maybe using slang, and we are not supposed to know slang, you know?

Ratna: Yes, once I was speaking with a security, not here in the university, in a shop. And I couldn't understand what he was talking about. He was one of these local people. And I couldn't understand him, you know. And I just said OK, OK, I leave.

Aini: Usually, I found that academic people are Ok.

Ratna: Yes, they speak the standard things, and very straightforward.

The participants illustrated the role of colloquial English and accents in communication with the local community. The participants differentiated between what they called 'standard' or 'straightforward' English and the indigenised Australian English. They related indigenisation of language and accents with the politics of inclusion and exclusion in everyday interaction contexts. In their perceptions, having the pragmatic capital to engage in local conversations on the one hand and the competence to speak indigenised discourses (local slang and colloquialism), particularly with a local accent was important in their negotiations of belonging and inclusion. Despite their expanded knowledge of the formal or 'standard' language, yet they talked about having limited flexibility in comprehending indigenous colloquial interactions. Their concerns underline the consequences of indigenisation of language and culture in immigrant-populated countries like Australia for integration of immigrant populations. Despite the scholarly recognition of multicompetencies (Cook 1999) of immigrants, monolingual and monocultural ideologies cultured among the public can result in marginalisation of minority groups and can contribute to having divided communities.

Employment prospects

Language proficiency is closely related to the employment prospects of skilled immigrants. Ability to communicate confidently with others is instrumental in accessing 'imagined communities' (Pavlenko and Norton 2007). For the participants in this study, all English language teachers, language proficiency was not as problematic as what they referred to as differences in accent, discourses or word choices. In what follows, Aini reflects on her daily experiences of interaction in English at her workplace, her 'non-native English language speaker's label, and how 'her different' English was impeding her integration and employment prospects:

> Aini: I am actually a sessional English teacher at Highland College, so most of my colleagues are local people. But we don't talk to each other often. It is very different from Malaysia. In Malaysia we like talking to each other. But here, they don't talk in the break time or lunch-time. We just get in to the office, and just say hi, very different from our culture. Basically, I really, really want to find close friends from Australia. But so far, I couldn't. I mean, I talk to some of them, but they are not really close friends.
>
> Shamim: Why? What do you think is the barrier?
>
> Aini: I don t know. Sometimes, I don't understand them. When they make jokes, it is very difficult to understand their jokes. What I am doing now, I'm learning now to understand their jokes, how to make jokes with them, how to respond. You know, just to response with a very sharp answer. Like oh no, that's good, really great.
>
> Shamim: [laugh] Yeah, get out, get out! (Lunch-time interactions)

Aini is concerned about her interactions with colleagues and feels excluded from their circle of friendship because of her different English. Immediately, she relates language with her employment prospects saying:

> What I observe is that all other teachers are locals. And for me, I can never imagine they'd hire me someday as a full-time staff member. Because they hired me as an emergency teacher to substitute their teachers when they cannot make it to come to class. Most of them, their education is not like me, I mean they only have a certificate in teaching but you know I am a PhD student in English teaching. I think their policy is to try to hire native speakers for full-time.

Aini spoke specifically about the field of TESOL, and the 'glass ceiling of working as on-call or sessional teacher and not a permanent teacher. She found legitimacy negotiation challenging and related her experience to the politics of difference at her workplace triggered by 'linguicism'. Shamim articulated the discriminative and marginalising power of the English language even in non-specialised fields:

> But even in jobs not teaching English, in their job ads, they always want strong communication skills and I never know what 'strong' means. I mean I think my English is good but sometimes I can't get those jobs. Once I applied for a part-time job outside university in a shop and I was rejected. I don't think that job needed much English at all. Sometimes I think it is only something when they want to reject you.

As non-native English speakers, the participants experienced real challenges on their ways to find employment even in non-teaching jobs. They felt that their audible differences (differences in how they sounded) were amplified within the community resulting in their marginalisation and limited access to employment.

Holliday and Aboeshiha (2009) warn against discrimination in the TESOL profession, the data above illustrates the existence of such discrimination. Shamim complained that even in non-TESOL jobs, the criterion of 'having strong communication skills' was confusing and undefined. Chen, too, during a lunch-time conversation related her pessimism regarding her employment prospects to language, saying:

> I was hopeful before coming here that with a PhD from Horizon University I could find an academic job in Australia, but now I think it is difficult. I think my English is not good enough, you know. I mean I tried to find a part-time job, but I couldn't.

The data discussed emphasises that language skills can easily turn to backdoors for discrimination. The impact of native speaker ideology on marginalisation of immigrants can be seen in TESOL profession more than other professional fields. The participants revealed how language was contributing to creating a glass roof to their professional recognition. Concerned with being judged against this idealised criterion, Ratna added:

> Ratna: The most difficult thing for me is that, you know, because I am an English language teacher, you know, I feel I expose myself to a lot of evaluation. I mean they say, oh you are an English teacher and your English is like this!
>
> Chen: [laughs] Yeah, they say, you are an English teacher! Really!

Pressure created by the criteria of native-like English fluency, accuracy and pronunciation for English on non-native English teachers to sound and write native-like causes undue additional workplace stress and negative feelings of being exposed to judgement, which may result in their self-isolation. In a context where reality has even passed the predictions indicating more than 80% of everyday interactions take place among non-native English speakers (Graddol 1996), and while significant scholarly work has taken place to shift the discourses of English language hegemony to flexibility for accepting and hearing an array of world Englishes (Graddol 1996), it seems questionable to still witness fixed native-like language models in the layers of community and in hiring trends.

Language, institutional identity and integration

As Gee (2007) reminds us, in our day-to-day lives we become engaged in multiple social interactions, take different social roles and accordingly construct and enact multiple social identities. Membership in an educational institution, therefore, demands that members construct, negotiate and (re)negotiate new social and professional identities which can enable them to be recognised as legitimate members within the institution. But these goals, as Ryan and Viete (2009) emphasise, 'are heavily mediated by the discourses in the new settings' (308). Institutional interactions are arenas for negotiation of social capital. In this study, the participants' negotiation of membership, legitimacy and identity is viewed as tied to their language use, choice of communication strategies and engagement in informal institutional interactions:

> I don't like to be mechanical [she is using this term as opposite of having a good sense of humour], I like my colleagues to know me as a fun friend, but my English is not enough and sometimes I don't know what themes they like to joke about and I am afraid I say something and they say she is rude, but they think I am very mechanical. I used to be a fun friend in my country. (Aini, focus group)

Construction and development of institutional identity involves a dynamic negotiation of the self in relation to institutions and to the communities that are embodied within those institutions. Language interactions are avenues for negotiation of institutional identity and as Aini mentions in the above excerpt lack of familiarity with the local and informal language patterns impede newcomers' identity negotiation.

In the context of this study, the participants worked towards shaping a 'legitimate Ph.D. student' identity as their institutional identity. They tried to negotiate legitimacy within the TESOL institution as the 'non-native' label by the institution imposed identities. The four participants in this study underwent several simultaneous transitions – from an expert academic or teacher to a graduate student, a native-speaker of their mother tongue to a non-native speaker of English, a legitimate member of their social circles in their own countries to a newcomer in Australia and a newcomer to their academic institution. Their institutional identities were shaped by these transactional and transitional processes. These identity transitions made the process of constructing a new and legitimate institutional identity challenging for the participants. They wanted to grow, to be heard and to be valued. They had different goals and agendas for continuing education and accordingly chose different approaches to engage in university and departmental interactions in order to negotiate their identities. The findings re-emphasise the role of language and institutional practices in identity construction.

Conclusion and implications

The discussions in this paper highlight the ties between language, identity and integration. It illustrated how space and identity are dynamically negotiated in informal everyday interactions. The participants in this study used a range of strategies to negotiate their institutional identities within the new context and to integrate into the target community. They desired to negotiate their spaces as valued members of the community bringing language, social and cultural capitals. However, often, the monolingual ideology dominating the language practices within their institution kept them from imagining themselves as multilingual and multicomponent members. The data highlighted how language and accent can turn to tools for othering non-native speakers in everyday community interactions. Lack of knowledge of local discourses and colloquial language contributed to the participants' intense feelings of marginalisation. Within highly and increasingly multicultural workplace and educational 'contact zones' such as what we experience in Australian contexts, there seems to be a need for further studies on the role of what I call *pragmatic capital* on institutional identity negotiation from a critical point of view. From a *critical pragmatic* lens, we need to search for ways to advocate institutions as 'social containers' to adapt strategies that can enhance *all* members' interactions and identity negotiation. By being critical in pragmatics, I intend to imply that in today's global contexts where multiculturalism and identity maintenance is advocated in the scholarly community, institutions need to hear the message and work towards raising their members' awareness to hear and legitimise the different, and to move beyond hegemonising language, culture and accent.

The data also reiterated previous researchers' concerns over a tendency for native speaker ideology in employment practices, particularly in the field of TESOL, disfavoring non-English speaking background English teachers. Participants expressed concerns that the lack of clarity around 'strong communication skills', often highlighted in job advertisements, might open doors to subjectivity and discrimination. Even as established English language teachers in their own countries and doctoral students in Australia, entering 'the glass door' and finding an entry level English teaching position in an English-speaking country seemed too out of reach for the participants challenged by the politics of native speaker ideology governing the institution. The real oppression experiences of the participants were far different from their initial naive imagined identities that once drove them to invest in this field. Their constant experiences of unmet expectations led them lose confidence in positioning themselves as valued multi-competent and multilingual members. They felt their social, language and cultural capitals were devaluated in the new context.

Everyday interactions are avenues for negotiations of language, identity and power. How politics of difference are understood and exercised within institutions immediately impacts integration experiences of members. The data presented in this paper, showcased negotiations of institutional identities through day-to-day engagement in institutional interaction. While institutions construct identities for their members, institutional identities are also dynamically reconstructed and negotiated by social members in institutional interactions. An understanding of the process of these dynamic negotiations among self, others and the institution provides insights into the ways institutional identities are constructed for new members. The role of organisations as the immediate contact points for integrating newcomers to the broader society was also highlighted in the data and discussions.

This study emphasised the significance of research into how new members to an institution with diverse language, cultural and socio-economic backgrounds, construct, develop and negotiate institutional identity. It further provided contexts for an interrogation into the ways the politics of language and culture are woven into the process of identity construction and social representations and the role institutional practices play in consolidating or marginalising their members, in amplifying or suppressing voices.

Acknowledgements

I wish to express my deep gratitude to the Editor of this special issue, Dr Shibao Guo, and the two anonymous reviewers for their insightful and constructive comments. The substance of this paper is indebted to their patience in meticulously reading the earlier drafts and providing me with feedback, and the flaws are all mine.

References

Bouma, G. 2000. *The Research Process*. 4th ed. Melbourne: Oxford University Press.
Bourdieu, P. 1993. *Language and Symbolic Power*. Oxford: Polity Press.
Bourdieu, P., and L. Wacquant. 1992. *An Invitation to Reflexive Sociology*. Chicago: The University of Chicago Press.
Cadman, K. 2005. "Towards a 'Pedagogy of Connection' in Critical Research: A Real Story." *Journal of English for Academic Purposes* 4 (4): 353–367. doi:10.1016/j.jeap.2005.07.001.
Canagarajah, A. S. 2006. "Negotiating the Local in English as a Lingua Franca." *Annual Review of Applied Linguistics* 26: 197–218.
Cervatiuc, A. 2009. "Identity, Good Language Learning, and Adult Immigrants in Canada." *Korean Journal of English Language and Linguistics* 8 (4): 254–271.
Cook, V. 1999. "Going Beyond the Native Speaker in Language Teaching." *TESOL Quarterly* 33 (2): 185–209. doi:10.2307/3587717.

DeVault, M., and L. McCoy. 2005. "Institutional Ethnography: Using Interviews to Investigate Ruling Relations." In *Institutional Ethnography as Practice*, edited by D. Smith, 15–44. Lanham, MD: Rowman and Littlefield.

Duff, P. 2003. "New Directions in Second Language Socialization Research." *Korean Journal of English Language and Linguistics* 3: 309–339.

Fotovatian, S. 2010. "Surviving as an English Teacher in the West: A Case Study of Iranian English Teachers in Australia." *TESL-EJ* 13 (4). http://www.tesl-ej.org/wordpress/issues/volume13/ej52/ej52a3/.

Fotovatian, S. 2012a. "Three Constructs of Institutional Identity among International Doctoral Students in Australia." *Teaching in Higher Education* 17 (5): 577–588. doi:10.1080/13562517.2012.658557.

Fotovatian, S. 2012b. "Negotiating Institutional Identity: International Doctoral Students in an Australian University." Unpublished PhD, Monash University.

Fotovatian, S., and J. Miller. 2013. "Constructing Institutional Identity in University Tea-rooms: International Doctoral Students' Experiences." *Higher Education Research and Development* 32: 345–367.

Gall, M. D., J. P. Gall, and W. R. Borg. 2007. *Educational Research: An Introduction*. Boston: Pearson Education.

Gee, J. P. 2007. *Social Linguistics and Literacies: Ideology in Discourses*. 3rd ed. London: Taylor and Francis.

Graddol, D. 1996. "The Future of English." *English Today* 52 (2): 61–87.

Guo, S. 2009. "Difference, Deficiency, and Devaluation: Tracing the Roots of Non-recognition of Foreign Credentials for Immigrant Professionals in Canada." *The Canadian Journal for the Study of Adult Education* 22 (1): 37–52.

Guo, S. 2010. "Toward Recognitive Justice: Emerging Trends and Challenges Transnational Migration and Lifelong Learning." *International Journal of Lifelong Education* 29 (2): 149–167. doi:10.1080/02601371003616533.

Guo, S. 2013. "Economic Integration of Recent Chinese Immigrants in Canada's Second-tier Cities: The Triple Glass Effect and Immigrants' Downward Social Mobility." *Canadian Ethnic Studies* 45 (3): 95–115. doi:10.1353/ces.2013.0047.

Guo, S., and M. Chase. 2011. "Internationalisation of Higher Education: Integrating International Students into Canadian Academic Environment." *Teaching in Higher Education* 16 (3): 305–318. doi:10.1080/13562517.2010.546524.

Holliday, A., and P. Aboeshiha. 2009. "The Denial of Ideology in Perceptions of Nonnative Speaker Teachers." *TESOL Quarterly* 43 (4): 669–689.

Kenway, J., and E. Bullen. 2003. "Self-representations of International Women Postgraduate Students in the Global University 'Contact Zone'." *Gender and Education* 15 (1): 5–20. doi:10.1080/0954025032000042112.

Kerekes, J. 2007. "Introduction to the Special Issue: High Stakes Gate-keeping Encounters and Their Consequences: Discourses in Intercultural Institutional Settings." *Journal of Pragmatics* 39 (11): 1891–1894. doi:10.1016/j.pragma.2007.07.013.

Kettle, M. 2005. "Agency as Discursive Practice: From 'Nobody' to 'Somebody' as an International Student in Australia." *Asia Pacific Journal of Education* 25 (1): 45–60. doi:10.1080/02188790500032525.

Li, P. S. 2003. "Deconstructing Canada's Discourse of Immigrant Integration." *Journal of International Migration and Integration* 4 (3): 315–333. doi:10.1007/s12134-003-1024-0.

Norton, B. 2003. "Bonny Norton Responds: On Critical Theory and Classroom Practice." In *The TESOL Quarterly Dialogues: Rethinking Issues of Language, Culture, and Power*, edited by J. Sharkey and K. Johnsons, 69–73. Alexandria, VA: TESOL.

Norton, B. 2006. "Identity as a Sociocultural Construct in Second Language Education." In *TESOL in Context, Special Issue*, edited by K. Cadman and K. O'Regan, 22–33. Vancouver, BC: University of British Columbia.

Norton, B., and K. Toohey. 2002. "Identity and Language Learning." In *Oxford University Handbook of Applied Linguistics*, edited by R. Kaplan, 115–123: Oxford: Oxford University Press.

Pavlenko, A., and J. P. Lantolf. 2000. "Second Language Learning as Participation and the (re)construction of Selves." In *Sociocultural Theory and Second Language Learning*, edited by J. P. Lantolf, 155–176. Oxford: Oxford University Press.

Pavlenko, A., and B. Norton. 2007. "Imagined Communities, Identity, and English Language Learning." In *International Handbook of English Language Teaching*, edited by J. Cummins and C. Davison, 669–680. Dordrecht: Springer.

Pennycook, A. D. 2004. "Critical Moments in a TESOL Praxicum." In *Critical Pedagogies and Language Learning*, edited by B. Norton and K. Toohey, 327–346. Cambridge: Cambridge University Press.

Phillipson, R. 2002. "Global English and Local Language Policies." In *Englishes in Asia: Communication, Identity, Power & Education*, edited by A. Kirkpatrick, 7–28. Melbourne: Language Australia.

Ryan, J., and R. Viete. 2009. "Respectful Interactions: Learning with International Students in the English-Speaking Academy." *Teaching in Higher Education* 14 (3): 303–314. doi:10.1080/13562510902898866.

Sawir, E. 2005. "Language Difficulties of International Students in Australia: The Effects of Prior Learning Experience." *International Education Journal* 6 (1): 567–580.

Shan, H., and S. Guo. 2013. "Learning as Sociocultural Practice: Chinese Immigrant Professionals Negotiating Differences and Identities." *Comparative Education* 49 (1): 28–41. doi:10.1080/03050068.2012.740218.

Smith, D. 2001. "Text and the Ontology of Organisations and Institutions." *Studies in Cultures, Organisations and Societies* 7 (2): 159–198. doi:10.1080/10245280108523557.

Solé, C. R. 2007. "Language Learners' Sociocultural Position in the L2: A Narrative Approach." *Language and Intercultural Communication* 7 (3): 203–216. doi:10.2167/laic203.0.

Wenger, E. 2000. "Communities of Practice and Social Learning Systems." *Organisations* 7 (2): 226–246.

Between the nation and the globe: education for global mindedness in Finland

Vanessa de Oliveira Andreotti[a,b], Gert Biesta[c] and Cash Ahenakew[b]

[a]Faculty of Education, University of Oulu, Oulu, Finland; [b]Department for Educational Studies, University of British Columbia, Vancouver, BC, Canada; [c]Faculty of Language and Literature, Humanities, Arts and Education, University of Luxembourg, Walferdange, Luxembourg

This article explores some of the tensions at the interface of nationalist and global orientations in ideals of global mindedness and global citizenship looking specifically at the Finnish context. We engage with discussions related to the social–political and historical context of national identity in Finland and outline the conceptual framework of an educational initiative related to the development of global mindedness through experiences of international mobility and partnerships. This conceptual outline presents a set of theoretical distinctions through which we seek to challenge humanist and universalist approaches to the question of (the formation of) global mindedness by arguing that the issue is neither about cognition or understanding nor about empathy and relationships but ultimately has to do with modes of existence and exposure. Similar to discussions in other small states, the historical trajectory in Finland illustrates how the encounter between the nation and the globe poses particular challenges for education as it runs the risk of reverting to ethnocentric rather than globally minded forms of national identity building. We argue that this risk cannot be addressed with the promotion of a mere understanding of or mere empathy for the other as an educational or political antidote but rather requires an existential approach.

Introduction

In recent years, educators, policy-makers and researchers have become increasingly interested in the significance of transnational mobility for the formation of a global outlook – often expressed with such notions as 'global citizenship' (e.g., Cabrera 2010), 'global engagement' (e.g., Paige et al. 2009), or the wider idea of 'global mindedness' (e.g., Kehl and Morris [2007] 2008; see also Andreotti 2010; Mannion et al. 2011). In both research and practice, there is a strong focus on cognitive change, that is, on the idea that, if certain conditions are met, contact amongst different groups will enhance mutual understanding and, through this, reduce prejudice and improve relationships. This line of thought, which goes back to Gordon Allport's contact hypothesis (see Allport 1954; see also Pettigrew and Tropp 2000), sees questions of transnational networking and interaction mainly in terms of understanding, that is, in terms of altering one's conceptions and perceptions. It thus conceives of the issue to be addressed as a learning task, that is, the task to learn *about* others in order to gain a better understanding which, in turn, will lead to more just and more equitable relationships. Putting it in this way reveals both the humanist and universalist assumptions guiding research and practice – assumptions, moreover, that often tend to overlook the wider socio-political and historical dimensions that shape the conditions for (mis)understanding and (dis)connection.

In this paper, we explore these issues through a discussion of a Finnish initiative aimed at the development of global mindedness through international exchange and mobility. Our contribution focuses on conceptual and theoretical issues and has the ambition to broaden the way in which initiatives such as the one under discussion can be understood and achieved. For this, we present a set of theoretical and conceptual distinctions through which we seek to challenge humanist and universalist approaches to the question of (the formation of) global mindedness by arguing that the issue is neither about cognition or understanding, nor about empathy and relationships, but ultimately has to do with modes of existence and exposure. We present our suggestions against the background of a discussion that looks at the wider socio-political history of Finland as an example of a small modern state which, whilst still in the process of establishing and consolidating its national identity, has been drawn into the flux of neo-liberal post-modernity. This particular historical trajectory creates specific challenges for the promotion of a more global outlook, not in the least because the very particular encounter between the nation and the globe that can be found in the Finnish case runs the risk of reverting to ethnocentric rather than globally minded forms of national identity building – a risk for which a mere understanding of or mere empathy for the other is unlikely to be a sufficient educational (and ultimately also: political) antidote.

The fear of small numbers

In his book *Fear of small numbers*, Arjun Appadurai (2006) offers a compelling explanation of why small numbers of immigrants often become the scapegoats in different types of national crises triggered by external and internal forces. His argument is based on the suggestion that there is an inherent ethnicist tendency in the construction of all ideologies of nationalism. These ideologies often rely on two interlocking tenets: the tenet of a national genius inherent in a singular national ethnos, and the idea of the sovereignty of the modern nation-state. According to Appadurai, the notion of 'distinctive and singular peoples grow[ing] out and control[ing] well defined national territories' (6) is always haunted by the denial of the process of construction of the national ethnos itself. Appadurai thus suggests that:

> the idea of a national ethnos, far from being a natural outgrowth of this or that soil, has been produced and naturalised at great cost, through rhetorics of war and sacrifice, through punishing disciplines of educational and linguistic uniformity, and through the subordination of a myriad of local and regional traditions. (4)

For Appadurai, the global fluidity of technology, weapons, peoples and images unsettles both of these tenets by blurring lines between 'us and them' and by destroying the illusion of national economic sovereignty, security and well-being, inflicting a deep wound in the narcissist nationalist project. This wound, so Appadurai argues, can trigger overwhelming anxieties and fears in majoritarian identities terrified about becoming minor, of minorities becoming major or of minorities/majorities morphing into an uncontrollable mass. Therefore, when social uncertainty is exacerbated by fears of increasing inequality, lack of security or loss of autonomy, and when the project of national purity/completeness is perceived to be jeopardised, narratives of majoritarianism and racialised nationalism can emerge even in (seemingly) inclusive, democratic and secular national states. For Appadurai, small numbers of people can unsettle big issues as economic globalisation triggers the blending of the latent logics of uncertainty (of self-determination) and incompleteness (of a homogeneous national ethnos), a toxic combination that can trigger a 'surplus of rage' and ethnocidal violence, which may be starting to surface in Nordic and other European contexts, as epitomised in Breivik's case in Norway in 2011.[1]

Appadurai's analysis is instructive not only for understanding the complex dynamics of nation building but also for revealing the inherent risks of any attempt to identify the nation as an ethnos or a 'we' in distinction from what the ethnos or we is not, that is, those who are other. Such issues can become particularly problematic when the building of the nation is itself characterised by historical trauma, as this intensifies the need for a strong(er) 'we' and stronger ethnocentric tendencies. Some of these dynamics can be seen in the history of the establishment of the Finnish nation, to which we now turn.

Building the Finnish nation

Finnish history is extremely complex. In the past 200 years, Finland was scarred by Swedish colonisation, Russian annexation and German occupation. A violent civil war less than 100 years ago turned brothers and neighbours into mortal enemies. One side's crushing victory and widespread famine at the time created both a deep collective wound and the motivation for a different future where teachers were seen as the 'enlightened candle'. Effective Finnish resistance to a Russian offensive in the Winter War and the end of WW2 gave rise to a nationalist project committed to class elimination based on a reciprocal social contract that involved social security (welfare), on the part of the state, and commitment to a project of a national ethnos, constructed primarily through formal education, on the part of Finnish citizens. Thus, schooling was formalised as the process that would heal the wounds of past subjugation and guide all Finnish people out of ignorance and poverty towards a shared collective future. However, oppressive historical memories and the cold war left their marks in terms of a constant (and repressed) feeling of (geographical, ideological, ethnic, cultural, linguistic) vulnerability which captured the national identity in a solid negative identification with Russia. Hence, the emergence of Finnish nationalism can be contextualised if we consider the contingent needs of a relatively small number of people living in a land of harsh climate, seemingly under siege: 'Swedes we are no longer, Russians we do not want to become, let us therefore be Finns!' Thus, 'Finland' needed to 'move on' from the pains of external oppression and of internal dismemberment, to protect itself in a volatile historical period in an inconvenient geographical location, and to provide its people with a way to overcome poverty. These needs created the conditions for the emergence of a strong social consensus around the meaning and direction of 'forward', of progress in a benevolent state, of ethnic egalitarianism, and of the role of education and of teachers within it: a project of an ethno-social democracy.

However, this type of strong social/national consensus relies partly on the elimination or domestication of internal dissent, and the construction and safeguarding of a positive sense of ethnic/national homogeneity. During the cold war, when Finland had its borders practically closed to immigration, the former manifested, for example, in secret police screening for Russian espionage, especially amongst intellectuals and foreigners. Higher Education also had an important role in the national consensus building, therefore the relationship of dependence between universities and the State limited academic scope for and possibility of critique and dissent. At this time, like other Nordic countries, Finland was involved in international development cooperation to 'export civilisation' through religious missions, especially in Namibia, Zambia and Tanzania (see Palmberg 2009). At a time when other European countries were facing problematic effects of former or existing colonial rule, Finland (and the Nordic region in general) developed a positive image as peacekeepers and exceptional examples of successful benevolent egalitarian nation states that did not depend on colonial violence,[2] theft, extortion and oppression, or internal/external corruption or exploitation to develop and succeed socially, politically and economically (see Vuorela 2009; Palmberg 2009; Rastas 2012). The notion of innocent exceptionality, which mutes critical debate, is as central to the construction of the Finnish ethnos as is the attachment to strong seemingly egalitarian consensus and avoidance/

elimination of conflict and dissent. Hence, 'discourses of nationhood and belonging serve to marginalise and exclude (or alternatively to subordinate and regulate) others' (Vuorela 2009, 5).

Finland was the last Nordic country to open its borders to immigration in the mid 1990s for economic and humanitarian purposes (see e.g., Mulinari et al. 2009). This was also a period of uncertainty when a severe economic crisis put the social-welfare capacity of the state at risk, reinforcing the feeling of national fragility. Therefore, relationships with Finnish-Others have been framed by a unique and complicated configuration of ideas, fears, vulnerabilities and collective memories, affirmations and denials about Finnish history and ethnic constitution, part and parcel of the construction of nationalism. With the economic crisis in the 1990s, Finland had to start to face itself more as part of and subject to (neo)liberal financial forces, not strictly controlled by the State. This opened contradictory possibilities. On the one hand, there was evident economic necessity to be a more active player in the international arena – Finland needed to become more outward-looking and engage in expanding the scope of possibilities for international economic engagements; on the other hand, this also meant the need to shift the dimension of national homogeneity towards a 'controlled' internationalisation: diversifying skills, languages, ideas and outlooks 'within' to address labour shortages, new areas of work and the demand for constant innovation.

Framed by (neo)liberal economic imperatives, the social and political changes that followed started to put into question the viability of a strong welfare state. Thus, historically established attachments to ideas of insularity/ independence (grounding the idea of national exceptionalism) and ethnocentrism (grounding national consensus and homogeneity) were gradually captured by populist groups that presented immigrants, plurilingualism and internationalisation in general as the root causes of social-economic scarcity and vulnerability (Vuori 2009), and political subjugation (often expressed as an erosion of freedom of expression; Rossi 2009), quickly making these ideas manifest as explicit racism and xenophobia (Rossi 2009; Rastas 2012). In this context, the perceived loss of national autonomy (caused by immigration and internationalisation) is associated with historical sentiments of opposition to past colonial rule, mobilising a discourse of traditional Finnish resistance to foreign oppression and subjugation.

Educating for global mindedness

The foregoing analysis of the rise and development of the Finnish nation provides an important backdrop for understanding the work of CIMO, the Finnish agency for International Mobility, and its attempts to contribute to the development of global mindedness. CIMO was created in 1991 as an independent agency under the Finnish Ministry of Education and Culture. Its general aim is to offer 'services and expertise to encourage international cooperation in education, culture, at work and among young people' (CIMO 2010, 11). CIMO administers several mobility, exchange, trainee and scholarship programmes, including European Union programmes like Life Long Learning, Erasmus, Comenius and Leonardo da Vinci. In its 2010 five-year strategy document, the concept of global mindedness was identified as a central tenet of CIMO's strategy. Strategically combining economic, nationalist and humanistic discourses, CIMO argues that bi-directional mobility is a way not only to address economic imperatives, but to enlarge frames of reference in ways that could counter existing growing opposing trends, and, as a result, enrich Finnish culture, and secure better international relationships at home and abroad.

The strategy booklet, entitled 'Strategy 2020: Towards a globally minded Finland' (2010) presents the need for a more international Finland that emerges as a result of demands created by global forces, including tougher competition, technological innovations, fast-paced change, interdependence, environmental fragility, migration of people, multiculturalism, increasing inequality, a shrinking public economy and increasing public deficit (3–7). The vision proposed in the document points to a 'genuinely international' Finland (3), with a high level of knowledge and skills, a country that is multicultural, creative and 'in the vanguard of knowledge, participation and creativity' (3). A globally minded Finland would offer equal opportunities for citizens (4), be a 'pioneer in intelligent technology' (5) and uphold values of universal and equal welfare, democracy, equality, social responsibility, justice and sustainability. Finland would achieve a more ethically 'sustainable image' (10) by being socially just and competitive, and encouraging global responsibility aiming for a 'just world with universal human rights and equality' (8), where all people could be educated and learn values and ways of life to help achieve 'a sustainable future and positive social change' (8). This would be achieved through increased social capital via collaboration and cooperation, increased competitiveness to improve well-being, increased creative and constructive interactions and networks, reliability and efficiency, participation in (inter)national debates and distribution of information, partnerships with developing counties, and attracting international interest in the Finnish language, culture, expertise, research, education and know how (7–10).

The booklet presents the strategy of international mobility and cooperation as a force for change towards global mindedness that can widen worldviews, increase skills, creativity and knowledge, strengthen international social networks, foster positive attitudes, boost social capital and competitiveness, promote Finnish culture, skills and knowledge abroad, tap into international know-how to improve knowledge and expertise, contribute to a sustainable future and to positive change, and enable human development in ways that would not be possible otherwise. As a result, global mindedness is conceptualised in the booklet as six interrelated characteristics: (1) being open-minded; (2) seeing the bigger picture; (3) having awareness of one's own prejudices; (4) being open to new things; (5) having a willingness to interact with different kinds of people; and (6) seeing difference as richness (3). In the context of recent political polarisations in Finland, it is interesting to note how CIMO's narrative was articulated in ways that strategically blended economic, social and cultural demands in response to concerns expressed by different social groups in Finland.

The way in which CIMO articulates its approach and rationale to questions of global mindedness clearly reveals the impact of a range of current agendas and discourses about globalisation and internationalism – agendas that strongly focus on an economic and social capital rationale which highlights the need for global connections in order to achieve long-term prosperity for Finland within an increasingly open and connected global marketplace. To this are added two further layers. One focuses on the 'global' values of justice, human rights and equality; the other on national culture and creativity. All this, in turn, feeds into a very particular definition of an agenda for the development of global mindedness that centres crucially on the individual and his or her willingness to be open, outgoing, and positive about the possibilities of being enriched by the encounter with otherness and difference. While the sentiments expressed here are not necessarily 'bad' – which is what makes them both attractive and problematic – the conception of global mindedness articulated here not only lacks a sense of specificity, but also seems to be unaware of the possibility that the encounter with what and who is other and different may not be experienced as enlarging and enriching, but as a threat – particularly a threat for a sense of national identity under siege. The conception of global mindedness articulated here, to put it differently, is one that perhaps may make sense in particular socio-historical contexts, but not in all contexts and perhaps particularly not if seen against the specific historical trajectory of the establishment of the Finnish nation.

Reconsidering and reconceptualising global mindedness: a proposal

The question the foregoing discussion raises is what kind of conception of and approach to the formation of global mindedness might be more sensitive to the specific historical conditions of the Finnish trajectory – bearing in mind that this trajectory in itself is not unique but, as our reference to Appadurai's work has indicated, may be representative of the dynamics of more smaller nation states that have developed more recently and that are faced with the dilemma of, in almost one and the same 'move' having to establish its own sense of national identity and having to connect up with the fast pace of globalisation. When we were invited by CIMO to develop an instrument to assess the impact of their work in the domain of global mindedness education, we thus had a wider ambition than only respond to an instrumental question, in that we wanted to engage more deeply and broadly with conceptions that would inform the creation of such an instrument. When we began to review the literature in the field, it became clear that this was a bigger issue than just with regard to CIMO's ambitions and initiatives. We found that existing approaches were limited in their conceptualisations of global mindedness and intercultural competence in three particular ways.

First, hierarchical binaries such as global versus local, self-centred versus other-cantered, citizen of the nation versus citizen of the world, were very common grounding ideas in several instruments, leading to one-dimensional conceptualisations of global mindedness (e.g., Kitsantas 2004; Morais and Ogden 2011). Second, instruments tended to organise the path towards global mindedness in terms of linear teleological developmental stages with each stage guaranteeing related competencies and behaviours (e.g., Nguyen, Biderman, and McNary 2010; Paige et al. 2009). Third, there was also a tendency to focus on the cognitive acquisition of knowledge about others or about the world as an indication of positive development (e.g., Pettigrew and Tropp 2000; Kehl and Morris 2008; Bennett 2009). We also noticed critical attempts to address the limitations of these conceptualisations through theoretical analyses (e.g., Zemach-Bersin 2009, 2012; Dervin 2009; Andreotti 2006, 2011a).

Drawing on post-structuralist, postcolonial and (neo)pragmatist conceptualisations of ethics, otherness and transnational engagements (see Biesta and Burbules 2003; Peters and Biesta 2008; Andreotti 2011b; Andreotti and Souza 2012) in developing an alternative framework, we wanted primarily to stress that the formation of global mindedness is not necessarily a process that operates through awareness and cognition. Our contribution aimed to problematise the old adage that travel broadens the mind, expressed in Allport's (1954) suggestion that, if certain conditions are met, contact amongst different groups will reduce prejudice and enhance mutual understanding. We wanted to be able to acknowledge, in other words, that knowledge or understanding of cultural otherness and difference is neither a necessary nor a sufficient condition for responsible engagement with the Other, and sometimes can actually hinder such engagement, particularly as Guo (2009) points out, when difference is exoticised, trivialised or framed through the lens of positivism or liberal universalism. We also wanted to create a conceptual model of global mindedness that took account of contextual factors in encounters with difference, moving away from a linear developmental understanding focusing on individual capacities towards situated contextual modes of engagement. And we wanted to stay away from a binary and one-dimensional representation of global mindedness so as to be able to highlight qualitative differences within engagement with cultural otherness and difference, and thus to conceive of global mindedness as a multi-dimensional construct. However, we also needed to wrestle with the normative tendencies in our academic orientations vis-a-vis CIMO's practical and political context and descriptive/prescriptive necessities.

We proposed a conception of global-mindedness as a multidimensional concept that is concerned with the ways in which individuals think about and engage with otherness and difference in contexts characterised by plurality, complexity, uncertainty, contingency and inequality (see Andreotti 2010). We started from Hannah Arendt's (1968) metaphors of tourism, empathy and visiting to refine distinctions between three qualitatively different ways to engage with the 'strangeness' of others and of the world itself (see Biesta 2006, 2010). In order to emphasise the problematic relationship between cognition and predictable behaviour, we conceptualised tourism, empathy and visiting neither as developmental stages, nor as capacities individuals can acquire, but rather see them as *dispositions*, that is, as acquired patterns of action (see Dewey 1922). Unlike capacities or competencies, dispositions develop, become latent and manifest in more complex and unpredictable ways, and individuals can have the three proposed different dispositions in differing degrees of 'strength', and manifesting at different points in time depending on contextual factors. Unlike developmental stages, individuals can acquire all three dispositions – so that they become part of a 'repertoire' of dispositions. *Empirically* our approach makes it possible to characterise the particular cognitive *configuration* of this repertoire at individual level at different points in time (thus allowing both for the characterisation of qualitative differences in global mindedness and for mapping change over time). *Educationally* it means that rather than aiming to shift individuals from one orientation to another – which would be the implication of a linear developmental understanding of global mindedness – the focus should rather be on *enlargement of the repertoire itself*.

We called our project the 'Global Mindedness Dispositions' (GMD) instrument. Tourism, empathy and visiting are used metaphorically (Arendt 1968) to conceptualise three qualitatively distinctive ways of engaging with cultural otherness and difference. Unlike parochialism which – literally and metaphorically – means to stay at home and not to engage with otherness and difference at all, tourism, empathy and visiting are all forms of engagement. They can therefore be seen as enactments of different conceptions or notions of global mindedness. Epistemologically, we associate the metaphor of tourism with objectivism – that is, to the idea that the world can ultimately be understood and described in one way. The metaphor of empathy is connected to relativism – that is, with the idea that we all have different *perspectives* on the world. The metaphor of visiting is connected to pluralism – that is, with the idea that we all live in different *worlds*. Empathy is therefore based on the assumption that it is possible to move oneself to the position of the other and see and understand the world from the other's perspective. Unlike tourism, which is the position of the spectator who, when encountering otherness and difference, in a sense already knows what he or she will find (which means that other cultures can only appear as other and different), empathy is based on the assumption that it is possible to bridge the difference between self and other through acts of understanding and interpretation (which means that, at the core, we can only be 'the same'). Empathy thus trades the position of the spectator for that of the native who identifies with the other culture so as to avoid the discomfort of being in an unfamiliar place. Visiting, on the other hand, tries to work through this discomfort. Unlike tourism, which always maintains a distance between self and other, visiting entails locating oneself in a different place, not with the ambition to think and feel like others in that place do, but to have *one's own thoughts, feelings and experiences* in a location that is different from one's own – a location where one is with and in the presence of others, exposed to the world, and open to being taught by unpredictable teachers and teachings (see Biesta 2013).

This means that while tourism ultimately *overrides* difference, and empathy aims at a *fusion* of perspectives, visiting has an orientation towards an *encounter* of worlds that is unscripted. While tourism and empathy in a sense contribute to the empowerment of individuals to engage with otherness and difference and thus literally make them stronger, visiting comes with an orientation towards *disarmament*, an 'opening up' of the individual so that the other – the human other, the world – can 'speak' and the visitor can be spoken to. While empathy aims at the development of *common* understanding, often informed by the idea of a common human identity and the possibility of consensus, visiting has an orientation towards *multiplicity*. In short: tourism eliminates difference; empathy confines difference; visiting enlarges difference. In terms of broader theoretical outlooks we might say, in sum, that tourism would be connected with ethno-centrism, empathy with ethno-relativism and visiting with existentialism (see Table 1).

While tourism, empathy and visiting are related to different ways of understanding, they are not just different perspectives on otherness and difference. They are, in other ways, not merely located at the level of cognition but have cognitive, affective and performative dimensions. They are about what we (claim to) *know*, about how we (are predisposed to) *feel* and about what we (are enabled or unable to) *do*. Tourism, empathy and visiting should therefore not be understood as different cognitive schemes, but as dispositions, that is, as *embodied possibilities for action*. Dispositions are different from capacities or competencies in that capacities and competencies are fully formed ways of acting, whereas dispositions are embodied *possibilities* for action. Capacities are, in other words, in the 'possession' of the individual who can either decide to deploy them in a particular situation or not, while the idea of dispositions as embodied possibilities for action makes it possible to acknowledge that how individuals will act in concrete situations always depends on the *interaction* between dispositions and situational characteristics.

Table 1. Conceptualising tourism, empathy and visiting.

Tourism	Empathy	Visiting
Objectivism (there is only one true account of reality)	Relativism (we have different perspectives on the same world)	Pluralism (we all live in different worlds)
Spectator: we always understand the other through our own knowledge, and we already know what the other is	Native: we can understand the world from the perspective of the other	Exposure: having one's own thoughts and feelings in a location that is different from one's own
Distance between self and other	Fusion of self and other	Encounter of self and other
Empowerment	Empowerment	Disarmament
Single understanding	Common understanding	Multiplication of understanding
Eliminating difference	Reducing different/plurality	Increasing difference/plurality
Ethnocentrism	*Ethno-relativism*	*Existentialism*

To understand why individuals will act in a particular way thus requires both an insight in the available dispositions and an insight in the ways in which individuals are affected by, perceive and interpret the characteristics of a particular situation, including the perception and the configuration of the power relations that are 'at work' in such situations. By seeing tourism, empathy and visiting as dispositions, it thus becomes possible to make sense of the fact that the same individual may act differently in different situations and also that such different responses are, in a sense, 'rational' – that is, they 'make sense' for the individual in the particular situation he or she is in.

While there are important differences between the three dispositions, we proposed the formation of global mindedness as a process in which one disposition is not superseded by the other. In this sense not only a linearly staged developmental understanding of global mindedness is rejected, but also does each disposition exemplify a different conceptual understanding of global mindedness. As visiting presupposes a different approach to knowledge than empathy, it requires a cognitive and/or affective critical dissociation from aspects of empathy. Similarly, as empathy presupposes a different approach to cultural difference than tourism, it requires a cognitive/affective critical dissociation from aspects of tourism. However, these cognitive and/or affective critical dissociations do not guarantee performative dissociations as action in individual situations will depend on the interaction between dispositions and situational characteristics.

Conclusion

We started this article by emphasising the importance of social-political and historical dimensions that shape the conditions for (mis)understanding of and (dis)connection with difference. Appadurai's analysis of the problematic and ambivalent relationship between nationalist discourses and 'difference' in the context of neoliberal globalisation sheds light on the difficulties of ethical engagements with difference at the interface between the nation and the globe. According to Appadurai, nationalist discourses depend on ideas of national self-determination and a homogeneous ethnos that are challenged by both the borderless expansion of financial capital and the heterogeneity of the nation reflected in increased migration as a result of globalisation. This dynamic can be observed in recent events in Finland where the populist mobilisation of discourses of resistance to economic globalisation and defence of national sovereignty have intensified hostility towards difference expressed as increased racism and xenophobia. Against this background, we offered a brief overview of an initiative of the Finnish Agency for International Mobility to promote a 'Globally Minded Finland' through a combination of economic, humanist and nationalist discourses that aimed to promote open mindedness through education and international travel. As researchers invited to engage with this initiative, we proposed a reconceptualisation of global mindedness that could expand educational debates about diversity beyond the focus on the call for more knowledge about the Other. The theoretical framework we described in this article consists of three travel dispositions represented in the metaphors of tourism, empathy and visiting. Each disposition consists of latent cognitive, affective and performative assemblages that are contingently mobilised. In the context of this special issue, this article draws attention to the challenge of enlarging possibilities of host populations to engage ethically and productively with difference within and outside of their national borders.

Notes
1. This analysis is expanded in a forthcoming paper.
2. The colonisation of the Sami is still repressed knowledge/history in Finland to date.

References
Allport, G. 1954. *The Nature of Prejudice*. New York: Addison-Wesley.
Andreotti, V. 2006. "Soft versus Critical Global Citizenship Education." *Policy and Practice: A Development Education Review* 3 (Autumn): 83–98.
Andreotti, V. 2010. "Global Education in the '21st Century': Two Different Perspectives on the 'Post-' of Postmodernism." *International Journal of Development Education and Global Learning* 2 (2): 5–22.
Andreotti, V. 2011a. "Engaging the (Geo)Political Economy of Knowledge Construction: Towards Decoloniality and Diversality in Global Citizenship Education."

Globalisation, Societies and Education Journal 9 (3–4): 381–397. doi:10.1080/14767724.2011.605323.

Andreotti, V. 2011b. *Actionable Postcolonial Theory.* New York: Palgrave.

Andreotti, V., and L. M. Souza, eds. 2012. *Postcolonial Perspectives on Global Citizenship Education.* New York: Routledge.

Appadurai, A. 2006. *Fear of Small Numbers.* Durham: Duke University Press.

Arendt, H. 1968. *Between Past and Future: Eight Exercises in Political Thought.* New York: Penguin Books.

Bennett, M. J. 2009. "Defining, Measuring, and Facilitating Intercultural Learning: A Conceptual Introduction to the Intercultural Education Double Supplement." *Intercultural Education* 20 (1–2): 1–13. doi:10.1080/14675980903370763.

Biesta, G. 2006. *Beyond Learning. Democratic Education for a Human Future.* Boulder, CO: Paradigm Publishers.

Biesta, G. J. J. 2010. "How to Exist Politically and Learn from It: Hannah Arendt and the Problem of Democratic Education." *Teachers College Record* 112 (2): 558–577.

Biesta, G. J. J. 2013. "Receiving the Gift of Teaching: From 'Learning From' to 'Being Taught By.'" *Studies in Philosophy and Education* 32 (5): 449–461. doi:10.1007/s11217-012-9312-9.

Biesta, G. J. J., and N. Burbules. 2003. *Pragmatism and Educational Research.* Lanham, MD: Rowman and Littlefield.

Cabrera, L. 2010. *The Practice of Global Citizenship.* Cambridge: Cambridge University Press.

CIMO. 2010. "Strategy 2020: Towards a Global-minded Finland." Accessed September 22, 2012. http://www.e-julkaisu.fi/cimo/strategy_2020

Dervin, F. 2009. "Transcending the Culturalist Impasse in Stays Abroad: Helping Mobile Students to Appreciate Diverse Diversities." *Frontiers: The Interdisciplinary Journal of Study Abroad* 18: 119–141.

Dewey, J. 1922. *Human Nature and Conduct. An Introduction to Social Psychology.* New York: Henry Holt.

Guo, S. 2009. "Difference, Deficiency, and Devaluations: Tracing the Roots of Non-recognition of Foreign Credentials for Immigrant Professionals in Canada." *The Canadian Journal for the Study of Adult Education* 22 (1): 37–52.

Kehl, K., and J. Morris. 2008. "Differences in Global-mindedness between Short-term and Semester-long Study Abroad Participants at Selected Private Universities." *Frontiers: The Interdisciplinary Journal of Study Abroad* 15 (Fall/Winter): 67–80.

Kitsantas, K. 2004. "Studying Abroad: The Role of College Students' Goals on the Development of Cross-cultural Skills and Global Understanding." *College Student Journal* 38 (3): 4–41.

Mannion, G., G. Biesta, M. Priestley, M., and H. Ross. 2011. "The Global Dimension in Education and Education for Global Citizenship: Genealogy and Critique." *Globalisation, Societies, Education* 9 (3–4): 443–456. doi:10.1080/14767724.2011.605327.

Morais, D., and A. Ogden. 2011. "Initial Development and Validation of the Global Citizenship Scale." *Journal of Studies in International Education* 15 (5): 445–466. doi:10.1177/1028315310375308.

Mulinari, D., S. Keskinen, S. Irni, and S. Tuori. 2009. "Introduction: Postcolonialism and the Nordic Models of Welfare and Gender." In *Complying with Colonialism: Gender, Race and Ethnicity in the Nordic Region*, edited by S. Keskinen, S. Tuori, S. Irni, and D. Mulinary, 1–18. Farnham and Burlington: Ashgate.

Nguyen, N. T., M. D. Biderman, and L. D. McNary. 2010. "A Validation Study of the Cross-cultural Adaptability Inventory Cross-cultural Adaptability Inventory." *International Journal of Training and Development* 14 (2): 112–129. doi:10.1111/j.1468-2419.2010.00345.x.

Paige, R., G. Fry, E. Stallman, J. Josi, and J. Jea-Eun. 2009. "Study Abroad for Global Engagement: The Long-term Impact of Mobility Experiences." *Intercultural Education* 20 (1–2): 29–44. doi:10.1080/14675980903370847.

Palmberg, M. 2009. "The Nordic Colonial Mind." In *Complying with Colonialism: Gender, Race and Ethnicity in the Nordic Region*, edited by S. Keskinen, 35–50. Burlington: Ashgate Publishing.

Peters, M., and G. Biesta. 2008. *Derrida, Deconstruction and the Politics of Pedagogy*. New York: Peter Lang.

Pettigrew, T., and L. Tropp. 2000. "Does Intergroup Contact Reduce Prejudice: Recent Meta-analytic Findings." In *Reducing Prejudice and Discrimination. The Claremont Symposium on Applied Social Psychology*, edited by S. Oskamp, 93–114. Mahwah, NJ: Lawrence Erlbaum Associates.

Rastas, A. 2012. "Reading History through Finnish Exceptionalism." In *Whiteness and Postcolonialism in the Nordic Region: Exceptionalism, Migrant Others and National Identities*, edited by K. Loftsdottir and L. Jensen, 89–105. Farnham and Burlington: Ashgate.

Rossi, L. 2009. "Licorice Boys and Female Coffee Beans: Representations of Colonial Complicity in Finnish Visual Culture." In *Complying with Colonialism: Gender, Race and Ethnicity in the Nordic Region*, edited by S. Keskinen, S. Tuori, S. Irni, and D. Mulinary, 189–205. Farnham and Burlington: Ashgate.

Vuorela, U. 2009. "Colonial Complicity: The 'Postcolonial' in the Nordic Context." In *Complying with Colonialism: Gender, Race and Ethnicity in the Nordic Region*, edited by S. Keskinen, S. Tuori, S. Irni, and D. Mulinary, 19–34. Farnham and Burlington: Ashgate.

Vuori, J. 2009. "Guiding Immigrants to the Realm of Gender Equality." In *Complying with Colonialism: Gender, Race and Ethnicity in the Nordic Region*, edited by S. Keskinen, S. Tuori, S. Irni, and D. Mulinary, 207–224. Farnham and Burlington: Ashgate.

Zemach-Bersin, T. 2009. "Selling the World: Study Abroad Marketing and the Privatization of Global Citizenship." In *The Handbook of Practice and Research in Study Abroad: Higher Education and the Quest for Global Citizenship*, edited by R. Lewin, 303–320. New York: Routledge.

Zemach-Bersin, T. 2012. "Entitled to the World: The Rhetoric of US Global Citizenship Education and Study Abroad." In *Postcolonial Perspectives on Global Citizenship Education*, edited by V. Andreotti and L. Mario de Souza, 87–104. New York: Routledge.

Constructing a theory of individual space: understanding transnational migration through the experience of return Chinese immigrants from Canada in Beijing

Yueya Ding

Department of International Education Research, National Academy of Education Administration, Beijing, China

> Drawing on life history research, this study critically examines the transnational experiences of return Chinese immigrants from Canada in Beijing. Through the accounts of their experiences, it explores different integration and reintegration strategies, including self-adjustment, lifelong learning and flexible citizenship. A native concept of 'space' is examined and a theory of individual space (IS) is constructed. The study demonstrates that immigrants' integration is a process of constant construction and reconstruction of their expected IS in various societies. This space defines the self and its relationship to others and the outside world. By spatial transformation, migrants break spatial limitations to seek a better future. The tension between IS and the society the migrant enters determines the ongoing characteristics of contemporary transnational migration.

Today, modern communication and transportation technologies allow transnational migrants to experience life in more than one place (Portes, Guarnizo, and Landolt 1999). Transnational activities and social networks can be successfully and easily sustained by migrants without the limitations of space and distance (Wong and Satzewich 2006). It is possible for migrants to keep close social ties with their homeland and at the same time build new connections with their host country (Lien 2008). Because transnationalism has changed the way migrants create economic, political and sociocultural connections between the host country and the homeland, their (re)integration is a complex process that deserves the attention of researchers.

In this context, China has become part of the transnational migration that was discussed above as an important source and host country. As one of the top source countries since the early 1990s, China has sent a large number of highly skilled migrants to different parts of the world, particularly to developed countries. Now China's booming economy is attracting some of them back. From 1978 to 2012, 1,091,200 people with overseas educational qualifications returned to Mainland China, most of whom returned to China in the past decade. In the year of 2012, the number reached 272,900 (Ministry of Education of the People's Republic of China 2013). These returnees, often referred to as *'haigui'* in Chinese, have brought social changes to Chinese society and meanwhile sparked heated debate. However, little has been written about the personal experiences of these transnational migrants. Drawing on life history research, this study critically examines the transnational experiences of return Chinese immigrants from Canada in Beijing. Through their stories, different integration and reintegration strategies are explored, and then a theory of individual space (IS) is constructed. It is hoped that the finding will shed light on the transnational migration in the age of globalisation.

Theoretical framework

Transnationalism provides the theoretical framework for this study. Vertovec (1999, 447) defines transnationalism as multiple ties and interactions that link people or institutions across the borders of nation-states. It is a kind of practice that requires regular and sustained transnational social contacts among nations over time, which may include a high intensity of exchanges, new modes of transacting, as well as a variety of activities that require continual cross-border travel and contacts (Portes, Guarnizo, and Landolt 1999). It is the scale of intensity and simultaneity of current transnational activities that constitute the essential distinctiveness of transnationalism.

With the increasing density and frequency of transnational practices and linkage, spatial distance has less and less connection with fixed national boundaries. The contemporary practice, according to political geographers, has altered the traditional definition of the space and time (Faist 2000). A fixed distance between two countries is gradually replaced by a floating distance determined by a transnational social network. A new social space is constructed that is not necessarily grounded in particular geographical places. The space combines various boundaries together into a single social field – a field combined here and there, absence and presence across ever-widening distances and spaces (Yeoh, Willis, and Khader 2003; Smith 2001). Faist (2000, 191) further clarifies transnational social space as 'a combination of ties, positions in networks and organisations, and networks of organisations that stretch across the borders of multiple states'.

Studies also point out how transnationalism influences not only the reconstruction of social space but also the migrants' adaptation and integration process in various host societies during their transnational lives (Ding 2010; Brittain 2009; Wiles 2008; Wong 2004). Migrants construct a transnational social network to sustain their feelings of allegiance to the home society, and tie family members who stay and those who emigrate by creating a tight and complex system of relationships and responsibilities (Gray 2003). It is possible for transnational migrants to keep close social ties with their homeland while at the same time build new connections in their host country (Lien 2008). The resources and supports from the transnational network help migrants break economic limitations from external macro circumstances, mitigate their culture shock and facilitate their adaptation into various local societies smoothly (Hagan 1998). The transnational network makes today's transnational migration more available, feasible and frequent than before.

The transnationalism discourse endows new paths to examine transnational migrants and their personal lives (Wong and Satzewich 2006). Portes (2003) has suggested that transnationalism should be considered a grassroots phenomenon that consists of individual cross-border activities. Studies find that the more migrants engage in maintaining their transnational social networks, the freer they move across countries (Ammassari and Black 2001). Levitt, DeWind, and Vertovec (2003) have stated that migrants' lives involve both observable and unobservable effects, especially in sociocultural aspects that are largely ignored by much of the early transnational migration research. The most noteworthy absences are these migrants' memories, stories and artistic creations, all of which are difficult to capture through traditional research methods. Nevertheless, they are critical for exploring transnational migration and should not be overlooked. The concrete, everyday changes in people's lives are the doorway into understanding transnationalism 'from below' (Portes 2003). Hence, this study aims to examine transnational migration at the individual level, focusing on how transnationalism exactly influences individuals' real life on their journey of transnational migration.

Life history research

Vertovec (1999) suggested that any investigation of migration should recognise the importance of the concrete, everyday changes in people's lives and comprise detailed studies of actual events. Because most migration stories happen over a long period of one's life or even across several generations, they need to be understood within a long-term autobiographical, biographical and family history context (King 2000). In light of these comments, life history research was conducted for this study.

In social sciences, life history is defined as a research approach that focuses on the partial or entire inner experience of an individual's life and how it reflects personal, institutional and social themes in a historical context (Cole and Knowles 2001). Life history research is based on the assumption that individual experiences are best understood through recounting and reconstructing a life story in the context in which it was lived. This approach helps focus on various life stages of individual migrants and holistically examines the integration process associated with various phases of their lives. This type of research also emphasises the interaction between individuals and the broader social contexts by framing their experiences in a wider social structure, allowing the researcher to situate participants' stories within the context of globalisation to observe their process of (re)integration into the local societies in which the individuals interact.

The fieldwork for this study was conducted in Beijing between 2008 and 2009. As China's political, economic and cultural hub, Beijing tends to be the first choice for return transnational migrants in China (Wang 2007). Criteria-based sampling and purposeful sampling were used to select participants. Recruitment message was posted on websites designed for returning migrants. Participants had to be permanent residents in the category of independent immigrants who spent a minimum of two years in Canada. They also had to have worked at least one year in China after returning from Canada to ensure they had accumulated sufficient experience as a transnational migrant but still had fresh memories of their life abroad.

Interviews are the main data collection method in this study. Life history studies favour depth over breadth. Some researchers in the field contend that a large number of life stories samples is unnecessary and possibly detrimental (Goodson and Sikes 2001). Following this principle, three participants were selected for the study. All interviews focused on the participants' personal life experiences relating to transnational migration, including pre-immigration experiences from China to Canada, adaptation experiences in Canada and reintegration in China.

Report of findings

The study's three participants, Tom, Helen and James (pseudonyms), all embarked on unique migratory paths. Their stories may not be the most typical compared with other Chinese returnees from Canada, but they are particular, authentic and special enough for deep exploration.

Tom, a 38-year-old TV programme editor, director and journalist, immigrated to Canada in 2002 and stayed in Toronto for about four years. In October 2006, he returned to China to work as the chief editor for Sunshine Movie & TV Planning Centre in Beijing. Helen is a senior technology consultant at Weiguang Co., a hi-tech company in Beijing. In 2000, at the age of 36, Helen and her family received permission to immigrate to Canada. The family arrived in Toronto and then moved to Halifax. Five years later, in February 2005, Helen's husband returned to China. After half a year, Helen returned with her son. James, 45, is now an associate professor at N University in Beijing. In 1990, he left China for Switzerland, where he studied at the University of Geneva. In 2000, he and his wife migrated from Geneva to Quebec. In 2006, they moved back to Beijing.

Helen, James and Tom submitted their Canadian immigration applications at the turn of the century, the peak time for Mainland Chinese immigrants to immigrate to Canada. For the first time since the 1970s, in 1998, immigrants from Mainland China outnumbered those from Hong Kong and Taiwan (Guo and DeVoretz 2006). Most immigrants from Mainland China belonged to the independent class, with most of them being highly skilled, young, educated, middle-class professionals. Helen, James and Tom fit all of these categories.

Immigrants moving from one country to another have various cross-cultural experiences. Bhatia and Ram (2001) confirmed that the integration process is a constant negotiation between here and there, past and present, homeland and host land, self and others. For my participants, three themes emerged out of their continuing negotiation with external social space: self-adjustment, lifelong learning and flexible citizenship.

Transnational migration as a process of self-adjustment

According to Searle and Ward (1990), self-adjustment in a new society consists of psychological and sociocultural adjustments. For migrants, self-adjustment, along with other strategies such as problem solving, detachment, positive thinking, tension reduction and withdrawal helps them adapt to a new society (Lazarus and Folkman 1984). Tom's cross-cultural experiences illustrate this process of self-adjustment.

In Tom's migratory story, the theme of self-adjustment emerged from the very beginning of his transnational migration journey. As a TV editor and journalist at one of China's largest TV station, Tom knew that the opportunity to work in Canada's media industry was relatively rare. Although he has a high level of education and training, his credentials could not be fully recognised by the host country (Guo 2009). When Tom arrived in Canada in November 2002, he decided to start what he thought would be a lucrative business – selling Chinese folk art and crafts. Unfortunately, his products did not sell very well and after only six months, Tom had to shut down his business:

> The fatal mistake I made was that, as a Chinese who started his own business overseas, I didn't ask or learn more about the local business system and rules. If I had, my chances of success might have been higher. But my two months'[1] understanding of Canada was kind of superficial and formed by traveling. So, I didn't change my mindset ... I still used my *Chinese eyes* and *Chinese brain* to think about Canadian stuff. My *Chinese way* was totally wrong ... It would work in China but did not in Toronto.

Tom learned that the approach he had used to develop distribution channels for his goods, which would have been effective in China, was not in Canada. In order to adapt to Canada, Tom realised that he had to alter his *Chinese wa*y to a *Canadian way* as soon as possible. He told me that it was through learning and gathering the 'right' information about his new society that he gradually adjusted his approaches to business marketing and also other aspects of Canadian society, including language fluency, culturally appropriate social skills, work skills and the ability to interact with host nationals (Searle and Ward 1990).

After the failure of paper-cuts business, Tom readjust his career development plan and worked at low-paying temporary jobs, most of which involved heavy manual or industrial labour. Then, after about a year of such employment, he found a position as a salesman. Tom did become a successful salesman before his return to China. He was successful at this job partly because of his positive thinking, a critical self-adjustment mechanism:

> One day, I came home from Steels Street and it was snowing heavily. Having walked about 10Km, I took off my boots as soon as I got home and found I couldn't take off my socks. [My feet were] bloody from walking so long in leaky boots through the snow. Blood and water were half-frozen together. I couldn't take my socks off ... Among so many hardships I have had, this was not a big deal. On the contrary, I was even excited. I thought, 'Okay, so this is hardship. Finally, I'm bloody' Ha ... [Tom laughs loudly], this was my real attitude at the time.

Tom believes that he adapted to the host society faster than other newcomers because of his upbeat response to hardship. He looked at his challenges as ways to experience a different lifestyle. Tom explained that for him 'a positive attitude was the right attitude'. Successful self-adjustment is an interactive process between the self and its individual psychological resources and the person's social circumstances, which include various catalysts for potential change (Lin 2008).

Even after his return to China in 2006, self-adjustment continued to be an important strategy for his reintegration into a familiar society. His self-adjustments involve interacting and negotiating with objective realities as he participates in the local community (Jarvis 2006). Besides changing his career plan several times in order to get an expected career development space in China, now he also needs to change from his *Canadian way* back to the *Chinese way*:

> I still remember I frequently said 'Thank you' to every one [after my arrival in Beijing]. My friends were bothered by it. They complained to me: 'Please do not say thank you to everyone at every moment anymore'. But you know, it is the etiquette that I learned in Canada. Three months after my return, I found that I didn't say 'thank you' as frequently as before. I don't say 'thank you' for a little favour. I just say 'thank you' when it is necessary.

Upon returning to China, Tom returned to his TV career, familiar social network and old lifestyle. However, he realised that he is not the same person who left his homeland four years earlier. Tom feels that now he has 'a transnational way of thinking' and has a stronger capability to adapt to new circumstances than before. His self-adjustment efforts were not only an important way to achieve economic self-sufficiency, psychological comfort and social security but also a necessary way to become a participating member in a global society.

Transnational migration as a process of lifelong learning

Research indicates that immigrants decide the specific nature and course of their integration (Essed 1996). Their interest and efforts to connect with mainstream society are influenced by their personal characteristics, original expectations and motives, all of which influence how they respond to the host society (Donkor 2004).

For Helen, her journey of transnational migration is a process of lifelong learning. Helen's learning curves were steep. When she moved to Canada she needed to improve her English, acquire specific employment skills, learn how to live in an unfamiliar culture, deal with complex and sensitive intergroup relations with unfamiliar social rules and customs, and learn how to negotiate within complex financial and social systems. At the initial stage of her life in Canada, Helen concluded that she adapted to Canadian society smoothly because she excelled in learning under new circumstances. She saw every situation in her daily life as a potential learning resource for her (Jarvis 2006).

One of the most important learning for newcomers is the host country's official language, which is an important indicator of successful integration. Helen chose two ways to improve her English: to use it in her daily life and to take English language classes. By the time she had been in Canada for two years, Helen took an advanced diploma programme in geographical information systems. She was confident the investment in education would improve her qualification as a professional in the local employment market. In order to excel in the programme, Helen quit her job and rented a room in a house near the school she attended. She went back home only on weekends. In 2004, upon her completion of the advanced diploma programme, Helen decided to earn a master's degree in the Civil Engineering at Dalhousie University.

As expected, all of her formal and informal learning not only helped Helen integrate into the host society but also opened up new professional opportunities in Canada and China. For example, after returning to China in 2006, she found that English became a vital tool in her work. In her current position at Weiguang Company, many of her project plans, such as those with the World Bank, need to be written in English. More importantly, her graduate degree from Canada is respected and valued greatly in China. The diploma from the advanced programme and the master's degree helped her find her current senior technology consultant position. She pointed out that her overseas education makes a great difference for her career development in China:

> The MA programme [in Canada] helped me return to my original specialised domain, return to water resources development [as I had studied in my undergraduate days] ... When they [the Weiguang Company] hired me as a

senior technology consultant, [in the interview] I said I was not sure if I could do it well. They said, 'We have reviewed your resume. You should be okay'. They also joked, 'We are just afraid you might not be willing to work for us here, considering your excellent overseas educational experiences'.

Helen's formal, structured learning coupled with experiential learning gave her a wealth of new skills and knowledge, which catalyses new ways of thinking and acting (Jarvis and Hirji 2006). Her English competence and overseas education qualifications, together with increased self-confidence, all contribute to and are reinforced by social recognition in the new environment (Williams and Baláž 2005).

In fact, all three participants spoke about learning as an important part of their successful (re)integration. Most of their learning occurred in informal settings – during everyday interactions and negotiations in the host society as Tom explained:

> You should ... [watch] TV, [imitate] their English on TV ... and so on. Actively communicating with people is a good way of learning too ... Don't be timid. Don't be afraid. Experience all kinds of scenes to experience; talk with people on street, with your neighbours, with the people on bus. Take part in all possible social events.

Transnational migrants as flexible citizens

In 1990, James first left China for Switzerland to study at the University of Geneva. At first, James decided to be majored in economics, which he thought would be valuable degree for employment; within a year he changed his major to chemistry:

> After my first year in the Department [of Economics], I realised the economic system in Switzerland differed from those in both Europe and America, which could limit me. It would be useless for me to work in Europe or North America ... So, I kind of have a thought about studying a major with more practical value, just like a hard currency that's acceptable around the world.

James' stories that follow clearly show that the vivid word *practical* has a tacit meaning of 'flexible'. As a Chinese student studying abroad, Chemistry could afford James more work options in more countries. Especially after James and his family immigrated to Quebec in 2000, his knowledge of science helped him find first employment in Canada, just as he had hoped. While still living in Switzerland, he secured a postdoctoral position at the University of Quebec. Selecting his major at the University of Geneva reflects his desire to be flexible, a significant part of his life philosophy and an essential principle for his reacting to a range of scenarios in the host society.

Even the migration decision from Switzerland to Canada, the principle of staying flexible was playing its role. James indicated that in Switzerland foreigners need to apply for their resident visas every year. Because of this James and his wife felt their status in Switzerland was unstable, a concern that inspired him to immigrate to Canada, where he and his family would no longer have a 'floating' status. Furthermore, when James' wife and son applied for Canadian citizenship before returning to China, James himself did not in order to keep his flexibility to move back to China. This was also one of his flexible strategies (Ong 1999).

Ong's notion of 'flexible citizen' also guided James' choice of returning to China after five years in Canada. In 2004, James' postdoctoral project at the University of Quebec was ending. He needed to think about this next stop. James expected a position as a researcher or scientist in a food corporation in Canada. Unfortunately, after looking for a job for more than 10 months, James had only a few interviews, none of which resulted in a job. Guo (2013) states that immigrants' negative economic and social integration experience can be attributed to a triple glass effect: glass gate, glass door and glass ceiling. A glass gate denies immigrants' entrance to guarded professional communities, and a glass door blocks immigrants' access to professional employment at high-wage firms. According to Guo, a glass ceiling prevents immigrants from moving up to management positions because of their ethnicity and culture. It seems that James was stuck at the glass door stage. He realised how the employment market in Quebec was limiting his career. He could have lowered his employment expectations and found an entry-level job, but did not because he knew he would be underemployed and unsatisfied.

The important factor that directly limited his employment opportunities in Quebec was his limited social network. He said:

> Local employment data showed that 70–80% of jobs were introduced by interpersonal relations, only 5–6% of the opportunities were offered purely based on your resume ... In my situation, the positions I was interested [in] were almost at high level. The best way is to contact directly with the general manager. But it was blocked. I had tried several times. My resume got no response. I needed someone to recommend me.

James' lack of local social resources limited his ability to develop his career in Quebec even though he had perfect education qualifications. His loss of his flexibility in the local employment market motivated him to move again, just as he left Geneva five years earlier.

In 2005, James visited N University in Beijing where he found a job opportunity through the Internet. N University was impressed with his post-secondary education in Switzerland and post-doctoral researching experiences in Canada:

> I found that they valued me ... I was offered a 140-square meter apartment, and received funding for my research project. This was very important for me too.

You know, ¥500,000 RMB (about $77,500 CAD) funding for my research project. As a researcher, ... with these two things, the attraction was huge.

An official document from N University in 2009 shows that the university has been enacting policies for recruiting talents from all over the world, including a bursary of ¥50,000 RMB ($7750 CAD) and ¥1,000,000 RMB ($155,000 CAD) worth of research foundation grants per year. And these were not the only benefits. After six months at his post, James had his office and lab, and joined in two important national research projects. N University's policies and friendly social environment gave James a flexible space for his career development, an opportunity that facilitated his decision to return to Beijing. Talking about his future plan, James stated that his ideal lifestyle is that his family lives in Quebec, and he would fly between Quebec and Beijing – like an 'astronaut' (Man 1997).

Constructing a theory of IS

The above discussion clearly demonstrates that self-adjustments, lifelong learning and flexible citizenship are important coping strategies in the process of integrating and reintegrating during transnational migration. When narrating their transnational experiences, participants frequently used the word 'space' – 'career development space' (Tom), 'the space left to us' (Tom), 'the space is too small' (James), 'not enough space' (Helen, Tom) and so on. Clearly, the notion of space is a core concept in the way they frame their stories. The participants also used a variety of words to describe their perception of the space, such as 'it made me asphyxiate' and 'suffocate' (Tom), 'on a new stage' (Tom), '[my husband] felt himself almost unable to breathe' (Helen), 'I am limited in it' (James), 'I found a larger stage (than in Quebec)' (James). Furthermore, the participants used spatial metaphors to describe their migration. Tom used a 'well' metaphor to describe his strong sense of space during his migration:

> I was a frog who had live[d] in a well [in China] for many, many years. I was familiar with the sky over the well. That was all what I saw. But I was eager to see the wider world. Then, the immigration gave me the chance. Canada is a new well under a new sky. I saw, felt, and experienced there until one day I said it was enough. Then, I went home, returned to the old well with some new things in my mind.

His language indicates that an imaginative or symbolic space exists in his mind and that has significantly shaped his integration process. His feeling of the space represents his personal status of integration. Spatial metaphors give the code of space a new meaning: transnational movement is a journey that allows participants to rediscover and redefine themselves. The 'space' represents their social existence in the world, affects their integration situations in their local society, shapes their expectations of the future and influences their self-evaluation.

Lefebvre (1991) argues that space, which is created by a human's social activities, constructs our lives. Space is not simply a container or neutral environment but a setting in which all human activities occur, whether material or spiritual. Researchers of transnationalism have developed Lefebvre's theory of space into a concept of transnational space to include 'a combination of ties, positions in networks and organisations, and networks of organisations that stretch across the borders of multiple states' (Faist 2000, 191). In other words, space indicates a dynamic social process more than a static notion of ties and positions.

Both Lefebvre's theory of space and Faist's transnational social space theory shed light on this study's native concept of 'space'. However, the native concept of space refers primarily to an individual level space, or we can call it IS. IS is individuals' social construction based on their special situation and relationship with society. It is influenced greatly by many factors including their gender, ethnicity, personality, values, competence and educational experiences. Because each of these factors is formed by the interaction between individuals and their macro social environment, the IS is also an outcome of individuals' social practice, negotiation, self-adjustment and reflection related to a particular physical place and by this way, all individual factors could attain their value, function and meaning.

IS represents individuals' overall socialisation – their social existence in the world, integration situations in the local society, expectations for the future and self-evaluation. IS is not the same as private or personal space though it may extend beyond a private personal space to a social and even macro public space depending on an individual's social practices. Figure 1 captures the differences between IS and other spaces.

Lefebvre (1991) used a spatial triad to explain the interplay of factors in the process of producing space. Lefebvre suggested that when producing space, we frequently encounter three different elements of space: the representation of space, representational space and spatial practice (SP). Representations of space reflect a conceptualised space that is conceived by the perceiver using power, knowledge and ideology. Representational space is a lived space that embodies everyday experience. SP refers to the practices. Lefebvre's concept has enhanced the understanding of how IS is formed and the impact that it has on a migrant's experiences. For this study, Lefebvre's spatial triad has been modified (Figure 2) to map the IS of the participants in order to introduce a theoretical explanation of what happens to an individual as a result of their transnational migration.

In Figure 2, IS is shaped by three pillars: SPs, perceived individual space (PIS) and conceived individual space (CIS). The SPs of the participants refer to what they act within the routes and regulations of the external world. The

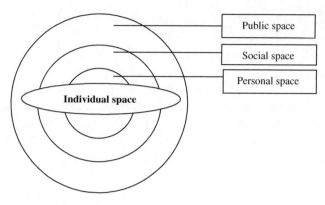

Figure 1. The extent of IS.

practices are affected by the relationship between participants' physical and social characteristics (e.g., gender, age, education, capital, experiences and networks) and the everyday rules and routes from the external world that are designed to be followed or navigated.

For example, Helen's learning, both formal and informal, is one of her key SPs in her transnational migration process. It happens in her everyday life, whether at school or eating dinner with her family. When learning and negotiating the rules and routines of a society, SP is the key component powering integration into the home and host societies.

PIS reflects the perceived social lives and status by the participants, which can be situational, based on relationships, and inclusive of various dimensions, such as family role, career status, social class, ethnicity, gender and social networks. PIS sculpts SPs. For example, Helen had to consider her social responsibility as a wife and mother in her family when making decisions about her career and the possibility of migration. In 2004, her husband went back to China to visit his parents, an experience that awakened his desire to return. After he moved back to China in February 2005, Helen stayed in Canada,

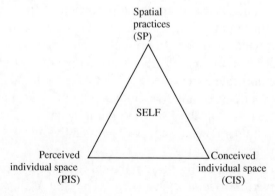

Figure 2. Structure of IS.

where she worked on her master's thesis day and night so that her family could be reunited as soon as possible. When she finished her thesis defence in October 2005, she returned to Beijing a week later with her son. She told me that without the influence of her husband, she might have chosen to stay in Canada.

PIS is also affected by an individual's social practices. Tom's PIS was formed by his financial and cultural integration into mainstream society. When Tom was in Canada, he found that no matter how hard he tried, the cultural gap between him and the host society was significant. He described that he felt 'marginalised' and devoid of 'social participation' and 'cultural sharing'. He felt he had lost his ability to participate in meaningful discourse. His reflections on his experiences in Canada show that PIS is affected by the macro society.

CIS refers to the participants' expectations regarding the 'self' – what they want their lives and their identities to be; it plays a substantive role in producing IS and greatly influences their decisions to migrate.

For transnational migrants, CIS supports and makes IS possible. For example, one dimension of James' CIS is his ambition to be a successful scientist and owner of a hi-tech company. During the migration from Switzerland to Canada, his professional goals were vague but became clearer once he started looking for work. After returning to China, his new post helped redefine his IS, the core of which became his desire to be a scientific researcher and entrepreneur. Now he centres his life and career on this core goal. The importance of other dimensions in CIS, such as cultural belonging, is exemplified by Tom and Helen's narratives, which mention the notion of being 'forever Chinese' when in Canada.

Compared with the other two elements of space, CIS is the least affected by the external social environment and depends more on the participants' expectations and self-value. CIS also plays an important role in the creation of IS as it provides the direction, faith, motivation and internal power that facilitates the struggle to attain goals and position planning in the origin and destination countries. CIS is the catalyst to integration into the host society. It was responsible for Tom's self-adjustment, Helen's lifelong learning and James' flexible citizenship.

Conclusion: IS and transnational migration

The theory of IS sheds light on the transnational experience of return Chinese immigrants from Canada in Beijing. Because immigrants have agents to decide how to react to given situations (Donkor 2004; Essed 1996), transnational migration is a constant negotiation between the micro IS and the macro social space or as Bhatia and Ram (2001) stated, a negotiation between internal and external worlds. Therefore, lifelong learning, self-adjustment and flexible citizenship are important negotiation strategies for the participants. Their migration stories reveal the hidden story line about the relationships among the self, others and external society. Migration can be a subjective choice by the participants themselves and is influenced by their relationship with external social circumstances (King 2000; Waldorf 1995). Through close interactions with the host society, their experiential world was (re)interpreted, (re)integrated and (re)transformed (Ross-Gordon 1998). Their original IS was deconstructed and then reconstructed. Therefore, migration is not only a way to exploring the host and re-exploring the home society but also a way to rediscover themselves. The more they understand about the external world, the more they learn about themselves.

Today, transnational movement is a useful strategy in breaking the economic limitations, political marginalisation and cultural blocks of migrants' external macro circumstances. In the context of transnationalism, migration becomes a strategy to relocate their position in a global society as an ambitious and high-grade talent. Through their spatial transformation, they break the limitations from external macro circumstances. The combination of transnationalism with the individual migrant's pursuit of space determines the ongoing characteristics of today's transnational migration.

Note
1. Tom had visited Canada for about two months before his immigration.

References
Ammassari, S., and R. Black. 2001. "Harnessing the Potential of Migration and Return to Promote Development: Applying Concepts to West Africa." *IOM Migration Research Series 5*. Geneva: International Organization for Migration.
Bhatia, S., and A. Ram. 2001. "Rethinking 'Acculturation' in Relation to Diasporic Cultures and Postcolonial Identities." *Human Development* 44 (1): 1–17. doi:10.1159/000057036.
Brittain, C. 2009. "Transnational Messages: What Teachers can Learn from Understanding Students' Lives in Transnational Social Spaces." *The High School Journal* 92 (4): 3–15. doi:10.1353/hsj.0.0027.
Cole, A. L., and G. J. Knowles. 2001. "Principles Guiding Life History Researching." In *Lives in Context: The Art of Life History Research*, edited by Ardra L. Cole and Gary J. Knowles, 25–44. New York: AltaMira Press.
Ding, Y. 2010. *Negotiating Individual Space: An Inquiry into the Experiences of Chinese Return Migrants from Canada*. Saarbrücke: VDM Publishing House Ltd.
Donkor, M. 2004. "Looking Back and Looking in: Rethinking Adaptation Strategies of Ghanaian Immigrant Women in Canada." *Journal of International Migration and Integration* 5 (1): 33–51. doi:10.1007/s12134-004-1001-2.
Essed, P. 1996. *Diversity: Gender, Color and Culture*. Amherst, MA: University of Massachusetts Press.
Faist, T. 2000. *The Volume and Dynamics of International Migration and Transnational Social Spaces*. Oxford: Oxford University Press. doi:10.1093/acprof:oso/9780198293910.001.0001.

Goodson, I., and P. Sikes. 2001. *Life History Research in Educational Settings: Learning from Lives*. Buckingham: Open University Press.

Gray, B. 2003. *Women and the Irish Diaspora*. London: Routledge.

Guo, S. 2009. "Difference, Deficiency, and Devaluation: Tracing the Roots of Non-recognition of Foreign Credentials for Immigrant Professionals in Canada." *The Canadian Journal for the Study of Adult Education* 22 (1): 37–52.

Guo, S. 2013. "Economic Integration of Recent Chinese Immigrants in Canada's Second-tier Cities: The Triple Glass Effect and Immigrants' Downward Social Mobility." *Canadian Ethnic Studies* 45 (3): 95–115. doi:10.1353/ces.2013.0047.

Guo, S., and D. DeVoretz. 2006. "Chinese Immigrants in Vancouver: Quo Vadis?" *Journal of International Migration and Integration* 7: 425–447. doi:10.1007/s12134-006-1014-0.

Hagan, J. M. 1998. "Social Networks, Gender, and Immigrant Incorporation: Resources and Constraints." *American Sociological Review* 63 (1): 55–67. doi:10.2307/2657477.

Jarvis, P., and N. Hirji. 2006. "Learning the Unlearnable—Experiencing the Unknowable." *The Journal of Adult Theological Education* 3 (1): 87–94. doi:10.1558/jate.2006.3.1.87.

Jarvis, P. 2006. "Beyond the Learning Society: Globalisation and the Moral Imperative for Reflective Social Change." *International Journal of Lifelong Education* 25: 201–211. doi:10.1080/02601370600697011.

King, R. 2000. "Generalizations from the History of Return Migration." In *Return Migration: Journey of Hope or Despair?* edited by Bimal Ghosh, 7–55. Geneva: IOM /UN.

Lazarus, R., and S. Folkman. 1984. *Stress, Appraisal and Coping*. New York: Springer.

Lefebvre, H. 1991. *The Production of Space*. Translated by D. Nicholson-Smith. Oxford: Basil Blackwell.

Levitt, P., J. DeWind, and S. Vertovec. 2003. "International Perspectives on Transnational Migration: An Introduction." *International Migration Review* 37: 565–575. doi:10.1111/j.1747-7379.2003.tb00150.x.

Lien, P. 2008. "Places of Socialization and (sub)ethnic Identities among Asian Immigrants in the US: Evidence from the 2007 Chinese American Homeland Politics Survey." *Asian Ethnicity* 9 (3): 151–170. doi:10.1080/14631360802349197.

Lin, L. F. 2008. "Hau qiao hua ren she hui shi ying nei zai ji li tan xi [Exploration of the Internal Social Adaptation Mechanism of Overseas Chinese]". *Around Southeast Asia*, 4: 63–67.

Man, G. C. 1997. "The Experiences of Women in Middle-class Hong Kong Chinese Immigrant Families in Canada: An Investigation in Institutional and Organizational Process." PhD diss., University of Toronto.

Ministry of Education of the People's Republic of China. 2013. *Jiao yu dui wai he zuo yu jiao liu jin zhan qing kuang* [The Development of International Education Communication and Cooperation]. http://www.moe.gov.cn/publicfiles/business/htmlfiles/moe/s7204/201302/148024.html.

Ong, A. 1999. *Flexible Citizenship: The Cultural Logics of Transnationality*. Durham and London: Duke University Press.

Portes, A. 2003. "Conclusion: Theoretical Convergencies and Empirical Evidence in the Study of Immigrant Transnationalism." *International Migration Review* 37: 874–892. doi:10.1111/j.1747-7379.2003.tb00161.x.

Portes, A., L. E. Guarnizo, and P. Landolt. 1999. "The Study of Transnationalism: Pitfalls and Promise of an Emergent Research Field." *Ethnic and Racial Studies* 22: 217–237. doi:10.1080/014198799329468.

Ross-Gordon, J. M. 1998. "What We Need to Know about Adult Learners." In *Program Planning for the Training and Continuing Education of Adults: North American Perspectives*, edited by Peter S. Cookson, 207–248. Malabar, FL: Krieger.

Searle, W., and C. Ward. 1990. "The Prediction of Psychological and Sociocultural Adjustment during Cross-cultural Transitions." *International Journal of Intercultural Relations* 14: 449–464. doi:10.1016/0147-1767(90)90030-Z.

Smith, M. P. 2001. *Transnational Urbanism: Locating Globalization*. Malden, MA: Blackwell.

Vertovec, S. 1999. "Conceiving and Researching Transnationalism." *Ethnic and Racial Studies* 22: 447–462. doi:10.1080/014198799329558.

Waldorf, B. 1995. "Determinants of International Return Migration Intentions." *Professional Geographer* 47 (2): 125–136. doi:10.1111/j.0033-0124.1995.00125.x.

Wang, H. 2007. *Zhong guo dang dai hai gui* [Contemporary Chinese Returnees]. Beijing: Chinese Development Publisher.

Wiles, J. 2008. "Sense of Home in a Transnational Social Space: New Zealanders in London." *Global Networks* 8 (1): 116–137. doi:10.1111/j.1471-0374.2008.00188.x.

Williams, A. M., and V. Baláž. 2005. "What Human Capital? Which Migrants? Returned Skilled Migration to Slovakia from the UK." *International Migration Review* 39: 439–468. doi:10.1111/j.1747-7379.2005.tb00273.x.

Wong, L. 2004. "Taiwanese Immigrant Entrepreneurs in Canada and Transnational Social Space." *International Migration* 42 (2): 113–152. doi:10.1111/j.0020-7985. 2004.00283.x.

Wong, L., and V. Satzewich. 2006. "Introduction: The Meaning and Significance of Transnationalism." In *Transnational Identities and Practices in Canada*, edited by Lloyd Wong and Vic Satzewich. Vancouver, BC: University of British Columbia Press.

Yeoh, B., K. D. Willis, and S. M. A. K. Khader. 2003. Introduction: Transnationalism and its Edges. *Ethnic and Racial Studies* 26: 207–217. doi:10.1080/01419870 32000054394.

'Talent circulators' in Shanghai: return migrants and their strategies for success

Yedan Huang and Khun Eng Kuah-Pearce

Department of Sociology, The University of Hong Kong, Hong Kong, People's Republic of China

> This paper argues for a flexible identity and citizenship framework to explore how return migrants, *haigui*, have readapted and re-established themselves back into Shanghai society, and how they have used their talents, knowledge and *guanxi* networks to optimise their chances of success. It argues that these return migrants, as talent circulators in their circulatory migration process, have adopted a flexible identity and citizenship, to confront their conflicting emotions and negotiated sacrifices for the well-being of their individual self and family as they expand their socio-economic and territorial space.

Introduction

The booming mainland Chinese economy in the decades since the 1978 Open Door Policy has created opportunities for highly skilled mainland Chinese professionals from the Diaspora to return to work in a capitalist-oriented Communist China.

One main reason for remigration is that these Chinese professionals, herewith termed talent circulators, feel that there are more opportunities and that their talents and professionalism will be better utilised and rewarded in China. Related to this is their frustration of continually being subjected to an invisible 'glass ceiling' in their adopted country.

The key consideration of this group is to develop a strategy to optimise their opportunities in China and yet, at the same time, retain their bond with their adopted country as they embark on a circulatory migration. Here, these talent circulators negotiate their identity and citizenship.

This paper will explore, through the use of the flexible identity and citizenship framework, how the talent circulators attempt to readapt and re-establish their career and social life in Shanghai through the deployment of their social capital and *guanxi* networks. It will also look at how they negotiate their identity in both China and overseas.

Talent circulators and flexible citizenship

In exploring the idea of flexible citizenship among these talent circulators, we follow the arguments advanced by various scholars such as Ong (1998), Ley and Kobayashi (2004) Wang and Wong (2007). Ong advances the argument that Chinese elites send their children overseas to 'gain access to an elite education that will benefit them in country of origin', and could also 'set up important business connections that could benefit their country of origin', which indicates the motive of migration is largely based on 'economic reasons rather than political rights or participation within what nation state they reside' (Ong 1998, 139). Likewise, migrant families move and relocate according to the specific needs of their members at various stages of their life cycle, which are often based on considerations of career developments, educational needs, childcare support, or providing for ageing or ailing parents. As such, the concept of 'home' has become 'extraordinarily complex' (Ley and Kobayashi 2004, 6), and home as 'stable and geographically confined is increasingly being challenged' (Wang and Wong 2007, 182).

Where the home is is now increasingly tied to the hypermobility of the migrants and citizens. As our study shows, with globalisation and hypermobility, non-organised voluntary return migration of skilled professionals who move back to their countries of origin as Mainland China after a period of settlement in overseas host societies has become a norm rather than an exception. Thus, traditional theories of return migration which takes return as the 'closure' and 'completion' of the migration cycle is now being challenged and the return movement is circulatory and 'continuous rather than completed' (Ley and Kobayashi 2004, 1).

This brings us to the issue of circulatory migration. Different from early generation of immigrants who took return back to their country of origin as the final destination, returnees in contemporary Chinese society are motivated more on personal and economic reasons, and many of them expect to re-emigrate to overseas after several years of settlement in their country of origin. In this case, the return of *haigui* is circulatory in its nature, as migrants are often 'locked into the global migration circuit that presupposes further opportunities to move to another destination' (Kuah-Pearce 2006, 226).

As transnational communities become more widely established worldwide, notions of 'home' and 'abroad' become blurred. Emigration and return migration are not isolated acts or events; instead, they are taken as 'interlocking parts of an open and wider on-going process of global mobility' (Ghosh 2000, 44–45). In her study of young Hong Kong transnationals, Janet Salaff, Wong, and Greve (2010) asserted that it is too limiting to speak of 'to remain or to return', as the two terms are merely artificial and interchangeable labels applied from different vantage points on the same big circle of transmigration movement. Ip (2012) further named this new trend of mobility as 'circulatory transmigration', which can be characterised by 'frequent commutes, short-term visits and sojourns of various family members in both the country of origin and destination, and sometimes relocation to a third country'.

Hypermobility and a circulatory and continuous form of migratory trajectory have led to a rethinking of one's home and one's identity that are no longer tied to geographical and nation-state boundaries. According to Schiller, Basch and Blanc-Szanton (1999) and Chan (1997), contemporary returnees can be taken as transmigrants, whose loyalty and sense of belonging are multiple and flexibly rooted in their host as well as original societies, and are highly contextualised in its nature, depending on the situation they are in. Ong argues for a flexible identity and flexible citizenship where individuals and governments 'respond fluidly and opportunistically to changing political-economic conditions' (Ong 1999, 6).

In our case study below, we attempt to show that the talent circulators have also adopted flexibility in their citizenship selection where they are both Chinese residents while holding to Canadian citizenship, adopting a hypermobile lifestyle jetsetting across the Pacific rim and reposition their relationship between the communist state and the communist-led capitalist development and operate within the Chinese cultural logic where they manipulated the family and gender relations to accumulate capital and attain higher social class (Ong 1999, 6). At the same time, they are also circulatory and consistently exploring where their home and loyalty are – territorialised and deterritorialised; and imagined and real at the same time.

Methodology and site of research

This study uses a qualitative research method, which is 'useful to investigate an issue in depth' and 'provides an explanation that can cope with the complexity and subtlety of real life situations' (Denscombe 2010, 55). The study's fieldwork, which was part of Huang's M.Phil studies, was conducted over five months in 2005. It included multiple case studies with indepth interviews, using a semi-structured questionnaire, of 12 *haigui* who had chosen Shanghai as their settlement destination. Some of the interviewees were recruited through Huang's personal social ties and networks. Others were obtained through a snow-balling method. All the informants of this study emigrated between the late 1980s and early 2000s and returned after 2000. Of the 12 informants, 11 of them have a Masters or Ph.D. degree (Appendix 1).

Shanghai is the chosen destination of most returnees because of its international commercial status, cosmopolitan outlook, western-style housing and good school networks. Furthermore, the preferential policies offered by the Shanghai local government have also been attractive to these talent circulators.

For example, in 2003 the implementation of the 'Ten-Thousand Overseas Talents Converging Program (*Wanming haiwai liuxue rencai jiju gongcheng*)' was aimed at attracting these talent circulators to leading positions in government agencies, higher education, scientific research, medical services, state industries and business organisations.[1] It successfully attracted 10,203 overseas scholars to return and contribute to this city within two years. Until 2010, about 25% of all returnees in mainland China lived in Shanghai (approximately 85,000) (Cao 2010, 2; Lu 2010, A1).

Talent circulators: *Haiou flying high*

According to the Ministry of Education (PRC), it is estimated that, from 1978 to 2012, 2.65 million Chinese students (either state-sponsored or self-funded) studied abroad. Of these, over 1 million have remained overseas.[2] This high rate of emigration resulted in a 'brain drain' and a shortage of skilled engineers, IT experts and other professionals needed for China's rapid development. These students-turned-migrants were 'criticised for disloyalty' to China by the government (Huang 2005, 58).

The economic boom since the early 1980s has led to a gradual reversal of the 'brain drain' trend to 'brain gain' with the return of *haigui* to big cities such as Shanghai, Beijing, Guangzhou and Shenzhen. Ley and Koyabashi have also indicated that such a trend is more appropriately regarded as a 'brain exchange', where emerging economies like China and India have provided incentives to attract professionals to their economy (Ley and Kobayashi 2005, 112) and return to their homeland when opportunities arose. Many also returned because of what they believed was a glass ceiling where there continued to be 'barriers to the upwards mobility of nontraditional yet qualified individuals (i.e., women, ethnic minorities, the disabled) in their working organisations' (Morrison, Schreiber, and Price 1995, 1). Chinese migrants in Canada also fall victim to this discriminatory practice (Salaff, Greve, and Li 2002, 450–464). Guo further argued that in addition to the glass ceiling, there were also the 'glass gate' and 'glass door' which effectively determined the types of jobs available to migrants right from the onset of their job-hunting. This is the 'triple glass effect' (Guo 2013).

Since the Open Door Policy, the Chinese who have returned to China after a prolonged stay in a western country are called '*haigui*' (海归), which literally means 'returning from across the ocean'. They are also referred to as 'sea turtles', the Chinese homonym is also *haigui* (海龟). The local Chinese draw a parallel between these return migrants and sea turtles, which migrate to the vast expanse of the ocean but eventually return to annually lay eggs on the same seashore where they were born. Here, we regard the *haigui* as talent circulators who, with their professional talents and social network skills, have the capability to circulate from one region to another around the globe where they are sought after by big multinational corporations.

These talent circulators choose to return to the Mainland on a voluntary basis. Return migration is regarded as a voluntary process which is contrasted with other categorises of return migration according to criteria such as the nature of their return (voluntary or involuntary), the levels of economic development in the home and host countries, the length of time spent back in their home country and the historical evolution of the migration process (Ghosh 2000, 9–10).

There are different types of *haigui* circulating in Shanghai and other Chinese cities based on their educational and overseas working experiences, their achievements in the job market and their differential treatment by the local society upon their return. On the one hand, there are the talent circulators – returnees who are well educated with high status jobs overseas and upon returning to China, are also appointed to high level executive positions. They are the professional 'golden collars' with an upper middle-class status who are regarded as the social elite of the local society.

The 'golden collars' are the target of large multinational and domestic corporations. As professionals, they possess desirable technological, management and financial skills as well as soft skills including language skills and social/personal connections that are deemed desirable for successful businesses in Mainland China's economy.

Among the 12 informants, apart from one still waiting for employment, there are five working in multinational corporations, three working as academics (one of whom started his own business in 2006) and three working in private enterprises. Four out of the employed 11 are directors of their corporations. These high performance talent circulators are the *haiou* (海鸥, seagulls), the most coveted group of *haigui*. They have been recruited or asked by their parent company in the west to return to the mainland to manage their business (Iredale, Fei, and Rozario 2003, 14). They belong to the 'expatriate' category and contribute great achievements in their fields of work, and enjoy high salaries and perks as foreign expatriate, including housing, car and membership to exclusive clubs. These *haiou* fly between the mainland and their host country and, like seagulls, they soar high in the sky and regard the sky as their limit. They are an extremely confident group of professionals who have a competitive edge over not only their local colleagues but also their western counterparts in terms of creativity, skills, knowledge, professionalism, administrative experience, and above all the language skills and social networks that enable them to move smoothly between the two cultures.

The *haiou* are also seen as 'golden collars' (*jinling*, 金领), occupying the middle and upper social strata in Chinese society (Wang 2008). They are considered to be the economic and social elite, making them winners in a competitive world and a rapidly developing China. They are seen by the Chinese Government and the general public as valuable assets that serve as a bridge to link foreign corporations with the Chinese Government and pave the way for foreign corporations in the Chinese market, because of their social networks on both sides. On the other hand, these *haiou* are not unlike an 'astronaut', as some of them return to Shanghai to work, but leave their wives and children in their adopted country to maintain citizenship in their adopted country and to ensure that their children receive a coveted Western education (Skeldon 1994, 11). Below is an example of the golden collar *haiou*:

Lu, a successful business executive, spent 15 years in the USA and was sent back to Shanghai in 2002 by a large US architectural agency to develop its business in the China market. He is a *haiou* and is provided with all the perks of an expatriate executive by his corporation. Lu valued his decision to become a talent circulator and returned to his homeland. His decision to return was made easier when he compared the opportunities open to him in the USA and those in the Mainland. Lu stated that:

> The architectural industry in the States has been fully developed, and all large-scale constructions have been stopped. However, it is completely the opposite in China. The architecture market in China is so big. I guess this growth will continue for at least a further 10 years. In fact, I've learned that many of my students in China have already built skyscrapers twenty to thirty floors high. I'm their former professor and I have only been able to work on townhouses of two to three levels during my stay in the US. I decided to return so that I could further develop my own career. I am now working harder than ever and I am very satisfied with my own accomplishments so far.

Similarly, another interviewee, Geng, also returned for the sake of personal development rather than economic necessity. He was a researcher with a Ph.D. in Medicine and had been doing scientific laboratory research in the USA and Canada for nearly 10 years. Although he was satisfied with his jobs and positions there, Geng could not see a promising future at his research institute overseas. He felt it would be very hard, if not impossible, for him to climb to the upper level of the academic ladder or to 'play a big role' during his stay overseas. He said:

> I am still a very traditional Chinese person, and I cannot tolerate the so-called 'glass ceiling effect' in western societies, as I worked harder than anyone else in the lab, but could not get promoted in my research institute, and my 'boss' (i.e. the research director) always took credit for the work I had done. I wanted to start my own medical research project and I believed I would have more potential opportunities for further development back in my homeland.

After his return in 2002, Geng became the project leader of a medical research institute in a local university and later started up a business in the biomedical industry in China. He has been enjoying the high-flying life of a typical talent circulator who travels back and forth between Canada and Shanghai for business as well as family affairs.

Another young informant, Xue, in his late 20s, found a job as an actuary with an international insurance company upon his return. He expressed his motivation to return to China:

> If I had remained overseas, I would have been pretty sure of what I would be doing in five years, ten years, and until I retire. I would not have faced any big challenges and uncertainties in my life. But I didn't really want my life to end up like that, which would be too boring. However, I knew it would be different if I chose to return to China for work: although I knew I would shoulder a lot more responsibilities and face a lot of uncertainties, I also knew I would have a lot of opportunities and excitement. Now I can't predict what exactly I will be doing in five or ten years, but the uncertainties will also give me many opportunities. That's what I want for my future.

Limited opportunities: Xiao haigui's woes

At the lower end of the professional scale are the 'Little Sea Turtles (*Xiao Haigui*)', who emigrate abroad for university education after graduation from high schools or universities in China. They all go to lower-ranking universities and are considered relatively unsuccessful as they have not managed to study at top-tier universities within China or abroad. They are of a younger age group and return to China upon completion of their studies. Members of this group do not have foreign work experience and do not get high-paying jobs in China. Those who fail to get a decent job with an average salary become 'seaweeds', *haidai*, reflecting their unsuccessful career and low status within the Shanghai community.

The rapid development of China has also offered younger talent circulators returning to the mainland the potential to launch a new career in various fields. Fifty per cent of our informants are of the younger age group – in their 20s. Of them, one is a technical consultant of a big foreign IT company, another works in a big foreign PR firm, one is a senior designer with a local-based cloth manufacturing company, one is a project researcher with a local urban planning and design research institute and one works as an actuary with an international insurance company. The youngest, Yu, 24 years old was unemployed at the time of the interview. This is also the case for many young Canadian Chinese of Hong Kong and Taiwanese descent who have increasingly returned back to Hong Kong and Taiwan for the same reasons (Chiang 2011; Salaff, Wong, and Greve 2010; Ley and Kobayashi 2005).

However, not all are successful. This is the case of the little sea turtles (*xiao haigui*, 小海龟). Among this group who go overseas to study, many do not gain admission to top-tier and even second-tier universities such as Peking University, Tsinghua University, Fudan University and Jiao Tong University, or even second-tier universities such as Nanjing University and Zhongshan University in China. They are seen as academically inferior and go overseas to obtain a second-rate degree from a foreign university.

In China today, an undergraduate or postgraduate degree from a second- or third-tier foreign university is considered a 'gold-plated' (*dujin*, 镀金) degree in contrast to a real gold (*chunjin*, 纯金) degree obtained from the top-ranking universities in the USA, UK, Australia, mainland China or Hong Kong. Therefore, these graduates are seen as inferior and not coveted by big foreign or domestic corporations.

Because of their inferior qualifications, they are unable to find a job in the country where they have studied. Many, therefore, have had to return to China after completing their studies. Upon returning to China, these little sea turtles also have difficulty finding good jobs. It usually takes several months to find a position that falls short of their expectations. Often, they are offered jobs and paid a salary of a local employee with no expatriate terms. To be trained overseas and then obtain a local terms of employment implies that they have sank to the bottom of the seabed and are treated as seaweed (*haidai*, 海带/海待), a return talent with no prospect of landing a good job. An example of a little sea turtle is Yu, our 24-year-old informant. Yu went to UK to study for an MBA degree for two years and his parents spent nearly RMB 500,000 on his tuition and living expenses. Upon returning to the mainland, he found that the companies willing to hire him were prepared to pay him only RMB 3000. He was disappointed with this as he expected an average minimum monthly income of around RMB 8000. He finds it difficult to make ends meet as he has to support his parents and save money for his marriage. He said:

> Such treatment is very unfair. My parents spent almost all their savings for my emigration and studies abroad, and since my return I'm now having to carry the costs of getting married and paying for my housing all by myself.

For the little sea turtles who managed to find a job, their salary is often no better than that of the graduates of local universities. Their qualifications, abilities and skills are often questioned by employers, the media and the local community and they are regarded as 'losers', not only in the eyes of the local public but also by themselves as well. Li, a postgraduate with a Master's degree in fabric design in France, changes her jobs twice in the first half of the year upon her return. She reported that:

> I am very disappointed at my present position as a factory secretary considering the high-level of education I received abroad. Maybe it is because there are too many little sea turtles like me on the job market in the mainland, and we are losing our competitive superiority compared with local graduates.

Cultivating social capital and utilising social networks

Scholars have long argued that to be successful in business in Chinese communities, there is a need to cultivate social capital and utilise and expand one's social networks. Return migrants possess social capital and network capital in the form of continued friendship with their former classmates, kinship-based personal and business friends (Wong and Salaff 1998). Upon returning home, they tap into their *guanxi* with these groups and use them to their advantage (See also Guo 2010, 309).

In the case of our informant Lu, upon returning to Shanghai he found that his qualifications, managerial and language skills became only useful once he had remastered the art of '*la guanxi*' (拉关系, literally 'pulling social connections') (MacInnes 1993, 346). As he mentioned:

> I used to take it for granted that I could make great accomplishments through my own efforts. However, I found it was a completely different story after I came back. In fact, I had to work upon the requirements of my customers and even had to modify the work over and over again until they were satisfied with it. Besides, I found myself just like a busy working dog as I have to work 14–16 hours a day here in Shanghai while I only needed to work 8 hours per day when I was in the States. Last, but not the least, I have to deal with the 'hidden rules' in running business in Mainland China, as I have tried my best to utilize my previously-built *guanxi* networks to develop my business.

Lu kept in contact with his old friends, former professors, classmates, colleagues and students and visited them regularly on his trip to China. Having this set of *guanxi* networks helped him in his decision to return as a talent circulator as his friends have introduced key businesspeople and government officials to him and enable him to conduct his business smoothly.

Professional skills and knowledge enabled him to gain entry into the market and a large corporation, but he attributed his success in business to 'soft power' in the form of the social capital and guanxi networks that he had amassed. In his words, 'I do not like to promote my business through social networking as it demands reciprocal actions on the receiver and the giver. But I need to do so in China'.

This was necessary as mainland Chinese 'have an inclination to form partnerships with people of similar backgrounds in ethnicity, kinship, place of origin and dialect' (Liu 2000, 121).

Thus, in Shanghai, he cultivated existing and expanded *guanxi* networks in the following ways: he invited one of his retired former professors to become an honorary consultant of his firm, so as to make it more convenient for him to enter the China market in the future. Besides, he also constantly accompanied potential customers or governmental officials from local or other provinces on business tours and dinners in order to consolidate his *guanxi* networks.

For those *haigui* who were unable to cultivate *guanxi*, it led to difficulties in their re-adaptation to their home society and even failure in their career. Informant, Li, spent nearly six months finding a job back in Shanghai after completing a master's degree in Fabric Design in France complained:

> It is quite difficult for returnees like me to find a suitable job here. Our situation is somewhat awkward, as we can 'neither reach the sky nor touch the ground' (*gao bucheng, di bu jiu*). Without *guanxi*, I have to compete with a large number of local-educated university graduates to get a job, and it seems I have hardly any advantage on the job market: Although I have an overseas degree, I do not have overseas working experiences, and language skills are not a problem for local graduates nowadays. More importantly, they are more familiar with the living and working environment and culture and maintain better social networks in local society than returnees like me.

Thus, in Mainland China, the art of establishing *guanxi* and the stores of *guanxi* available to return migrants greatly influences their success in career development as they seek to settle down in their homeland once again.

Making sense of returning home: Haigui and their transnational social life
Fragmented relationship

Many highly successful *haigui* have unsuccessful transnational social relationships with their spouse and family. In our study, only two out of the 12 informants considered themselves as being successful in both career and family/social life. The talent circulators often adopt a flexible strategy, living the life of an astronaut while holding onto their adopted nationality as well as minimising the disruption to their children's education by leaving their family behind in the adopted home. One-third of our informants are astronauts and maintain a transnational relationship with their spouse and children, a situation similar to the Hong Kong migrants to Canada in the 1980s (Johnson 1994, 134).

Such relationships become fragmented and problematic. For Lu, feelings of guilt and isolation have taken their toll on his marriage and parental role. He said:

> In my eyes, the long distance separation between a couple is a typical *haigui* problem. It is a very sensitive issue. To be frank, I do have problem with my wife, and I am uncertain about our future. Some of my friends choose to return to their home country with the family, others re-emigrate abroad so they can be reunited with their family in the long-term. In my case, both my wife and I have a decent and stable career, despite being in different countries. That is one key reason why it seems so hard for either of us to give up our current career simply to enhance family contact.

Lu, as with other astronauts who migrated to Canada, Australia and New Zealand, experienced problems of a fragmented family and the Pacific shuttle syndrome (Ley and Kobayashi 2005, 115). It is not uncommon for marriages and father–children relationships to break down after a prolonged period of separation. In rare cases, children act as a bridge and facilitate communication between their parents through cheap and lengthy online chatting. Lu felt grateful that he was able to maintain contact with his eight-year-old daughter through the Internet:

> A frosty relationship between a married couple may affect their relationship with their children. My wife knows that well and she taught our daughter how to write emails and chat online. Since then, I have been able to learn from her about their life in the United States, and I write to her by email about what I am doing here in Shanghai, with pictures sometimes. She will pass on my message to her mother, which has thus enhanced the relationship between my wife and I to some extent.

Quest for personal space

For the single unmarried return migrants, they face another problem related to personal living space, having to live in the same household as their parents. Here, the private individual who 'finds no space for self-expression' in such a hierarchical society, 'might resist the enculturation process ... [and even] create a social and spiritual dissonance [resulting in] emerging tensions' between an individual and society (Kuah-Pearce 2006, 225). It was a struggle for these singletons to balance their personal needs with the expectations and needs of their parents. Pan wanted to create her personal space:

> I do not think it is a good idea to live with my parents forever. It would be better for the elder generation to have their own lives, and leave more room for my future self-development. I have already told my parents that I shall rent an apartment outside after I have worked for another two years and have some money at hand. I am actually looking forward to my dream apartment where I can finally have my own space and night life. I take it as a sign of my independence. However, I will surely go to my parents' for dinner during weekends, as I am their only daughter.

In another case, Wang, a university professor who lives with his parents, also wants to establish his own life and personal space and has to escape to his office for personal solace. He stated:

> Although I am regarded as an expert in the field of Psychology, it is still difficult for me to deal with my parents. It is possibly due to the fact that they are very traditional Chinese parents who seldom reveal their true feelings and tend to take 'control' and 'worry' as an expression of love ... Sometimes I have to use 'I am busy at work' as a reasonable and acceptable excuse to escape from this situation.

Towards flexible citizenship and identity

In an age of globalisation, population mobility across national boundaries has continuously increased. The pattern of migration has been changed in terms of spatial preferences, cultural identities and attachments to places. Greater spatial mobility of diasporic individuals, according to Ma, has given rise to 'multiple and flexible personal identities that tend to change with shifting circumstances' (Ma 2003, 32).

One form of multiple identity, according to Ong, is 'flexible citizenship', where 'new strategies of flexible accumulation have promoted a flexible attitude towards citizenship' (Ong 1999, 17).

As talent circulators, these *haigui* are pragmatic individuals who want the best of both worlds. So, they adopt a policy of flexible identities and multiple territorialities with multiple homes.

According to Ley and Koyabashi (2005), a Canadian passport provides peace of mind for these return migrants returning to Communist China. The passport also represents ease of travel to and from China which is essential for maintaining a transnational family structure. Nearly half of the informants possess a Canadian or US passport. Three of them have indicated that they will return to Canada or the USA after they have amassed sufficient wealth. The main considerations are better living conditions, better social security and to spend more time with their family. Others want to return for a better education for their children.

Among them, being an American or a Canadian represented one set of identity and citizenship. There are other layers of identity, notably cultural identity. Along with globalisation, the Chinese abroad have experienced a state of migranthood that is 'both flexible and unpredictable where notions of home and nationality are concerned', and also 'a prelude to a new kind of mobility and personal responsibility' (Wang 2007, 177). Accordingly, home is global and local; territorialised and deterriotorialised to cope with their quest for a flexible citizenship.

Home is global

After returning to Shanghai, they feel that they are regarded as 'too westernised' by the local Chinese because of their Western mannerisms and western values and cultural traits, creating a cultural gulf between themselves and their local counterparts. Feeling unable to integrate fully into Shanghai society, they form a local *haigui* club to socialise and exchange business information and news of their adopted country. As transmigrants, they feel strangled and caught 'in-between', fortunate to have two cultures, yet accepted by none. These return migrants, thus, have established a new identity for themselves and seek to redefine where home is. Informant Lu said:

> I think I prefer to call myself a global citizen. I don't think I can simply identify myself as Mainland Chinese, American Chinese, Chinese or American. My identity actually shifts under different conditions when I face different groups of people. If I am asked I tell local Americans I came from the Mainland but am now a US citizen; when I am asked by a local Chinese person here in Shanghai

about where I come from, I declare myself as a *haigui* who had lived in the United States for over ten years before I came back to Mainland China. In reality, however, few local Chinese can tell from our daily contact that I am actually a 'sea turtle'. (Huang 2008, 152)

Home is still China

For five of the *haigui* in our study, they express nostalgia and a sense of nationalism for China even though they have lived overseas for two to nine years. They express pride in the success of China's space expedition to the moon and the 2008 Beijing Olympics. This group is unable to become fully integrated into the host society, in contrast to the return migrants of the 1.5 generation who embrace western lifestyles and values and have become fully integrated into their adopted country (Chiang 2011; Ip 2011).

For Geng, his home continues to be in China. He stated that:

> Although I was rather well-off working at a university lab when I was in Canada, I hardly made any real friends and didn't build up any deep-rooted relationships with the local white Canadians. It would be ok if I went out for dinner or tea with my non-Chinese colleagues, but I never invited them home. Instead, I only invited my Chinese friends to my home, where we could chat freely in Chinese.

Another felt that the host society saw them as being 'too Chinese' and questioned their loyalty to their adopted country. According to Zang, who had spent nearly five years in the United Kingdom, pursuing his studies and part-time jobs said:

> Mainland China is always my homeland in my eyes no matter where I stay. This feeling was extremely strong when I studied in UK. After all, China is where I was born and raised and where my parents are still living.

The early sociological paradigms on migration assumed that the first migration stop in a host society was the final destination of the migrants, and therefore focused on assimilation, cultural pluralism and multiculturalism policies that aimed to integrate the migrants into the host society. Today, migration flows have become not only thicker and denser but also faster and more fluid, culminating with the emergence of global circulatory migration, where migrants circulate from one destination to another with no end destination (Kuah-Pearce 2006, 225). Return migrants oscillate in circular mobility between the diaspora community and their homeland. They regard both as home. Home is their world, which transcends political boundaries and territoriality (Shen and Chiang 2011; Chiang 2011). Against this backdrop, contemporary theories on international migration have turned to focus on 'transmigrants' – the development of multi-threaded relationships and multiple identities in this process of transnational migration (Schiller, Basch, and Blanc-Szanton 1999, 26–49).

How do return migrants look towards flexible identities and multiple territorialities? Having a transnational family serves as a reminder to the return migrants that their identity is rooted in two cultures and two or more countries. It is not uncommon for return migrants to commute frequently between their two homes to visit the family and then to return to work as well as travelling frequently across the globe for business and leisure pursuits. The multiple movements and multiple modalities have an impact on how this group of return migrants view themselves not only in China but also in their adopted country.

As more return migrants resettle in Shanghai and other parts of China, they adopt a pragmatic approach towards a flexible identity. They continue to hold on to their naturalised national identity and foreign passports but at the same time, express sentiments towards their cultural identity.

Back home in China, these highly skilled westernised return migrants play a significant role in bridging cultures as they bring 'their vast wealth of knowledge, experience, financial clout, socio-economic capital and networks' to the receiving diasporic community and the host society (Kuah-Pearce 2006, 237). This helps minimise tensions and conflicts.

Globally, given the fact that the return migrants are no longer rooted in one geographical location and one culture, it is imperative to understand how they attempt to reposition themselves within the circulatory migration circuit and the identity that they will ultimately assume. According to Chan, they can be seen as transmigrants with multiple roots or consciousness but without a fixed physical home (*chonggen*, 重根) (Chan 1997, 206–207). With the ability to move around freely, these Chinese transmigrants tend to be footloose, less fixed in space and more fluid in place attachment. They view mainland China as one stop in the circulatory migration circuit, until the next opportunity arises to make the next stop.

Conclusion

This paper has explored return migrants as talent circulators who, because of their talents, are able to circulate from one region to another. In our case, they circulated first from China to Canada and the USA; and today from Canada and the USA back to China, pausing at this point, and awaiting opportunities to move again in a circulatory migrational trajectory.

As *haigui*, they have come to realise the worth of their talents in the professional and business world. Yet at the same time, they have also realised that talent and knowledge is only a part of the success equation. They need to kickstart Chinese cultural elements, and in this case, *guanxi* networks and to amass social capital to continue their successful journey and soar to greater heights in the pursuit of their career.

Returning to Shanghai has come with a price. These *haigui* experience a fragmented social and familial relationship. Some marriages break down while a gulf emerges between themselves and their children. Is this trade-off worth it? Familial relationship with parents comes under scrutiny and the returning singleton *haigui* have to adapt once again to parental demands and some find it difficult to readjust to this.

Finally, as talent circulators, they are pragmatic and want the best of both worlds. As such, they adopt a flexible identity and multiple territoriality approach where they continue to hold on to their foreign citizenship to minimise their risks in a communist country and yet portray their cultural identity as being Chinese to take advantage of their ethnicity in a Chinese state. At another level, depending on their success in integrating into the host society, some have expressed a stronger sense of identity and sentiments towards the host society that they have come to call home, whilst others cling on to their 'Chineseness'.

In the final analysis, in light of their transnationality, in which experiences of territoriality and deterritoriality overlap and consume each other, the *haigui* pose challenges to our understanding of how the connections between the diasporic Chinese community and mainland China should be re-evaluated. Here, the location of the individual self needs to take into account the concepts of flexible identity and multiple territorialities to which this group of transmigrants subscribes to.

Acknowledgements

We would like to thank the editor of this special issue, Professor Shibao Guo, and the two anonymous reviewers for their comments that were beneficial to our revision. Yedan Huang would like to acknowledge the University of Hong Kong for a research postgraduate studentship to complete her M.Phil studies.

Notes

1. For further details, see the official website of the project 'Shanghai 10,000 Overseas Talents Converging Programme, 2010'. http://egov.21cnhr.com/wanren/index.jsp, last accessed July 15, 2010.
2. Jiaoyubu: 2012 nian chuguo liuxue renshu jin 40 wan (Ministry of Education (PRC): China has sent out nearly 400,000 students, *liuxuesheng* abroad in 2012). *Official Website of the People's Daily (Overseas Version)*. http://edu.haiwainet.cn/BIG5/n/2013/0301/c232659-18231504.html (last accessed 22 May, 2013).

References

Cao, J. J. 2010. Shanghai jiasu rencai guojihua [Talents in Shanghai are Increasingly becoming Internationalized]. *Guangming Ribao* [Light Daily], 1 June, page 2.
Chan, K. B. 1997. "A Family Affair: Migration, Dispersal and the Emergent Identity of the Chinese Cosmopolitan." *Diaspora* 6 (2): 195–213. doi:10.1353/dsp.1997.0005.
Chiang, L. H. N. 2011. "Return Migration: The Case of the 1.5 Generation of Taiwanese in Canada and New Zealand." *The China Review* 11 (2): 91–124.

Denscombe, M. 2010. *The Good Research Guide for Small Scale Social Research Projects*. Maidenhead: Open University Press.
Ghosh, B., ed. 2000. *Return Migration: Journey of Hope or Despair?* Geneva: International Organization for Migration.
Guo, S. 2013. "Economic Integration of Recent Chinese Immigrants in Canada's Second-tier Cities: The Triple Glass Effect and Immigrants' Downward Social Mobility." *Canadian Ethnic Studies* 45 (3): 95–115. doi:10.1353/ces.2013.0047.
Guo, S. 2010. "Return Chinese Migrants or Canadian Diaspora: Exploring the Experience of Chinese Canadians in China." In *Migration, Indigenization and Interaction: Chinese Overseas and Globalization*, edited by L. Suryadinata, 297–320. Singapore: World Scientific.
Huang, X. J. 2005. *Guiguo huaqiao de lishi yu xianzhuang* [History and Current Conditions of Returned Huaqiao]. Hong Kong: Hong Kong Social Sciences Publishing House.
Huang, Y. D. 2008. "Return Migration: A Case Study of 'Sea Turtles' in Shanghai." M.Phil, The University of Hong Kong, unpublished.
Ip, M. ed. 2011. *Transmigration and the New Chinese: Theories and Practices from the New Zealand Experience*. Hong Kong: Hong Kong Institute for the Humanities and Social Sciences, University of Hong Kong.
Ip, M. 2012. *Here, there, and Back Again: A New Zealand Case Study of Chinese Circulatory Transmigration*. Accessed August 13, 2013. http://www.migrationinformation.org/feature/display.cfm?ID=878.
Iredale, R., F. Guo, and S. Rozario, eds. 2003. *Return Migration in the Asia Pacific*. Northampton: Edward Elgar.
Johnson, G. 1994. "Hong Kong Immigration and the Chinese Community in Vancouver." In *Reluctant Exiles?: Migration from Hong Kong and the New Overseas Chinese*, edited by R. Skeldon, 120–138. Hong Kong: Hong Kong University Press.
Kuah-Pearce, K. E. 2006. "Transnational Self in the Chinese Diaspora: A Conceptual Framework." *Asian Studies Review* 30: 223–239. doi:10.1080/10357820600897655.
Ley, D., and A. Kobayashi. 2004. *Back to Hong Kong: Return Migration or Transnational Sojourn?* Accessed April 10, 2010. http://www.instrcc.ubc.ca/History485_2008/Ley_Kobayashi.pdf.
Ley, D., and A. Kobayashi. 2005. "Back to Hong Kong: Return Migration or Transnational Sojourn?." *Global Networks* 5: 111–127.
Liu, H. 2000. "Globalization, Institutionalization and the Social Foundation of Chinese Business Networks." In *Globalization of Chinese Business Firms*, edited by H. W. Yeung and K. Olds, 105–125. Basingstoke: Macmillan.
Lu, Z. 2010. Quanguo sige haigui zhong yige zai shanghai [One out of Four *haigui* in China is in Shanghai]. *Xinmin Wanbao* [Xinmin Evening News], 28 January, page A1.
Ma, L. J. C. 2003. "Space, Place, and Transnationalism in the Chinese Diaspora." In *The Chinese Diaspora: Space, Place, Mobility, and Identity*, edited by L. Ma and C. Cartier, 1–50. Boston, MA: Roman & Littlefield.
MacInnes, P. 1993. "*Guanxi* or Contract: A Way to Understand and Predict Conflict between Chinese and Western Senior Managers in China-based Joint Ventures." In *Research on Multinational Business Managemen and Internationalization of Chinese Enterprises*, edited by D. McCarty and S. Hille, 345–351. Nanjing: Nanjing University Press.
Morrison, A. M., C. Schreiber, and K. Price. 1995. *A Glass Ceiling Survey: Benchmarking Barriers and Practices*. Greenboro, NC: Center for Creative Leadership.

Ong, A. 1998. "Flexible Citizenship among Chinese Cosmopolitans." In *Cosmopolitics: Thinking and Feeling beyond the Nation*, edited by P. Cheah and B. Robbins, 134–162. Minneapolis, MN: University of Minnesota Press.

Ong, A. 1999. *Flexible Citizenship: The Cultural Logics of Transnationality*. Durham, NC: Duke University Press.

Salaff, J., A. Greve, and L. Xu. 2002. "Paths into the Economy: Structural Barriers and the Job Hunt for Skilled PRC Migrants in Canada." *International Journal of Human Resource Management: Special Issue on globalization and HRM in Asia Pacific* 13: 450–464.

Salaff, J., S. L. Wong, and A. Greve. 2010. *Hong Kong Movers and Stayers: Narratives of Family Migration*. Urbana: University of Illinois Press.

Schiller, N. G., L. Basch, and C. Blanc-Szanton. 1999. "Transnationalism: A New Analytic Framework for Understanding Migration." In *Migration, Diasporas and Transnationalism*, edited by S. Vertovec, 26–49, Cheltenham: Elgar Reference Collection.

Shanghai 10,000 Overseas Talents Converging Program. 2010. *Programme Objectives*. Accessed July 15, 2010. http:// egov.21cnhr.com/wanren/index.jsp.

Shen, J., and L. H. N. Chiang. 2011. "Chinese Migrants and Circular Mobility: Introduction." *The China Review* 11 (2): 1–10.

Skeldon, R. 1994. "Reluctant Exiles or Bold Pioneers: An Introduction to Migration from Hong Kong." In *Reluctant Exiles?: Migration from Hong Kong and the New Overseas Chinese*, edited by R. Skeldon, 3–18. Hong Kong: Hong Kong University Press.

Wang, Cangbai, and Wong Siu-lun. 2007. "Home as a Circular Process: The Indonesian-Chinese in Hong Kong." In *Beyond Chinatown: New Chinese Migration and the Global Expansion of China*, edited by Mette Thuno, 182–209. Copenhagen: NIAS Press.

Wang, F. Z. 2008. "China Goes on the Road to Lure 'Sea Turtles' Home." In *Reuters*, 17 December. Accessed April 28, 2010. http://www.reuters.com/article/2008/12/18/us-financial-seaturtles-idUSTRE4BH02220081218.

Wang, G. 2007. "Liuxue and Yimin: From Study to Migranthood." In *Beyond Chinatown: New Chinese Migration and the Global Expansion of China*, edited by M. Thunø, 165–181. Copenhagen: NIAS.

Wong, S. L., and J. Salaff. 1998. "Network Capital: Emigration from Hong Kong." *British Journal of Sociology* 49: 358–374. doi:10.2307/591388.

Appendix 1. Profile of informants.

No.	Name	Gender	Age	Educational attainment	Country of emigration	Year of out	Year of return	Occupational background
1	Lei	F	39	University undergraduate (English)	USA→Canada	1993	2003	Executive assistant of a local investment consultant company
2	Geng	M	42	Postdoctoral degree (Medicine)	USA→Canada	1993	2002	Project leader of a local university medical research institution and later started a biomedical business
3	Lu	M	43	Master's degree (Architecture)	USA	1988	2002	Director of China market of an overseas-based architecture firm
4	Zheng	M	27	Master's degree (Computer Science)	Singapore	2002	2004	Technical consultant of a big foreign IT company (Shanghai branch)
5	Pan	F	26	Master's degree (Comparative Literature)	USA	2001	2003	Client executive of a big foreign PR company (Shanghai branch)
6	Zang	M	32	Master's degree (Director of Theatre Performance)	United Kingdom	2001	2005	CEO of a local-based cultural media company
7	Li	F	26	Master's degree (Fabric Design)	France	2002	2004	Senior designer of a locally based cloth manufacturing company
8	Yu	M	24	Master of Business Administration (MBA)	United Kingdom	2002	2005	Waiting for employment
9	Zhou	M	27	Master's degree (Environmental Engineering)	Germany	2000	2005	Project researcher of a local urban planning and design research institute

Appendix 1 (*Continued*).

No.	Name	Gender	Age	Educational attainment	Country of emigration	Year of out	Year of return	Occupational background
10	Xue	F	29	Doctoral degree of Statistics & Actuarial Science	USA	1998	2005	Actuary of an international insurance company
11	Wang	F	33	Doctoral degree of Clinical Psychology	Australia	1992	2003	Teaching staff of a local famous university
12	Zhu	M	40	Master's degree (Economics and Finance)	USA→Hong Kong	1987	2001	Director of China market for an overseas-based investment bank

Index

Note: Page numbers in *italic* refer to figures
Page numbers in **bold** refer to tables

acceleration of migration, the 2
APEGGA (Association of Professional Engineers, Geologists and Geophysicists of Alberta) 16–17
Appadurai, Arjun 102–3, 107, 112
Arendt, Hannah 109

barriers for migrants 10, 16–18, 36, 40–1; in the employment market *19,* 19–20, 58; in language 15–16, *16,* 18, 23, 94–5, 97; for women 11, 61 *see also* deskilling and devaluation of migrants' prior experiences and qualifications; triple glass effect, the
body shopping 51–2, 56–60
Breivik, Anders 103

Canada and immigration 2–3, 8–12, 35–6
case study of Chinese immigrants in Canada 7, 8, 10–16, 18–19, 21, 26–9; barriers faced by *16,* 16–18, 25–6, 28; education levels of *13,* 13–14; and employment *19,* 19–20, **20,** 21–5, **22**
case study of ESL teachers' identity and integration in the Australian labour market 87–94, 96–8; and language barriers 94–6, 97
case study of how entrepreneurial female Chinese immigrants overcame barriers in the Canadian labour market 37–8, 39–44
case study of self-identity of multilingual students in a Mandarin–English bilingual programme 65, 66–7, 68–71, 76–81, *77;* through transnational flow of images from popular cultures *71,* 71–6, *72, 73, 75,* 81–2
case study on Indian immigrants working in IT in Canada 50, 53, 55–60
case study on the strategies for success of return Chinese migrants to Shanghai 133–45, **148–9**

case study on the transnational experiences of return Chinese immigrants from Canada 115, 118–24; and IS 124–8, *126*
CCR (credential and certificate regime) 40
Chinese education system, the 38–9
CIMO (Finnish agency for International Mobility) 105–6, 107
circulatory migration 132–3
CIS (conceived individual space) *126,* 127
cognition and predictable behaviour 109–11, **111**
Cold War, the 104
comparison of the Canadian and Chinese national flags 79
Confucianism 38
contact hypothesis 102
cultural gulf for returned migrants 142–3, 144–5

'democratic racism' 11–12
design of case studies 89
deskilling and devaluation of migrants' prior experiences and qualifications 16, 21, 55–6, 97–8; affect on social mobility 2, 10–11, 27; non-recognition of prior qualifications 27, 40, 88
differentiation of migration, the 2
downward social mobility of migrants 2, 10–11, 27

economic immigration 9–10
education and global mindedness 4, 105–6
education policies and neoliberalism 35
empathy as a metaphor 109–10
'entrepreneurial self,' the 34, 35, 44–5, 62
entrepreneurship of women immigrants in Canada 33–4 *see also* case study of how entrepreneurial female Chinese immigrants

INDEX

overcame barriers in the Canadian labour market
ESL teachers in the Australian labour market *see* case study of ESL teachers' identity and integration in the Australian labour market
essential skills initiative of the Canadian government 8

Fear of small numbers (book) 102
fears in majority identities of a nation 102–3
female immigrants in Canada 11, 21, 27, 36, 60–1 *see also* case study of how entrepreneurial female Chinese immigrants overcame barriers in the Canadian labour market
feminisation of migration, the 1–2
Finnish nation, the 103–6, 112
flexible citizenship 132, 141–2, 144, 145
Foucault, Michel 32
Frisch, Max 44

gendered networks through body-shopping 60
'generic workers' and the instability of neoliberalism 34
globalisation and transnational migration 1
global mindedness 101, 102, 106–7, 111; and education 4, 105–6; reconsiderations to the framework of 107–11, **111**
GMD (Global Mindedness Dispositions) 109
guanxi networks 139, 144

haigui (talent circulators) 134–8, 140, 142, 144–5
haiou group of *haigui* 135–6
Harajuku Lovers (sketch book) 72, *72–4, 73*

identity as a process of becoming 66–7
IE (method of inquiry of institutional ethnography) 37
immigration to Finland 105
institutional identity construction by migrants 96–7, 98
IS (individual space) theory 124–7, *126*

labour: and mobility 49–50, 51–3, 57–60, 61; and neoliberalism 34–5, 45, 50, 51, 52, 61–2 *see also* downward social mobility of migrants
labour shortages and immigration policy 10
language and identity formation 3–4, 86
language barriers 15–16, *16,* 18, 23, 94–5, 97
language proficiency for new immigrants 86, 94, 121
life history as a research approach 117–18
lifelong learning and transnational migration 121–2

LINC (Language Instruction for Newcomers to Canada) 24–5
living space for unmarried returned migrants 141
Longitudinal Survey of Immigrants to Canada 21

meritocracy as an educational ideology 38, 39, 40, 44
migrant ties with the homeland 115, 116–17
mobility and transnationalism 101–2
mobility of labour, the 49–50, 51–3, 57–60, 61
multilingualism of immigrant children 65–6

native concept of the space, the *see* IS (individual space) theory
neoliberalism 32–3; and the labour market 34–5, 45, 50, 51, 52, 61–2
networking and social capital 138–9
non-recognition of the prior qualifications of migrants 27, 40, 88
notions of 'home' and 'abroad' 132–3

Open Door Policy, the 131, 134

PIS (perceived individual space) 125, 126, *126,* 127
pluralism in Canada 11
points system for Canadian immigration 9–10, 11, 36
politicisation of migration, the 2
post-structuralism and identity 66–7
proliferation of migration transition, the 2

recruitment agencies and a compliant workforce 50–4, 57–60, 61–2
recruitment agencies in the developing world 51, 56–7
Remembrance Day (Canada) 77–8
return migration of Chinese expatriates 5, 115–16, 131–2 *see also* case study on the strategies for success of return Chinese migrants to Shanghai; case study on the transnational experiences of return Chinese immigrants from Canada
rhizoanalysis 70–1, *71*

scapegoating of immigrants 102–3
self-adjustment and transnational migration 119–21
skills initiatives for migrants *see* essential skills initiative of the Canadian government
social capital for new immigrants 86
social space and transnationalism 116, 124–5
SP (spatial practice) 125–6, *126*
Stefani, Gwen 72

152

INDEX

Strategy 2020: Towards a more globally minded Finland (booklet) 106

talent circulators *(haigui)* 134–8, 140, 142, 144–5
TESOL (Teaching English as a Second Language) 85–6 *see also* case study of ESL teachers identity and integration in the Australian labour market
tourism as a metaphor 109, 110
transculturation 67–8
transnationalism and migration 1, 4–5, 68, 86, 101–2, 115–17; and flexibility as citizens 122–4, 141–4, 145; and IS (individual space) 124–8, *126*; as a process of lifelong learning 121–2; as a process of self-adjustment 119–21; and social space 116, 124–5
trends in migration 1–2
triple glass effect, the 28, 55, 61, 87, 123, 134, 136

visiting as a metaphor 109, 110

women and neoliberalism 33
worldwide migration figures 1

xiao haigui (sea turtles) 137–8